Wholehearted School Leadership

Relationships are the heart of great teaching, great leadership, and our greatest predictor of achievement. This book provides you with the tools and a values-based framework to ensure you're prioritizing relationships and rewiring your school for courage, justice, learning, and connection! Each chapter includes strategies and reflective exercises to guide your leadership work. Written by an educational administrator and researcher with experiences in intercultural and technology-mediated contexts, this exciting new book provides a compelling vision for the complex and evolving landscape of schools. Refreshingly honest and relevant, this book will make you laugh, think, notice, and prioritize what matters most in schools—students and those who support them. It is a must-read title for school leaders and a powerful choice to read with your leadership team.

Kathryn Fishman-Weaver is an educator, author, and international lecturer. She is the Executive Director of Mizzou Academy, a global and blended K-12 lab school at the University of Missouri and an Associate Teaching Professor in Community Engagement and School Leadership. She also serves as a Court Appointed Special Advocate (CASA) for youth navigating the foster care system.

Also Available from Routledge Eye on Education

(www.routledge.com/eyeoneducation)

Coaching Education Leaders: A Culturally Responsive Approach to Transforming Schools and Systems
Nancy B. Gutiérrez, Michelle Jarney, and Michael Kim

Fostering Parent Engagement for Equitable and Successful Schools: A Leader's Guide to Supporting Families and Students
Patrick Darfler-Sweeney

Finding Your Path as a Woman in School Leadership: A Guide for Educators, Allies, and Advocates
Kim Cofino and Christina Botbyl

A Leadership Playbook for Addressing Rapid Change in Education: Empowered for Success
Teresa L. San Martín

Improving Teacher Morale and Motivation: Leadership Strategies that Build Student Success
Ronald Williamson and Barbara R. Blackburn

Teaching Women's and Gender Studies: Classroom Resources on Resistance, Representation, and Radical Hope (Grades 9–12)
Kathryn Fishman-Weaver and Jill Clingan

Teaching Women's and Gender Studies: Classroom Resources on Resistance, Representation, and Radical Hope (Grades 6–8)
Kathryn Fishman-Weaver and Jill Clingan

Brain-Based Learning with Gifted Students: Lessons from Neuroscience on Cultivating Curiosity, Metacognition, Empathy, and Brain Plasticity: Grades 3–6
Kathryn Fishman-Weaver

When Your Child Learns Differently: A Family Approach for Navigating Special Education Services with Love and High Expectations
Kathryn Fishman-Weaver

Wholehearted Teaching of Gifted Young Women: Cultivating Courage, Connection, and Self-Care in Schools
Kathryn Fishman-Weaver

Wholehearted School Leadership

Rewiring our Schools for Courage, Justice, Learning, and Connection

Kathryn Fishman-Weaver

NEW YORK AND LONDON

Designed cover image: Getty Images

First published 2025
by Routledge
605 Third Avenue, New York, NY 10158

and by Routledge
4 Park Square, Milton Park, Abingdon, Oxon, OX14 4RN

Routledge is an imprint of the Taylor & Francis Group, an informa business

© 2025 Kathryn Fishman-Weaver

The right of Kathryn Fishman-Weaver to be identified as author of this work has been asserted in accordance with sections 77 and 78 of the Copyright, Designs and Patents Act 1988.

All rights reserved. The purchase of this copyright material confers the right on the purchasing institution to photocopy or download pages which bear the support material icon and a copyright line at the bottom of the page. No other parts of this book may be reprinted or reproduced or utilized in any form or by any electronic, mechanical, or other means, now known or hereafter invented, including photocopying and recording, or in any information storage or retrieval system, without permission in writing from the publishers.

Trademark notice: Product or corporate names may be trademarks or registered trademarks, and are used only for identification and explanation without intent to infringe.

Library of Congress Cataloging-in-Publication Data
Names: Fishman-Weaver, Kathryn, 1981- author.
Title: Wholehearted school leadership : rewiring our schools for courage, justice, learning, and connection / Kathryn Fishman-Weaver.
Description: New York, NY : Routledge, 2025. |
Series: Routledge eye on education | Includes bibliographical references.
Identifiers: LCCN 2024058753 (print) | LCCN 2024058754 (ebook) | ISBN 9781032852133 (hardback) | ISBN 9781032852126 (paperback) | ISBN 9781003517122 (ebook)
Subjects: LCSH: Educational leadership.
Classification: LCC LB2805 .F486 2025 (print) | LCC LB2805 (ebook) | DDC 371.2/07--dc23/eng/20250213
LC record available at https://lccn.loc.gov/2024058753
LC ebook record available at https://lccn.loc.gov/2024058754

ISBN: 9781032852133 (hbk)
ISBN: 9781032852126 (pbk)
ISBN: 9781003517122 (ebk)

DOI: 10.4324/9781003517122

Typeset in Palatino
by Deanta Global Publishing Services, Chennai, India

Contents

Support Material	vii
Meet the Author	viii
Acknowledgments	ix
Introduction	1

PART 1	**LEADING FOR COURAGE AND JUSTICE**	**15**
I	LEAD FOR COURAGE OVERVIEW	23
	1 Commit to High Expectations	27
	2 Celebrate Community Wisdom	31
	3 Keep Showing Up. Keep Listening.	40
	4 Relationships Are the Heart of Great Leadership	48
	5 Cultivate Gratitude	57
II	LEAD FOR JUSTICE OVERVIEW	63
	6 Commit to Antiracism	74
	7 Hold Space for Healing	90
	8 Foster a Sense of Belonging	101
	9 Practice Inclusion	111
	10 Advocate for Inclusion	124

Continuing to Lead for Courage and Justice	132

PART 2	LEADING FOR LEARNING AND CONNECTION	139
	III LEAD FOR LEARNING OVERVIEW	145
	11 Advance Agency and Opportunity	149
	12 Support Learner-Led Projects	160
	13 Leverage Emerging Technologies	168
	14 Lean into Brain-Based Leadership	179
	15 Diversify Your Professional Learning	191
	IV LEAD FOR CONNECTION OVERVIEW	199
	16 Practice Cultural Learning and Reciprocity	207
	17 Build Accountability Through Grace	214
	18 Communicate Care Across Cultures	223
	19 Progress Is a Team Process	231
	20 Expand Learning, Reduce Barriers	240

Continuing to Lead for Learning and Connection   257

The Brave Leadership Needed to Rewire Our Schools   261

Support Material

The reproducibles in this book are also available on the book product page online, so you can easily print them for use. To access these downloads, go to www.routledge.com/9781032852126 and click on the "Support Material" link.

- Lead for Courage Overview
- Concept Study: Lessons from our First Classrooms
- Lead for Justice Overview
- Concept Study: Trauma-Informed School Leadership
- Concept Study: What Is an Upstander?
- Lead for Learning Section Overview
- Concept Study: Strengths-Based Perspectives in a Digital World
- Lead for Connection Overview
- Concept Study: Youth Participatory Action Research (YPAR)
- Concept Study: The Cognitive Triangle as a Support Tool

Meet the Author

Kathryn Fishman-Weaver, PhD (she/her) began her career as a special education teacher in a sunny classroom in Oakland, CA. Since then, she has taught and led programs in special education, gifted education, English language arts, and teacher preparation.

Currently she serves as the Executive Director of Mizzou Academy, the K-12 lab school in the University of Missouri's College of Education and Human Development. The school serves approximately 7,000 students from over 60 countries.

Kathryn holds a PhD in Educational Leadership and Policy Analysis, a Master's in Special Education, and a Bachelor's in Sociology. A prolific and celebrated author, she has written numerous books in education including, *Wholehearted Teaching of Gifted Young Women* (2018), *When Your Child Learns Differently* (2019), *Brain-Based Learning with Gifted Students* (2020), *Connected Classrooms* co-authored with Stephanie Walter, and a book series on *Teaching Women's and Gender Studies* in the middle and high school classroom co-authored with Jill Clingan.

An avid local volunteer and advocate, a sought-after speaker on inclusive practices in schools, and a career educator, Kathryn's work has a broad reach. Her work has been cited by the US Department of Education and she has led educational conferences around the world. When Kathryn isn't at school, her favorite place to be is in the water. She loves both pool and open water swimming and stand-up paddleboard.

Acknowledgments

Book writing is a community project, and this title is no exception. Throughout the following chapters, I draw on the experiences, lessons, and friendships I have developed at each of the schools where I have worked. These schools have shaped me into the educator and school leader I am today. I am thankful to still work and learn with students and colleagues from each of these school communities.

I am forever grateful to the student leaders who continue to teach us a better way forward and am especially indebted to my first class in Oakland, California. The insights of those early elementary children can be seen across the pages of this book. Their influence has persisted for over 20 years, guiding many of my decisions and philosophies in education.

As a leadership book, I owe a special appreciation to our leadership team at Mizzou Academy. This group includes our "Fab4 Admin Team" with Stephanie Walter, Angie Hammons, and Tami Regan. What a gift it is to work with these amazing women. Together, we lean on each other's strengths and have developed the kind of friendship that comes from years of working through hard things together and seeing our efforts positively impact students and teachers. Many of these successes are because of the smarts and care of our broader leadership team: Barbie Banks, Alicia Bixby, Lisa DeCastro, Lee Fent, David Prats, Amelia Howser, Jacquelyn Kay, Karen Scales, Greg Soden, Brian Stuhlman, and Chevi' White. These leaders in teaching, learning, school counseling, technology, curriculum, and human resources bring expertise, purpose, and humor to big projects, student support, and the everyday work of doing school. While not all named here, our instructional technologists, developers and designers, support staff, instructional specialists, and students are the heartbeat of leadership and innovation in my school system. I am grateful for the lessons they continue to teach me and for the opportunity to share some of this wisdom in the following chapters.

In my humble opinion, our Mizzou Academy teachers and partner teachers are hands down the best. They represent a phenomenal group of compassionate, creative, and dedicated educators. Spending time in their classrooms, both online and in-person, is one of the greatest joys of my career. In the upcoming chapters, I am thrilled that you, too, will get to "visit" some of these classrooms and "meet" some of our incredible students. These classrooms are led and supported by faculty leads Dr. Ta Boonseng, Jill Clingan, Dr. Sherry Denney, David Graham, Jeff Healy, Lou Jobst, Kimberly Kester, Jeff Kopolow, Brennan Ransdell, Ericca Thornhill, and Dr. Jason Williamson. Every day, this team takes teacher leadership to the next level.

So many of the teachers and school leaders named above spent time thoughtfully reviewing chapters, offering insights, and encouraging my writing process. Although named above, I am grateful for the extra time Karen Scales and Jill Clingan spent thoughtfully reviewing my first draft of this manuscript. These two language arts leaders reminded me that compassionate feedback is a best teaching practice, and that editing can be an act of love.

Additionally, Kaci Conley and Matt Miltenberg both partnered with me on chapters or concept studies in this book. Kaci is a former student of mine, although our faculty and I all agree that she taught us more than we taught her. You will have the gift of learning alongside Kaci in our chapter on inclusion. Similarly, Matt Miltenberg has left his fingerprints all over the sections on mental health and upstander behaviors. More importantly, his influence continues to guide care practices in my school system.

As my family knows, school leadership doesn't stop at the end of the school day. There are many nights when I am responding to messages late into the evening and mornings when I start work before the rest of my house is even awake. And yet, my family supports this work wholeheartedly. When it comes to writing, my family are my first readers, my early testers, my sounding board, and my favorite cheerleaders. Their support extends well beyond my writing projects. Often, we spend Sunday dinners preparing materials for special activities at school. When I tell her about student or faculty needs, my mom shops for the young people and adults at my school as if they were her own. This book, this work, and certainly this author would not be the same without the care and support of my immediate and extended family. They tell me that they are my biggest fans, but the truth is, I am theirs.

Finally, the editorial team at Routledge is fantastic to work with. Heather Jarrow is a masterclass in enthusiastic and responsive support. On more than one occasion when my worries about this project became a productive block, her confidence about the book gave me the boost I needed. Despite breaking many of the forms he sent me and responding to straightforward questions with creative "concept art," Dr. Sean Daly was patient, good-humored, and a wealth of information throughout the publishing process. The design and copyediting professionals worked their magic transforming my rough ideas and sketches into this beautiful book you are holding. The Routledge Eye on Education collection is regarded as among the best in professional learning resources for educators and school leaders, and it is my joy to have this title included there.

> **A Note About Identity and Permissions**
>
> All student names used in this book are pseudonyms. While I stayed true to the lessons these young people taught me, specific identifying details were combined or obscured to create composite characters. In addition to student leaders, I also leaned on the lessons of school administrators, staff, teacher, and community leaders. These people have been instrumental in my growth as a professional and I am grateful for their example and mentorship. In the instances where their real names were mentioned, they were added with expressed permission and my gratitude.

Introduction

This book tells the story of finding my way as a new school leader. It is purposefully set in this interconnected moment in education.

On my first day as a school administrator, I was filled with bright anticipation and shadowy imposter syndrome. I walked into my new office and was met by an oversize mahogany desk. Reluctant to take my place there, I held my first meeting in two chairs facing *the desk*. The desk didn't fit my leadership style or me. However, I quickly learned that school leadership doesn't wait for you to sort out your feelings about furniture.

Within the first hour of that first day, teachers, support staff, counselors, and other administrators came to me needing decisions. A teenager panicked and left in the middle of an exam. This is against our testing policies. Should she get a retake? Two international students in our online program have fallen behind in their math class. They live on separate continents and haven't met previously, is it okay if we pull them together for academic intervention? A senior didn't submit his required service project for honors credit by the deadline, but he needs that designation for his scholarship. What are his next steps? There is an angry dad on the phone [no information yet], may I transfer the call to you?[1]

I knew the ways I responded to each of these situations would speak volumes about who I was and what I valued as a school leader. My experiences in the classroom and my academic research on hope, heart, and high expectations (see particularly *Wholehearted Teaching*, 2018) helped me navigate those first decisions and many of the decisions that came after. Oftentimes leadership is about responding to change or uncertainty and then navigating a way forward. Leadership is not a static position, rather it is a constant process of becoming. In his book on human-centered leadership, Dr. Peter Stiepleman (2023) writes, "So much of the professional literature presented to leaders is the curation of a perfect image, but we are all imperfect..." His work aims to "lift the learning and to lift imperfect leaders. That way, when you hear the term imperfect, you'll see strength, strength from the candor needed to recognize imperfection as a real advantage" (pp. xvi–xvii). Being imperfect is about being a learner. It is about becoming. My book offers an honest account of what that process can look like.

This is a book for school leaders who are still figuring it out. Spoiler alert—all leaders are still figuring it out. In the following stories, I share openly about times I learned, stumbled, ventured something new that didn't work, and then something new that did. I believe we should normalize the experience of leaders learning, becoming, fumbling, and trying again. Yes, the field is long, and sometimes the rules of the game shift right under our feet. However, leadership is a team sport. When we stumble, we can often find vision in the strong relationships we have built and collective expertise of our team. Teams and collaboration are central to this book, as are values, vulnerability, and learning. I encourage you to read through this book with your team. The vignettes, strategies, and reflective exercises lend themselves to productive teamwork. Whether you are in your first year in school leadership, your tenth, or your twentieth, my hope is that the following pages offer you relevant ideas, relatable stories, and meaningful questions, and that these chapters help you better serve and support the students and staff in your care.

Using a narrative approach, this book presents a values-based leadership philosophy for serving in the intercultural and blended landscape of today's schools. Some of the stories are informed by my earlier research on wholehearted teaching (2018) and connected classrooms (2022). An extensive reflective journal tethers the narrative, inviting leaders to engage in their own reflective practice and lean into wholehearted approaches to school leadership. In addition to the reflective journal, I also drew on my weekly newsletter to my team. Each Monday, I open these newsletters with a reflective letter to our faculty and staff. The tone of the letters, just like the tone of this book, is conversational and real. My hope is that this book feels like how we would talk about school, leadership, or teaching in the hallway, over lunch, or early one morning before the students arrive. While not an epistolary text, this book offers a similar closeness for our conversation about leadership.

Context and Research Setting

I hold a PhD in educational leadership and policy analysis and am trained as a qualitative researcher. While most of my research employs participatory action research (PAR) with school communities, this book draws on the qualitative practices of autoethnography. According to Bochner and Ellis (2006), autoethnographers attempt to show "people in the process of figuring out what to do, how to live, and the meaning of their struggles" (p. 111). Autoethnography is, of course, autobiographical. It draws on the researcher-writer's own lived experiences in a way that is "grounded in active self-reflexivity. [It is an] observational data-driven phenomenological method of narrative research and writing that aims to offer tales of human social and cultural life that are compelling, striking, and evocative" (Poulos, 2021, pp. 4–5). Autoethnography draws on personal experiences to help fill gaps in research or narratives (Adams & Manning, 2015). Personal stories are often the shortest distance between people.

School stories matter. Leadership stories matter. Our lives are story rich. We also know that stories are didactic. They are among our oldest and most treasured teaching tools. The vignettes and stories I share in the following chapters give the Wholehearted Leadership Framework dimensionality. They also begin to add context to four important gaps in educational literature.

First, they offer knowledge from a place of becoming. Our leadership literature seldom includes primary-source stories of early- to mid-career school leaders; yet this is often the time when leaders are in the most need for mentoring and guidance. I hope these stories are a refreshing and relatable offering for school leaders at all points in their career. Further, I hope that early- to mid-career professionals feel seen and affirmed by the questions I was asking and experiences I had at similar moments in my own career.

Second, this framework does not treat equity and justice as special issues in school leadership; instead it affirms that these are integral to effective school leadership. We live, teach, and lead in schools that welcome students and families from many different cultural backgrounds and lived experiences. If a leadership practice doesn't align to our moral compass or work for one or more of our student populations then it doesn't work for our school. Wholehearted leaders affirm the inherent dignity and humanity of every student and family in search of a place to learn. They do so by safeguarding the legal and moral right of all students to receive a free and appropriate public education (US Department of Education, n.d.). They extend this commitment to the academic, social, and athletic opportunities available in their school community. This work is grounded in understanding the historical and persistent social inequities that leaders must continue to address within our field.

> *If a leadership practice doesn't align to our moral compass or work for one or more of our student populations then it doesn't work for our school. Wholehearted leaders affirm the inherent dignity and humanity of every student and family in search of a place to learn.*

Third, my experiences in school leadership draw on highly relevant competencies for schools today. My work has been grounded in online and blended methodologies across global contexts. The skills our school team have developed and experiences I've had navigating technology-mediated instruction and working across multicultural and multilinguistic school communities are highly pertinent topics for current schools and school leaders. I share more about the unique context of the school system I lead below.

Finally, I believe it is important to bring women's voices and experiences into the school leadership literature. "Historically, little attention has been given to the experiences and perceptions of women superintendents in the educational administration literature" (Garn & Brown, 2008, p. 49). In a recent census, the

"United States Census Bureau has *characterized the superintendency as being the most male dominated executive position of any profession in the United States*" (as cited in Garn & Brown, 2008, p. 51, my emphasis). As Garn and Brown go on to describe, "The lack of female superintendents is more striking when one considers data from the 2003–2004 School and Staffing Survey that indicate 75% of teachers were women." It is important to acknowledge that we have seen a growth in recent years of women in the top executive position in schools (Gresham & Sampson, 2019) and significant growth in women principals (Women in Academia, 2023). However, that growth is not commensurate with other sectors or with the percentage of qualified principal candidates working in schools. It is further stilted for women of color and women from other historically and continuously marginalized backgrounds.

In sharing my own positionality, it is important to note that I do not serve in a traditional superintendent position. This continues a historical trend that "that women have assumed leadership roles as county and state superintendents or established their own specialized schools, but men have traditionally dominated district superintendencies" (Garn & Brown, 2008, p. 50). While women's representation in the principalship has improved significantly—57.4% of the nation's principals were women in 2020–2021—this trend persists there, as well (Women in Academia, 2023). When it comes to the principalship, women are more likely to lead private schools, lower-income public schools, and city schools. They are also significantly more likely to lead elementary schools than they are high schools. In public schools, only 35.5% of high school principals are women (Women in Academia, 2023). To be clear, this book is not only for those leaders whose names are listed at the top of their school or district organizational charts. Teacher leaders, department chairs, principals, assistant principals, curriculum coordinators, support staff, home-school coordinators, and all who are working within our schools to bring about positive change are critical leaders in this field. That said, as we explore school leadership and seek to improve our own practices, we must also study the historical and social conditions that continue to impact our schools and school structures as well as the ways power and privilege intersect with change, leadership, and systems.

Mizzou Academy

During my autoethnographic process I served in two school administrator roles. First, I served as the Director of Academic Affairs and Engagement where I oversaw teaching and learning and served as the principal of our middle and high school. Next, I moved into the Executive Director position of our school system, where I continue to oversee all departments including Business, Development, Academics, Technology, and Support Services. These roles were both situated in Mizzou Academy, an online and blended school system housed in the University of Missouri's College of Education and Human Development. Mizzou Academy serves students from all 50 states in the United States and 60+ countries around the world. During my time in this role, we also opened our elementary school and a second middle school program.

At the onset of the COVID-19 pandemic in 2019, our team was uniquely situated to offer online educational support to local and international schools. This book addresses some of the lessons my team and I learned during this period in our global history. It also invites school leaders to make space to process their own experiences during this difficult and innovative time in schools. The work our school does around online and blended learning has continued to hold relevance since the pandemic. A 2023 report by the University of San Diego offers three persistent post-COVID trends in K-12 education:

1. Using online learning to students' advantage.
2. Strategically adopting educational technology in schools for in-person instruction.
3. Making accommodations for neurodiversity.

(School of Leadership and Education Sciences, 2023)

This book addresses each of these trends and offers strategies for school leaders to adapt and iterate toward each of these important realities in K-12 education.

During my tenure with Mizzou Academy, we experienced rapid international enrollment growth. We also developed new elementary and middle school programs, launched our co-teach programs which offer blended programming to partner schools, and increased partnerships and support with local public schools. Our student population is culturally, linguistically, and geographically diverse. The experiences and insights I have gained working in this context are relevant to diversity, equity, and inclusion (DEI) initiatives across schools and districts. "Research suggests that efforts to expand school racial and socioeconomic diversity can yield positive outcomes for students from all backgrounds," asserts a 2023 report by the US Department of Education (Cardona & Rodríguez, 2023, p. 2). "School diversity is associated with increased social mobility, civic engagement, academic success, empathy, and understanding" (p. 2). Many of the stories draw on the lessons I learned traveling and working across geographical borders.

Just as you will read more about my development as a school leader, you will also notice the ways my relationship to specific places has changed over time. For example, I have spent several months working in-country with students and teachers in Brazil. Along the way, many of the schools I work with in South America have shifted from being places I visit to communities I know well. Critical moral geography (see Aitken, 2001) is a theoretical framework that addresses the political and ideological constructions of place and space. This concept has important implications for my work in global and online education, where place can be distributed, blended, and virtual. My unique experiences in school leadership have given me interesting material to consider what it means to think of school as a place. In writing on this topic, David Smith (2007) asserts that, "Places are created by human action and motivated by moral values, but their material expression cannot itself have normative standing. The function of a place constructed for a particular purpose can change with societal context" (p. 9). I shared in the introduction that this book is set in a unique global moment in education. As we work together through these stories and exercises we'll return to the idea of place, space, morality, and ethics in schools. And we'll do so through the context of both my own school experiences and yours.

Wholehearted Leadership Framework

It has been a decade since that first awkward meeting looking at a large mahogany desk. As I reflect on the lessons I learned in my early years in school leadership, I am struck by how much our teams have accomplished, how much the field has changed, and how the most important things in school leadership will always be constant. These experiences and lessons contributed to my emerging framework on *Wholehearted Leadership*. The Wholehearted Leadership Framework highlights the conditions needed to cultivate courage, justice, learning, and connection in our schools and leadership practices.

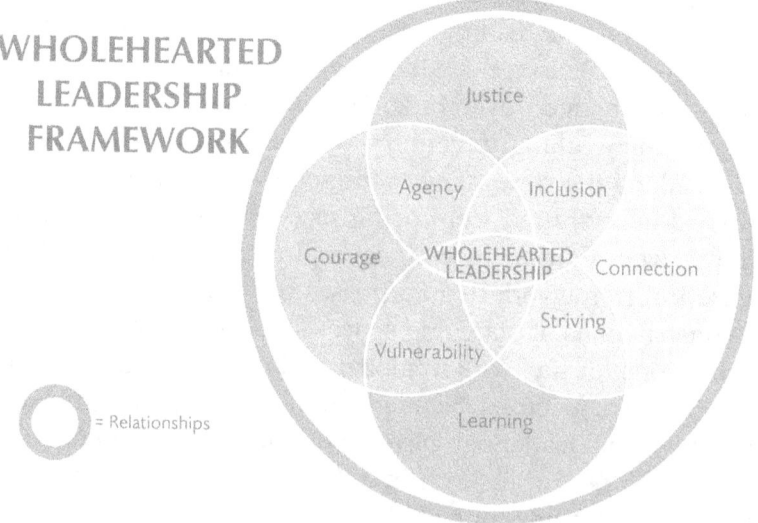

Our most important leadership work often happens within and between the ways these themes interact with each other. For example:

- ♦ Courage + Justice = Agency
- ♦ Justice + Connection = Inclusion

- Connection + Learning = Striving
- Learning + Courage = Vulnerability
- Relationships × (Courage + Connection + Learning + Justice) = Wholehearted Leadership

> ### 📖 Key Vocabulary
>
> - **Agency:** The power (and control) you have to think for yourself, make independent choices, and act in ways that enact change, shape your experiences, and help you fulfill your potential.
> - **Courage:** A willingness to act on your beliefs even when you are unsure of the outcome or that outcome might be personally difficult. This work is often characterized by strength of heart.
> - **Vulnerability:** From the Latin word for "wound," the state of being open to judgment, discomfort, or pain. It is rooted in authenticity and disclosure and essential for connection.
> - **Inclusion:** A commitment to access, belonging, welcome, full participation, and representation for all people within your school and broader communities. Inclusion is grounded in action, intentionality, and respect for the diverse lived experiences and identities of every member of your community.
> - **Learning:** To successfully stretch toward a new skill, goal, desired result, or specific objective. Learning is often the product of effort, skill, and courage.
> - **Striving:** Pursuing work that is both personally and intellectually fulfilling and challenging. In my school, we also refer to this as stretching. Striving is work that combines care and knowledge of self with goals and achievement. This flow state often leads to creativity, innovation, and courage.
> - **Connection:** To bring in close (proximity) and provide access through care, empathy, equity, and/or technology. Connection requires intentional learning about the unique and specific affective and academic needs of your school community. It also requires an understanding that these needs and the tools we may use to bring others into

> conversation change over time. Connection is grounded in communication and learning.
> - **Wellness:** The regular and intentional practice of developing and prioritizing practices that support mental, physical, and spiritual health. Wellness is sometimes characterized as moving beyond surviving to thriving.
> - **Wholehearted Leadership:** A values-based framework for cultivating the conditions needed to lead for courage, justice, learning, and connection in our schools.

How to Use This Book

The narrative structure of this book is designed to keep pace with the whirlwind of school leadership. This is a text you can pick up and put down as student, faculty, and community needs emerge. It is also a professional learning book that can carry you and your leadership team through the school year. Part 1: Leading for Courage and Justice, and Part 2: Leading for Learning and Connection fit nicely into semester studies. The four distinct sections (courage, justice, learning, and connection) can be leadership themes for each quarter of the school year.

Each chapter can be used as a unique leadership team meeting theme. Depending on the length of your meetings, you could have your team read the chapter content in advance of your meeting and then work through the reflective exercises together. Alternatively, you can work through the full chapter content together. The chapters utilize a consistent structure:

- The chapters open with a story from my own practice.
- Next, I connect that story to strategies and research for your practice.
- Finally, I close with reflective exercises for you and your leadership team.

In this way, every chapter is actionable for your own context.

By the end of this book, you and your team will have direction and strategies to move forward thoughtfully *with the important work of rewiring our schools for greater courage, justice, learning, and connection.*

I close each chapter with reflective exercises. This reflective work matters. "Human beings are not built in silence," writes Paulo Freire, "but in word, in work, in action-reflection" (1970). Reflection is one of the drivers that moves us from reading a text to changing or implementing a practice. In our book on connected classrooms (2022), my colleague, Stephanie Walter, and I described it as the power of the pause. "In this space, [you can] take a deep breath, and think through what you are accomplishing, and how it aligns with your set intentions and goals. That, in turn allows [you] to move forward thoughtfully" (Fishman-Weaver & Walter, 2022, p. 9). By the end of this book, you and your team will have direction and strategies to *move forward thoughtfully* with the important work of rewiring our schools for greater courage, justice, learning, and connection.

Inviting Your School Community to This Conversation: Reproducibles

To help build common language, consistent framing, and wholehearted learning goals, this book includes a number of reproducibles available as free downloadables at Routledge. These ten reproducibles include four overviews and six concept studies. These are intended for collaborative professional learning with your teams. Without requiring a full book study, these materials give you a way to share your learning with your broader staff.

Overviews

The overviews outline key concepts, introduce essential vocabulary, and offer reflective questions for dialogue. The questions and definitions can be used to further collaborative reflection and learning at your all-team meetings. The overviews are built on the four key components of this text.

- Lead for *Courage* (pgs. 24–26)
- Lead for *Justice* (pgs. 64–66)
- Lead for *Learning* (pgs. 146–147)
- Lead for *Connection* (pgs. 200–202)

Concept Studies

Much like the narrative chapters, the concept studies begin with a vignette that moves toward practice and reflection. These are not case studies per say, meaning that it is not the specific case or story that drives the learning. Instead the stories are intended as a vehicle to explore concepts from the Wholehearted Leadership Framework. Mental health, and student and staff support are themes that run throughout these six concept studies. These paramount concepts from the Wholehearted Leadership Framework require community learning to implement. Therefore, these concept studies invite your teams to consider how their commitments can work for courage, justice, learning, and connection. Below are the six concept studies:

- Lessons from Our First Classrooms (pgs. 38–39)
- What Is an Upstander? (pgs. 119–123)
- Trauma-Informed School Leadership (pgs. 67–73)
- Strengths-Based Perspectives in a Digital World (pgs. 176–178)
- Youth Participatory Action Research (YPAR) (pgs. 203–205)
- The Cognitive Triangle as a Support Tool (pgs. 253–256)

These reproducibles offer a great learning tool to shape an all-team or PLC meeting. It is possible in sharing these reproducibles that more members of your community will want to join your administrative and leadership team in a fuller exploration of the whole book.

Note

1 The stories from these two paragraphs were adapted from a 2017 essay I wrote for the National Association for Secondary School Principals (NASP) (Fishman-Weaver, 2017).

References

Adams, T. E., & Manning, J. (2015). Autoethnography and family research. *Journal of Family Theory & Review, 7*(4), 350–366.

Aitken, S. C. (2001). *Geographies of young people: The morally contested spaces of identity*. Routledge.

Bochner, A. P., & Ellis, C. S. (2006). Communication as autoethnography. In G. J. Shepherd, J. St. John, & T. Striphas (Eds.), *Communication as… perspectives on theory* (pp. 110–122). SAGE.

Cardona, M. A., & Rodríguez, R. J. (2023). *The state of school diversity in the United States*. www2.ed.gov/rschstat/eval/resources/diversity.pdf

Fishman-Weaver, K. (2017, August 9). *September 2016 viewpoint*. NASSP. www.nassp.org/publication/principal-leadership/volume-17-2016-2017/principal-leadership-september-2016/september-2016-viewpoint/

Fishman-Weaver, K. (2018). *Wholehearted teaching of gifted young women: Cultivating courage, connection, and self-care in schools*. Routledge.

Fishman-Weaver, K., & Walter, S. (2022). *Connected classrooms: A people-centered approach for online, blended, and in-person learning*. Solution Tree Press.

Freire, P. (1970). Chapter 3. In *Pedagogy of the Oppressed*. The Seabury Press.

Garn, G., & Brown, C. (2008). Women and the superintendency: Perceptions of gender bias. *Journal of Women in Educational Leadership, 6*(1). http://digitalcommons.unl.edu/jwel/62

Gresham, G., & Sampson, P. (2019). Women superintendent research: 2014–2016 dissertation literature review content analysis. *Athens Journal of Education, 6*(4), 257–270.

Poulos, C. N. (2021). *Essentials of autoethnography*. American Psychological Association.

School of Leadership and Educational Sciences. (2023). Emerging trends in education in a post-Covid era. solesstories.sandiego.edu/degree-of-difference/emerging-trends-in-education-in-a-post-covid-era.

Smith, D. M. (2007). Moral aspects of place. *Planning Theory, 6*(1), 7–15.

Stiepleman, P. L. (2023). *An imperfect leader: Human-centered leadership in (after) action.* Rowman & Littlefield.

US Department of Education. (n.d.). *Free appropriate public education under Section 504.* www2.ed.gov/about/offices/list/ocr/docs/edlite-FAPE504.html#:~:text=FAPE%20Provisions%20in%20the%20Individuals,ranges%20residing%20in%20the%20state

Women in Academia. (2023, December 28). *The status of women as school principals in the United States.* www.wiareport.com/2023/01/the-status-of-women-as-school-principals-in-the-united-states/

Part 1

Leading for Courage and Justice

Student and teacher leadership is one of the most powerful and important forces in transforming our schools and communities. School leaders play a vital role in cultivating and safeguarding a culture where these community voices and ideas are valued.

During my career, I have taught and led in a variety of public school classrooms and programs including a multigrade program for elementary students with disabilities, secondary math and finance classrooms, and all levels of high school language arts. Across these positions I engaged in action research and community-based pedagogies. Engaging in sense-making and public literacies with my students shaped many of my later practices as a school leader.

> *Student and teacher leadership is one of the most powerful and important forces in transforming our schools and communities. School leaders play a vital role in cultivating and safeguarding a culture where these community voices and ideas are valued.*

Before taking the academic director position, I served as the chair of an equal opportunity gifted education program. While working in this role, I led a longitudinal study (from 2009 to 2015) with my students that explored the tenuous transition from high school to college, a period we affectionately called "the precipice." In this original wholehearted teaching study, a group of high school seniors described the interdependence between courage, vulnerability, and connection as such:

> It takes courage to be vulnerable enough to empathize with others. One must be open and transparent because that is the only way... [to] develop meaningful relationships with others. Being honest and truthful is the only way to build trust. But, we will be the first to admit that it is difficult at times to be honest. Certainly, telling others your secrets and sensitive information is hard, but we think the real challenge is being frank and honest with yourself... The first step then, is to tell ourselves the truth, and that takes strength and vulnerability because sometimes the truth is not what you want to hear. Overall, though, we think that vulnerability is the basis of empathy and that the outcome of being vulnerable and raw is that others will connect with you... Oftentimes, people are very guarded, and it is hard to tell if you actually mean something to them and if they are being truthful with you. Thus, we believe that everyone should practice being vulnerable. If we all did that, the world would be a much more understanding place.
>
> (Fishman-Weaver, 2018, pp. 49–50)

As high school students, the group quoted above taught me important lessons about teaching and leadership. These students have gone on and applied these concepts to their own lives and fields of study. Today, some are practicing medicine and law. Others are working in the sciences, the arts, and a few are working in education.

Since that study, we have all navigated many precipices: a new school year, a new curriculum, a new global moment. As school leaders, sometimes we know the precipice is coming; it looms in the near distant future and is marked on the calendar. Other times, the precipice gives no forewarning. We walk into what we thought was an ordinary leadership team meeting, we answer a phone call from a stakeholder, something unexpected happens in our community, and afterward, everything is a little different. How do we find our way forward? In this book, I argue that courage, justice, connection, and learning are an important compass for navigating our next moves.

In this first section, we explore what it means to lead for courage and justice, acts that are often rooted in student and community leadership. For me, these chapters build on the belief that wisdom is ubiquitous, and they continue some of the conversations my students started all those years ago.

******

As I work with school leaders around the world, it is clear that the classrooms we are building look different from the classrooms we learned in ourselves. These spaces are more technologically mediated, global, and connected and yet the heart of these spaces and our best practices is still relationships. What does effective school leadership look like in this moment? How can we couple agency with vulnerability as we rewire our schools for courage and justice? What processes should we use to make sound daily decisions in these layered spaces? This section explores how we can use courage and justice as a pathway forward.

Social work researcher and international author Brené Brown (2008) reminds us that courage is "a heart word." Leading with courage asks that we stretch beyond what is easy to see and hear; that we approach our classrooms, our districts, and each other with compassion and resilience. Navigating the barrage of questions that come your way as a school leader requires a clear moral compass and the courage to follow it toward justice. Justice is action that makes right or whole; it leads to fairness, equity, and humanity. In our work on teaching Women's and Gender Studies in the middle and high school classroom, Jill Clingan and I wrote that in its deepest sense, justice is rooted in love and inclusion. (Fishman-Weaver & Clingan, 2022). In the introduction I shared that wholehearted leaders affirm the inherent dignity and humanity of every student and family in their school community. They do so by safeguarding the legal and moral right of all students to receive a free and appropriate public education (US Department of Education, n.d.), that is filled with academic, social, and enrichment opportunities, and marked by belonging and joy.

Leading for justice is grounded in action, morality, and continued learning about the historical and persistent social inequities within our field. This includes understanding the ways students of color, especially African American and Latine students, LGBTQ+ students, students with neurodiversities and disabilities, multilingual students, and under-resourced students have either been denied access to the full opportunities available in their schools or actively segregated from these experiences. These chapters take a forward focus, offering leaders tools and mindsets to replace punitive practices with asset-based approaches. They focus on responsive services, restorative justice, and practices that commit to inclusion, high expectations, and psychological safety.

> **Restorative Justice**
>
> With roots in Indigenous peacekeeping traditions (Marsh, 2020), *restorative justice* is a philosophical framework that seeks to strengthen relationships, address issues of justice and equity, and repair harm (Reimer & Parker-Shandal, 2023). Restorative justice offers an alternative to punitive and exclusionary discipline practices. However, it isn't just a discipline framework, it is a paradigm shift in how school leaders build school climate and inclusive practices. Restorative practices include naming emotions (affective statements), affirming emotions, and thinking critically about emotional responses (affective questions); in-the-moment meetings to foster awareness, connection, and responsibility (impromptu conferences); purposeful conversations to process, plan, and heal together in circles (groups or circles); and formal meetings to respond to specific actions/behaviors and plan next steps (formal conferences) (Starzecki, n.d.).
>
> In a 2020 policy brief for the National Education Policy Institute, Anne Gregory and Katherine Evans write that

restorative justice has the potential to shift school culture and "prioritize relational pedagogies" (p. 3). They go on to say that:

> Responsive Restorative Justice in Education (RJE) practices build accountability, promote social-emotional growth, and support positive behaviors in schools. *However, if an RJE effort does not also address the need for preventative practices to transform school climate, the singular emphasis on behavior management may distort the initiative and preclude the opportunity to promote interconnectedness and well-being.*
>
> (p. 9, my emphasis)

To date, restorative justice has shown promise in reducing suspensions and beginning to narrow some of the racialized disparities in discipline practices in schools. However, to truly transform school climate, produce systematic change, and advance holistic justice practices, school leaders must critically explore the ways policy and practice contribute to both specific and generalized patterns of inclusion/exclusion and opportunity/barriers. This begins with some hard questions about how we lead, teach, and relate to and with one another.

One of my mentors, Dr. Mary Laffey, is a retired assistant superintendent and a leader in her Catholic faith. She has spent several decades working in public schools as a teacher, principal, and district leader. One afternoon we met over sandwiches. I was worried about a vulnerable student in our school system and asked if she would brainstorm wraparound support with me. As always, she said yes, right away. We talked about support plans, community-based partnerships, and care. Yet, I continued to feel worried for my student and his family. They were navigating trauma, separation, and difficulties that I couldn't even imagine. Of course, this was affecting his school work and behavior. While Dr. Laffey helped me put together a more robust action plan, I knew it wouldn't be enough to alleviate all the challenges and pain he was going through.

I put down my sandwich. "Could I ask you a personal question?"

Dr. Laffey nodded.

"Do you pray for your students?"

"Of course, everyday. You might not tell them, but many of the ways you send care are between you and God. These can happen in the quiet of your heart."

My own family's faith traditions have taught me that oftentimes prayer is action. How we show up for each other, particularly in the most uncertain and difficult moments, is a form of prayer. It makes sense that this, too, is a kind of courage. And, as Dr. Laffey knows, it is rooted in a resolve that grows from the quiet of your heart. Anais Nin, the French-American essayist, famously wrote that "Life shrinks or expands in proportion to one's courage." The same is true of teaching and school leadership. Our capacity to enact change, to make a difference, and to rewire our schools shrinks or expands in proportion to our courage.

The earliest references to the word courage come from 12th century Old French (*corage*) meaning heart or our innermost feelings. In Latin the root is *cor* or simply heart. As the word evolved through Old and Middle English, it took on layers of bravery and boldness (Etymonline, n.d.). I think of Dr. Laffey and all the school leaders working boldly on behalf of their students, advocating relentlessly for the best interests of young people. This difficult work is followed by quiet moments when you close your door and sometimes bow your head at the face of our tremendous task and its inherent uncertainty.

Without fail, a moment later there is a knock on that same door. Sometimes it is a student in tears, sometimes it is a distressed teacher, sometimes it is a frustrated parent. These members of our school communities arrive with questions they might not yet be ready to fully articulate. Asking for help is an act of courage; so, too, is answering the door to uncertainty. Each time we swing open that door, we have the opportunity to invite someone in with compassion, resilience, and a readiness to move forward together.

References

Brown, B. (2008). *I thought it was just me (but it isn't): Making the journey from "What will people think?" to "I am enough."* Avery.

Etymonline. (n.d.). *courage | Etymology of courage by etymonline.* www.etymonline.com/word/courage#:~:text=1300%2C%20corage%2C%20%22heart%20(,kerd%2D%20%22heart%22).

Fishman-Weaver, K. (2018). *Wholehearted teaching of gifted young women: Cultivating courage, connection, and self-care in schools.* Routledge.

Fishman-Weaver, K., & Clingan, J. (2022). *Teaching women's and gender studies: Classroom resources on resistance, representation, and radical hope (Grades 9–12).* Taylor & Francis.

Gregory, A., Evans, K. R., & National Education Policy Center (NEPC). (2020). *The starts and stumbles of restorative justice in education: Where do we go from here?* National Education Policy Center. https://files.eric.ed.gov/fulltext/ED605800.pdf

Marsh, C. (2020, December 15). *Honoring the global Indigenous roots of restorative justice: Potential restorative approaches for child welfare.* Center for the Study of Social Policy. https://cssp.org/2019/11/honoring-the-global-indigenous-roots-of-restorative-justice/

Reimer, K., & Parker-Shandal, C. (2023, February 22). Restorative Justice in Education. In *Oxford research encyclopaedia of education.* https://oxfordre.com/education/view/10.1093/acrefore/9780190264093.001.0001/acrefore-9780190264093-e-1828.

US Department of Education. (n.d.). *Free appropriate public education under Section 504.* www2.ed.gov/about/offices/list/ocr/docs/edlite-FAPE504.html#:~:text=FAPE%20Provisions%20in%20the%20Individuals,ranges%20residing%20in%20the%20state

I

Lead for Courage Overview

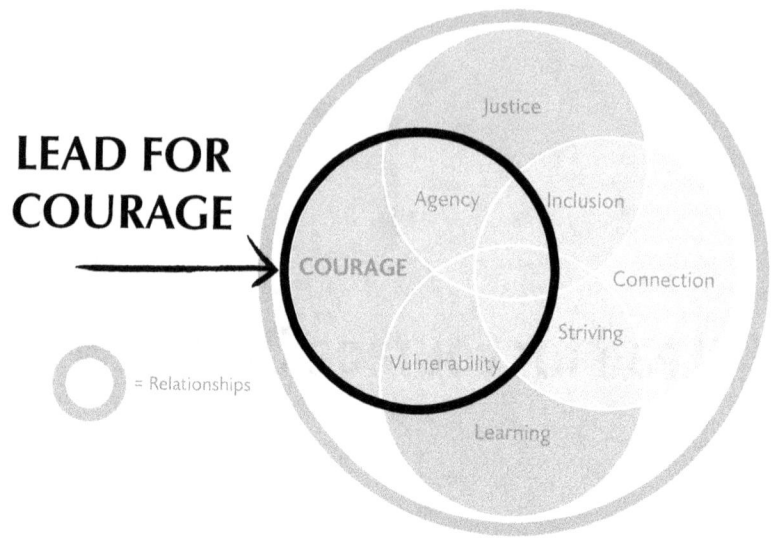

LEAD FOR COURAGE

Wholehearted Leadership Framework Focus Areas—*Agency, Vulnerability, and Relationships*

Tethering Ideas:

- Commit to high expectations.
- Celebrate community wisdom.
- Keep showing up. Keep listening.
- Relationships are the heart of great leadership.
- Cultivate gratitude.

 Key Vocabulary

- **Cultural Reciprocity:** A mutual appreciation and respect for differing cultural traditions, ways of knowing, and practices. This work begins in understanding your own cultural identities and traditions and then seeking to grow in understanding and respect of identities and traditions that are different from your own. With an emphasis on

working together, cultural reciprocity builds active engagement, collaborative approaches, and respectful knowledge sharing.
- **Brave Space:** In brave spaces, community members commit to inclusivity and dialogue. In these co-created learning environments, leaders support members in taking healthy risks, including emotional risks. Here students and staff have the agency to make their own decisions about participation, challenge, and disclosure (Ali & NASPA, 2017; Arao & Clemens, 2023).
- **Empathy:** An ability and willingness to understand the feelings of another person.
  - **Cognitive Empathy:** Perspective taking, using logic and knowledge to understand another's emotions.
  - **Affective Empathy:** Attending, responding to, and absorbing the underlying conditions and feelings of another.

Lead for Courage Guiding Questions

1. Who are your student, teacher, and staff exemplars at leading for courage? What can you learn from them?
2. How can you lean into *strong vulnerability* to better support your school communities?
3. What does it look like to honor student, teacher, and staff agency? How can you find more ways to *say yes* to the great ideas these community members bring to you?
4. What are the lessons you have carried forward from your early experiences in the classroom?
5. What does it look like to teach and lead as though *all children are our children*?
6. How can you center relationships and connection in your leadership practice?
7. What gratitude practices will you implement in your school communities?

8. What positive practices are currently taking root in your school communities and how can you nurture this growth?
9. How do your personal and professional learning goals align with the needs of your school community?
10. As a school leader, what does cultural reciprocity mean to you?

References

Ali, D., & National Association of Student Personnel Administrators (NASPA). (2017). Safe spaces and brave spaces. In *NASPA Policy and Practice Series*. www.naspa.org/files/dmfile/Policy_and _Practice_No_2_Safe_Brave_Spaces.pdf

Arao, B., & Clemens, K. (2023). From safe spaces to brave spaces. In L. Landerman (Ed.), *The art of effective facilitation: Reflections from social justice educators* (pp. 135–151). Routledge.

1

Commit to High Expectations

Our first group of students often leave a lasting mark on our teaching, leadership, and philosophy of education. This chapter builds on a conversation with an educational leader about our early teaching experiences. These experiences affirmed that all children are our children. This chapter calls on school leaders to teach and lead for the futures they want to see. It also reminds us that teaching and leading with high expectations is an act of love.

> **Key Concept:** All children are our children. Teach and lead for the futures you want to see. This practice reminds us that high expectations are an act of love.

It's been 20 years since I met the first-grade scholars who would become some of my most important teachers. Often it feels like everything important I know in education I learned in that first year.

My first teaching position was to set up a self-contained classroom for early elementary learners with disabilities. Our school was in a multilingual, urban school district. The decisions and mistakes I made that first year taught me about context, culture, and equity. The relationships we built taught me about pedagogy, expectations, and strengths-based approaches. Below are four lessons I learned that first year which continue to inform my work in teaching and school leadership.

Strategies for Practice

1. **High expectations are an act of love.** As a new teacher, I tried to set up a literacy-rich environment with stories representing the lived experiences of my students. I believed that if we read and wrote regularly enough, that together we would become scholars. However, when it came to my student population, I learned that not everyone shared my beliefs about rigorous and relevant curriculum. In that first year, I discovered a prevalence of low, false, and misguided expectations surrounding my students. This shadow hung around us when families told me what specialists, doctors, and others had told them their children could and couldn't do. In that first classroom I learned the power teachers, students, and families have in speaking back to deficit-based frameworks. My students again and again distinguished themselves as scholarly readers, writers, mathematicians, and leaders.
2. **Classroom community is built on love.** Most acts of love don't require advanced scholarship or technical training, and this may be one of the reasons it's something I got right in that first year. We built our classroom community through songs sung, hugs given, stories shared, and lots of laughter. Affirming and celebrating the cultural wisdom young people bring to our school community means centering the possibilities young people have for greatness and genius, not on our terms, but on theirs. Dijano Paris offers important scholarship on *culturally sustaining pedagogies* to honor the multilingual and multicultural pluralism of our schools. This wisdom is essential in offering what he calls a "loving critique forward" (Paris & Alim, 2014).
3. **Be relentless in pursuing equity and inclusion.** Like many self-contained classrooms, our classroom was a reclaimed corner of the building—a space that wasn't intended to be a classroom but became one. Almost immediately, it became

clear that if I wasn't relentless in pursuing inclusion, my students would not interact with their general education peers. To disrupt the separate education of my students with disabilities, I knocked on doors, made phone calls, asked, begged, and partnered with anyone who would listen. We launched science and art expeditions with the general education K-1 team, and math partnerships with our sixth grade student leaders. We were the first self-contained class in our district to adopt a new rigorous math program, we hosted a service dog in training, we launched a wiffle ball league, and we filmed a documentary on caring. I am sure I also said yes to initiatives that flopped, but as I think back I'm struck by how often saying "yes" or saying "us, too" led to projects that mattered. Teaching is advocacy.

4. **Relationships are the heart of great teaching.** In the whirlwind of school, relationships tether us to each other and to our purpose. In that first year, I celebrated birthdays, shared meals, visited homes, got to know siblings, parents, and grandparents, played in the teacher–student basketball game, laughed, cried, and grew with an exceptional group of young people.

As a first-year teacher, I was a livewire of energy—rapidly alternating between trepidation and optimism. In fact, I can still feel the racing in my pulse as I remember what it felt like to navigate that year. On many of my best days as a school leader, my mind flutters back to that sunny corner of a school building and the 13 seven-year-olds who ignited in me a current of hope, heart, and high expectations.

Reflective Work for Continuous Learning

My own work learning with students and leaders from the disability community has led to incredible opportunities I could have never imagined in that first year. For example, I had the opportunity to facilitate a multi-day conference on inclusion and neurodiversity for a school in India. I authored a course series on inclusive practices for children with disabilities for our state department of education. Most importantly, though, I have made countless friendships with students, staff, and families who bring different talents, abilities, and experiences to our school communities. I am a better educator, leader, and human being for the lessons I have learned through these relationships.

The following reflective questions and exercises shine light on the lessons you learned in your early years in the classroom. I encourage you to work on these questions both individually and in dialogue with your teams.

1. **Assess new teacher needs.** Teacher support and retention are important indicators of wholehearted leadership.
    - How are the new teachers in your building or district doing?
        - What data will you draw on to answer this question? What data is missing? How can you better connect with this group?
    - What do you wish a school leader would have done to support you in your first couple of years in the classroom?
2. **Support teacher mentorship.** Who is particularly skilled at mentoring new teachers in your building or district?
    - Take a moment to write them a thank you note today. This work matters.
    - How can you create more space for them to engage in this important work?

References

Paris, D., & Alim, H. S. (2014). What are we seeking to sustain through culturally sustaining pedagogy? A loving critique forward. *Harvard Educational Review, 84*(1), 85–100.

2

Celebrate Community Wisdom

The most important ideas for our school communities often come directly from our school communities. As I finished my first year as a school principal, I had an important conversation with a member of our support staff. That conversation inspired the opening to this chapter, the importance of leveraging community wisdom and expertise, and my leadership "protocol to yes."

> **Key Concept:** Leverage community wisdom and expertise. The most important ideas for our school communities often come directly from our school communities.

The band has packed up their instruments. The leftover cake is boxed for us to bring back and share at school. The happy graduates and their proud families are on their way home. This auditorium which, just an hour ago, was bustling with noise, energy, and the endless clicks of cameras, is now quiet. I am sitting with our registrar, Jean Zenner, snacking on leftover dinner mints and catching my breath.

There is reflective electricity in the air, and Jean seizes the moment to both check-in and share some feedback. She starts by asking me about my first year in the principalship. After a few musings, she pauses and then says, "Could I share something with you?"

Jean often brings me new perspectives about how our staff and students are feeling.

"Of course."

"We've all noticed that you say yes a whole lot more than the last principal. I wonder if that is something you want to address."

I smile, my eyes crinkling at her observation. "Yes."

We laugh.

Jean wanted me to feel empowered not to say yes so often. However, I assured her that I was both intentional and comfortable with saying yes. Here are some things I had said yes to recently:

- Teacher: Can I bring my son to our faculty meeting?
- Student: Can we launch a class project to address food insecurity in our city?
- Teacher: Can I start a new science club?
- Student: Can I make a video instead of writing an essay?
- Teacher: Can we change the final exam from objective-based questions to a performance-based speech?
- Student: Can I have a do-over?
- Teacher: Do you have five minutes?

There is a deeper philosophy around saying yes. This philosophy puts trust in people, acknowledges that all experiences are valid, and gives the benefit of the doubt. It is also rooted in shared leadership and acknowledges that sometimes the best way forward is through listening to a new approach. Shared leadership is a partnership (Hughes & Pickeral, 2013). It requires a balance of power and a belief in communities. Shared leadership opens up decision-making power by recognizing that all members of the school community have important ideas to offer, questions to ask, and perspectives that can move our school communities closer to our mission and values. Shared leadership also recognizes that all members of the school community matter in their own right. We each come to school with our unique lived experiences and needs. Creating wholehearted school communities means seeing each member of our school communities as an individual.

In his work on school leadership and organizational change, Ramazan Atasoy (2020) writes that the most effective principals "pay attention to each individual's needs and take heed of actions related to moral values and beliefs. They often point out cooperation, collective task achievement, sharing experiences, control and freedom in decision-making and delegation of authority" (pp. 257–258).

There are a few times when policy, budget, or other circumstances mean I have to say no, but it's not an answer I give lightly. On my best days, when I say no, I go back to the *protocol to yes* questions (listed on pg. 36) and look for other ways to affirm our people. In all of this, I recognize that there is a bigger picture to saying yes. The underpinning of many questions we ask our leaders is: *Am I valued?* Using different words, teachers and students ask me this every day, and on that I am committed to a resounding yes.

Wholehearted leaders believe in their teams and know that their leadership can influence school culture. They strive to foster a culture of belonging and a vision for achievement. Leading with courage leverages community expertise and wisdom in ways that can transform schools. This begins with active listening and asking teachers, students, and staff for their ideas. Lao Tzu, an ancient Chinese philosopher, said that: "A leader is best when people barely know he exists, when his work is done, his aim fulfilled, they will say: we did it ourselves." By using kindness, listening, and logic to achieve common goals, a philosophy of saying yes to community genius can produce dramatic positive results for schools.[1]

Strategies for Practice

As leaders, we have a responsibility to role model the practices we want to see. This means not asking members of our team to do a task we aren't personally willing to do. Whether it's picking up trash on the soccer field, admitting to a mistake, or leading a Saturday study session, if we want to see it, we need to be willing to put in the work. At the same time, this doesn't mean having all the answers. Just as we teach students, one of our most important skills is knowing how to find the answers. In leadership, the best answers often come from our teams and our communities. Saying yes to the genius within your school community can lead to new strategies, solutions, and approaches. I have found that often these new ideas are smarter and more effective than my original ideas. Saying yes can lead to people getting what they need to more effectively learn or teach. Finally, hearing yes is affirming and affirmation builds confidence, camaraderie, engagement, and success. Below are two specific strategies for leveraging community wisdom.[2]

1. **Remember, team projects aren't about you.** As school leaders, our focus is on students and those who support them. This means projects aren't about us at all. As you put together project teams, try to take your own feelings and pride out of the project. Instead focus on the goal and its impact. Team projects experience the most success when everyone is working toward a common goal or vision. Be generous in giving others credit for a job well done.
2. **Be transparent about your learning.** It can feel vulnerable to admit that you have made a mistake or need help. Sometimes leaders worry that doing so will make them seem less competent. However, it turns out our teams often recognize this honesty as a critical component of competence. Being transparent builds trust. I can recall several examples when school and district leaders humbled themselves to ask for help or share transparently about a mistake they had made. When done with sincerity, this not only increased my respect for them, but also created the capacity to course correct and implement better solutions.

As school leaders, we want to cultivate brave spaces. In these spaces, learning and creativity can flourish. A precondition for a brave space is the safety to take healthy risks, make mistakes, and try again. Great leaders work with great teams. Be forthcoming when someone on your team has a talent or perspective you can learn from. Share openly about what you are learning and when you need help.

💡✏️ Reflective Work for Continuous Learning

Saying yes relates to one of my fundamental beliefs in education—that wisdom is ubiquitous. Saying yes signals, *I hear and value you, your ideas are important, and* you *are important.* In their 2013 report for the National School Climate Center, William Hughes and Terry Pickeral wrote "Successful schools require the substantial engagement of those who make it a community." This includes students, families, teachers, and staff.

> *Saying yes relates to one of my fundamental beliefs in education—that wisdom is ubiquitous. Saying yes signals,* I hear and value you, your ideas are important, and *you* are important.

In my first teaching job, our school's head custodian launched an important mentoring program for boys. This program gave the young men who participated invaluable opportunities in service and leadership. The more time I've spent in schools, the more I know that our support staff are often our most inspiring role models for community-based leadership. Our principal said yes to his idea to launch a mentorship and leadership program for boys and young men in our school. I saw firsthand how this initiative made a profound difference for participants.

In 2021, a group of Grade 8 students at the school I lead wanted to do something meaningful to support the unhoused population in their São Paulo community. They conducted independent research and learned that socks were one of the key needs of the housing-insecure population. Socks were repeatedly listed as a priority item at homeless shelters and agencies in their local community. Their school coordinator said yes to the idea. The project had a ripple effect in the central United States where our faculty and staff were inspired to launch a sister drive. Over the next two months our student, faculty, and staff groups collected over 600 pairs of socks which were delivered to people navigating housing insecurity in both Missouri and São Paulo.

Below are some reflective questions and exercises to consider ways to honor the genius in your school communities.

1. **Set a protocol to yes.** As a leader, what values, beliefs, and practices do you consistently want to affirm? Below is a protocol I use to help me get to yes more often. After reviewing my list, author your own set of questions.
   - Do I trust our students and teachers?
   - Do I believe that all experiences are valid?
   - Can I give the benefit of the doubt?
   - Am I committed to making time for people?
   - Is this consistent with our values of courage, learning, justice, and connection?
   - Am I willing to try a new approach?
2. **Increase agency.** How can you give students, staff, and teachers more agency in your school or district?
   - What are the barriers? Are these barriers addressed in your protocol to yes?
   - What are the possibilities? Are the possibilities worth the risks?
   - Why is agency important for teachers and staff? How can you give your teams more agency in your school or district?
     - What are the barriers? Are these barriers addressed in your protocol to yes?
     - What are the possibilities? Are the possibilities worth the risks?
3. **Connect with experts who lead with heart.** Who are the students, teachers, and staff who are already exemplars at leading with heart?
   - How do you know they are experts?
   - What can you learn from them?
   - Who is missing from your list and how can you better connect with that group and their great ideas?

Notes

1 I first shared these opening stories in a 2016 blog post on LinkedIn titled "The Most Important Word in School Leadership."
2 These strategies are adapted from a 2018 article I wrote for *Edutopia* on community-based leadership.

References

Atasoy, R. (2020). The relationship between school principals' leadership styles, school culture and organizational change. *International Journal of Progressive Education, 16*(5), 256–274.

Fishman-Weaver, K. (2018, November 8). Practicing community-based leadership. *Edutopia.* www.edutopia.org/article/practicing-community-based-leadership

Hughes, W. H., & Pickeral, T. (2013). School climate and shared leadership. In T. Dary & T. Pickeral (Eds.), *School climate: Practices for implementation and sustainability.* A School Climate Practice Brief, Number 1. National School Climate Center.

Concept Study: Lessons from Our First Classrooms

There are several students who were powerful teachers to me in my first years in the classroom. When making decisions about courage and inclusion, Luiza and Maya are two students whose stories still serve as an important guiding light for me.

When I first met Luiza in the early 2000s, she was seven years old. She took me by the hand, beamed *Hola Maestra*, and walked me down the hall of our public K-8 school. Luiza helped lead the way for greater mainstreaming initiatives in our K-1 programs. She did so by being exactly who she is. Luiza was the first student with complex disabilities that many of our general education teachers had taught in their classrooms. Because of her kindness, teachers loved when Luiza was mainstreamed in their classes. They often told me that when Luiza was present, the whole class grew in kindness and friendship. Her example made our school community more inclusive and more open to mainstreaming.

Maya, a six-year-old and newcomer to the United States, was already learning English as a third language when she joined my classroom. Despite her young age, she was the family's primary translator. They had recently moved to a predominantly Spanish-speaking community and she would translate between her mother's native Indigenous language to Spanish with neighbors and community organizations and then to English as she and her family navigated school and health care. When I think about the incredible strengths our multilingual students bring to our schools, Maya is often still one of the student leaders I remember.

Questions for Consideration

1. Which students were your most important teachers in your first two years in the classroom? What did they teach you and how can you use those lessons today?
2. Write your top five list of lessons learned from your early years in the classroom. If you were to share this list with your team, would these lessons surprise them or align with your decisions and actions today?

3

Keep Showing Up. Keep Listening.

How can school leaders use love and dialogue to co-create solutions in uncertain times? This chapter, situated in the COVID-19 context, builds on lessons I have learned about connection, worldview, and active listening. In a culture where leaders often feel pressure to have all the answers, listening to learn can be an exercise in vulnerability. So too, can showing up authentically. As you lean in to vulnerability, you give your team permission to do the same.

> **Key Concept:** In uncertain times, keep showing up with love, listening, and dialogue.

It was February 2020, and I was in a first grade classroom in Santos, SP, a coastal city in the southeast part of Brazil. A group of six-year-olds and I sat in small plastic chairs, working on a Carnival-themed identity project. At the close of the lesson, the children wrapped their arms around each other, donning the brightly colored masks we had just decorated, and sang a song to the tune "If You're Happy and You Know It." That evening as we walked out of school, the international program coordinator shared with me that a cruise ship had been docked all week "because of a flu."

*****

Five weeks later, school buildings around the world closed. In response to COVID-19, the field of education transitioned to online, distance, and crisis teaching. What happened next is a collective global story of previously unimaginable proportions. At home in the United States, my team and I started working with our local public schools on online solutions for the fall. In partnership with our local school district, we helped open the largest elementary school in the state of Missouri. Three months after the planning began, we opened this new public elementary school with more than 80 teachers and nearly 2,000 students.

Where was this school? What did "classroom" mean during this time? In this new liminal reality, learning happened within and between our students' homes. As I think back to that time, it's hard to believe it happened. The realities of this global moment called on us to reimagine space and place in ways that shifted what we know about where learning happens. One of my mentor teachers, Marilyn Toalson, taught me that if you teach and lead long enough, you will teach through major local and global events. The work you are doing in schools, the students you are with, and the teachers in your community will become part of your historical memory of that time. During COVID, educators engaged in noble work to teach and support students in unprecedented ways. My own memory of that time is punctuated by specific students, school leaders, and family members.

Early on we started negotiating new kinds of dialogue. I remember driving to the central office administrative buildings to zoom in for community dialogues with live Q&A. As a school leader, I wanted to communicate reason, compassion, and planning. I also wanted to be transparent that there were parts of this plane we were building while flying. In her work on leadership, Brené Brown (2024) reminds us that clarity is essential. "Over the past several years," she writes, "my team and I have learned something about clarity and the importance of hard conversations that has changed everything from the way we talk to each other to the way we negotiate with external partners. It's simple but transformative: Clear is kind. Unclear is unkind."

During COVID, I worked with incredibly talented school administrators. We all acknowledged that we would make mistakes. And we did. However, our schools also got a lot right. From delivering lunch, breakfast, hot spots, and library books to kids in their neighborhoods, educators and leaders were relentless in caring for students. Many of those things we got right were born from deep listening. In addition to community dialogues, we also hosted regular listening sessions with teachers.

I remember one particularly challenging session a few months into the school year. The teachers were frustrated, scared, exhausted, and angry, and they let us know. Dr. Susan Deakins, a talented district leader, facilitated this session. Dr. Deakins has a gift for connection. I remember being struck by her capacity to communicate love and reality in stressed times. She validated that teachers were being asked to teach in impossible circumstances and she still communicated high expectations. "We won't get everything right," she told the team, "but we will keep students first in all our decisions." She didn't make pretenses about having all the answers. In fact, I observed that her transparency about what she knew and what she didn't was disarming. She built on the relationships she had established with her teachers over the years and brought everyone into a dialogue about this new school reality that we were co-creating.

Brazilian educational philosopher Paulo Freire (1970) writes that:

> Dialogue cannot exist… in the absence of a profound love for the world and for people. The naming of the world, which is an act of creation and re-creation, is not possible if it is not infused with love. Love is at the same time the foundation of dialogue and dialogue itself.

As we were naming this new reality in education, active listening became our most important lifeline for student and teacher support. Listening was the act of love that helped us all log in for yet another unknown day.

Strategies for Practice

During COVID-19, my school team was instrumental in mitigating educational disruptions for thousands of local students in our public schools and also for international schools across our global learning community. Today, with some distance between that time, I can appreciate some of the lessons we learned, and I can celebrate how we lived, taught, and led though challenges. Today, when I reflect on this time, I can marvel at what students and school leaders were able to accomplish without a guidebook. When we were in the midst of it, though, it was hard to see through the worry. I worried about wraparound services. I worried about access. I worried about the health and safety of my loved ones, including the many students in my care.

One of my core commitments during the pandemic was to keep showing up. *Showing up* looked like answering that teacher's message right away, logging in for a kindergarten read aloud, sitting down with a coordinator to talk through curriculum, celebrating the media center specialist who was out delivering books again. Showing up also meant deep listening. Showing up requires the kind of listening that hears not only what is being said but what is being felt. The tools for this kind of listening include love, dialogue, and strong vulnerability. These are what I observed Dr. Deakins use to guide her team through that tense teacher meeting, as well as the many intense meetings that followed. These same tools can support you and your school communities in uncertain times. Below are four strategies to implement this in practice.

1. **Practice Strong Vulnerability.** Strong vulnerability is a tethering concept in my research on *wholehearted teaching* (Fishman-Weaver, 2018). Through my wholehearted teaching study, we found that although vulnerability is difficult to practice, it is also often the most direct path to greater connection.

   It is inherently difficult to speak truth to power, truth to bullies, truth to self. This difficulty, this vulnerability, is often indicative of change potential. When we take the risk and make the hard but right choice, we often see great rewards, such as stronger connections, safer schools and communities, and more courageous peer groups. When courage becomes part of the classroom culture, courageous acts are contagious.

(Fishman-Weaver, 2018, p. 162)

As you practice vulnerability, you give your team permission to do the same.

During COVID-19, I had to lean into not knowing, even when that was frightening. As you practice vulnerability, you give your team permission to do the same. While this work carries risk, I have found that the response is almost always compassion, connection, and courage. It also helps to remember that you are the author of your own story, and you get to make the choices about what is safe for you to share. The times when I let colleagues into the worries or weights on my heart offer a humanizing invitation for them to do the same. Often the stories that are difficult to share lead to greater connection. In your next team communications, let your colleagues into something true in your heart.

2. **Celebrate collective wisdom.** This chapter included specific lessons I learned from my colleagues—from the way Dr. Deakins led her team, to Marilyn Toalson's reflections on teaching. I am constantly learning from the professionals in our school systems. One of the ways to cultivate a culture of lifelong learning is to be forthcoming in what you are learning, including what you learn from each other. Over the next couple of weeks, pay attention to the concepts, great ideas, and insights of your team. Take note of these and report on them in your team communications. Give credit by name.
3. **Take the lead from our student leaders.** One of my favorite strategies for creating a culture of leadership and care is to celebrate student leadership. The student leaders in my own school system are organizing initiatives to support the housing-insecure population in São Paulo. We have middle schoolers who have partnered with cancer hospitals to perform music and collect food. And we know fourth graders who care in quieter ways, who reach out to someone new in the cafeteria to say, "Sit here. There is room for one more at

our table." Seek out these examples and name them in your student and staff meetings, celebrate them in your school newsletters, and hold them up as examples for us all.
4. **Create processing space.** This chapter built on the work of Brazilian educator and philosopher Paulo Friere, who writes about the role of heart (or love) in dialogue. Creating processing space is an act of care. In addition to scheduling such time, it is also important to create norms for productive, wholehearted dialogue. This work is important during and after all major events such as a change in leadership or community crisis. The purpose of dialogue isn't to find an answer or even a point of agreement. It is, in the words of Paulo Freire (1970), "name the world to change it." As you schedule processing dialogues, remember that in a dialogue the purpose is to learn from each other, to hold different perspectives and realities up to the light, to consider new questions, and to find ways forward together.

Reflective Work for Continuous Learning

In the spring of 2021, one of our Lead English Language Arts teachers, Jill Clingan, taught us about *chiaroscuro*, a technique artists use to represent both light and shadows. While she was teaching about the arts, I remember thinking that this concept was timely for how we were processing crisis teaching. My historical memory of leading in schools during COVID-19 is complicated. As Marilyn said it is colored by the students, families, and teachers I worked with at the time. It is video conferences and all those surprises that can (and did) happen when you have a class of 25 six-year-olds zooming in from home. It is stories of triumph, projects that worked, and relationships that carried us through. It is educators and school leaders who pressed forward, who innovated, and who found new ways to connect. It is light and shadows. Gradually we came back together. School buildings reopened, then closed, then reopened, and eventually they stayed open. Just like the students, teachers, and leaders, the buildings that reopened were changed.

*****

In the spring of 2024, I returned to our partner school in Santos, SP. I visited the now fifth graders I had worked with before the world shifted. In anticipation of our visit, the students prepared interactive projects to teach us about Brazil. In a delightful turn of events, three students taught us about the cultural and artistic traditions of Carnival, bringing in brightly colored masks for us to try on. They turned on lively music and we danced the samba together. It was late in the evening when we left school that day. As we headed out into the night, a teacher pointed to a famous port "where cruise and cargo ships come and go."

It was at this moment that I realized, while some spaces felt familiar, they weren't exactly as they had been before. This was in part because we hadn't returned to schools as we had been before. We were changed and so were our schools. We didn't reopen what was—instead, we opened up a new awareness of what matters in learning spaces. In our best moments, we opened a growing sense of what might be.

- **Take a long view.** Sometimes it helps to look back. Compare your school community today with that of your community three years ago.
  - What new practices are underway?
  - What positive changes have taken root?
- **Mark what you've overcome.** What challenges have you and your teams overcome? Be specific. How do you know that you are on the other side of these challenges?
  - Is there more healing work that needs to take place? If so, what might that look like?
- **Create a celebration survey.** Ask ten leaders (broadly defined) in your school communities to share two celebrations from the last semester. Add your own two and compile the list together.
  - How will you mark these celebrations?
  - What trends do you notice across the list?
  - How can you leverage these strengths?

References

Brown, B. (2024, February 22). *Clear is kind. Unclear is unkind.* https://brenebrown.com/articles/2018/10/15/clear-is-kind-unclear-is-unkind/

Fishman-Weaver, K. (2018). *Wholehearted teaching of gifted young women: Cultivating courage, connection, and self-care in schools.* Routledge.

Freire, P. (1970). Chapter 3. In *Pedagogy of the Oppressed*. The Seabury Press.

4

Relationships Are the Heart of Great Leadership

Adapted from my leadership journal during my school travels in South America, this chapter reminds leaders that just like teaching, the greatest predictor of school leadership is the quality of relationships.

> **Key Concept:** Relationships are the heart of great teaching, great leadership, and the greatest predictor of achievement.

A teacher is reading over the shoulder of one of her eighth grade students. From across the room I hear her exclaim "Great work, Ana!" I turn around as their hands clap together in an enthusiastic high five. A few minutes later, Ana shares her essay with me. She's written on the importance of friendship. Her teacher was right—it is excellent and important work.

As a global school district, we are actively reimagining what it means to teach and learn across and in blended geographic borders. This is programmatically, ideologically, and logistically complex and big. Yet at the end of the day, it is the small interactions and daily decisions that matter most. It is the connection between one student and someone in their school community who cares for them.

DOI: 10.4324/9781003517122-8

During this visit to partner schools in Brazil, my team and I took copious programmatic notes. In our reflective evening sessions, though, I noticed that we always started by remembering small moments, brief interactions like the one between Ana and her teacher.

*****

I am sitting in the hallway with a group of middle school students, helping them record a video on Newton's laws of motion. One of the group members is visibly nervous. His peers tell him, "You can do this!" and "Let's do a run-through together. We've got this." I watch as they go through their lines a couple times together. When the team pushes the record button, I hold my breath, and they nail it. "Ótimo!"[1] I tell the student who was so nervous and now beams.

Courage, justice, connection, learning, and relationships—whether you are working with one student or 3,000, these are the elements that matter most in education. Like the more complicated infrastructure of larger cities, the bigger the program, the more moving parts there are to organize. Educational programs include curriculum, grades, assessments, logistics, differentiated lesson plans, etc. However, during these school visits, I was reminded that the greatest predictor of student success isn't data, logistics, or assessments. Just like teaching, the greatest predictor of school leadership is the quality of relationships.

> ...the greatest predictor of student success isn't data, logistics, or assessments. Just like teaching, the greatest predictor of school leadership is the quality of relationships.

I look out over the São Paulo skyline. Tonight it is all bright lights and rain. Focusing my gaze on the distance, I think of the 7,000 students in our school district. There is so much data to track and there are so many critical moments of connection that can't quite be quantified. Big data sets, just like big ideas, are understood by breaking them down into smaller pieces. You look for ways to tether your existing knowledge to new knowledge. You find connection points, each dotting its way to bigger constellations of meaning. I look out at the city view again. The rain blurs my focus and all the lights run together. Just then a colleague calls me inside with a question from a teacher.

Strategies for Practice

1. **Learn student names.** One of the quickest ways to build bridges between you and another person is to know their name. Principals and central office administrators have many names to learn. Large schools, districts, and even big undergraduate lecture classes contribute to a challenging volume of names. I get it. It is hard. Wholehearted leaders accept the challenge. Sometimes in school and classroom visits we don't know everyone's names yet, so we have to get to work straightaway.

   The Baker/baker paradox suggests that if we meet someone and learn they are named Baker we might not remember their name. However, if we meet someone and learn they are a baker we are more likely to remember their profession. It is the same word associated with the same person, yet one (the profession) conjures an image and prior knowledge connection while the other (the name) doesn't (as cited in Brod, 2021). You can use the Baker/baker paradox to your advantage by asking students to tell you something interesting about them as they tell you their name. Put the two bits of information together:

   - Lorenzo speaks Spanish.
   - Zoe likes photography.
   - Kristen is a cheerleader.
   - Joshua plays the piano.
   - Rania is from Tunisia.

   This has double advantages. First, it helps you learn names, and second it gives you something to build on after you learn the person's name.

   Let students know that their names matter to you because they matter to you. Tell students that it is hard to learn all their names but that you are committed to working on it until you get it. And then be good to your word. When students see me trying to learn 30 new names they help me with clues, laughter, and lots of encouragement. These are all indicators of positive school culture.

As a school administrator, I visit a lot of classrooms, including classrooms in our partner schools around the world. Whenever I spend time in a new classroom, I share a little bit about myself and ask students to do the same. I tell our students that I want to get to know them and their names. Then I work really hard to do just that.

I spend a few minutes at the start of each lecture going around using the Baker/baker strategy trying to learn the students' names and an interesting fact about each of them. Later, if I can't remember a student's name, I apologize and ask them to remind me.

In addition to bridging humanity, learning and using student names also supports engagement. Everyone likes to be recognized, affirmed, and named. *The cocktail party effect*, first discovered by Colin Cherry in 1953, refers to the ways that relevance can refocus our attention in high sensory situations (Haykin & Chen, 2005). These situations might include a cocktail party, a middle school cafeteria, or a rousing biology debate. What is one of the most effective focus triggers in these situations? Your name. In a world where there are so many calls for our attention, hearing your name can bring you back to the present moment and refocus your attention on the task at hand. This is an imperative skill in schools.

As a blended school district, much of my team's correspondence is digital. We utilize a myriad of tools to stay connecting including Zoom, Teams, WhatsApp, text, and Slack. Our teacher training includes meaningful lessons on humanizing online communication, and the heart of this lesson is about relationships. Often, in the online setting you must amplify your voice and find new ways to speak compassion into your feedback.

It isn't just the names that matter, it is the person behind the name, their culture, and their humanity. For these reasons, pronunciation matters, too. Don't allow students or staff to let you off easy by shortening their names or giving you an easier nickname. Ask them to correct you and work with you until you get it right. Caring enough to learn names and get them right is an exercise in humanity. This also goes for spelling and diacritics. How many of us have received an email, certificate, or cup of coffee with our name misspelled? I know, for me, when this happens, I always feel a little unseen. The cumulative effect of having your name mispronounced or misspelled can contribute to feeling not just unseen but unknown. This is something our school communities can commit to getting right.

The root word for courage comes from Latin, meaning heart strength. A related word I saw practiced during our school visits is encouragement, *meaning to make strong or give hope.*

2. **Practice en<u>courage</u>ment.** The root word for courage comes from Latin, meaning heart strength. A related word I saw practiced during our school visits is *encouragement*, meaning to make strong or give hope. In our schools, students and teachers live this out in countless daily ways. Administrators, families, teachers, and students all have the potential, through their relationships, to build students up and support learning. During this particular visit, I saw many examples of how care can transform frustration into engagement or loneliness into connection (Kumar & Epley, 2023). I saw this from caring teachers and caring friends. I remember a teacher leader telling me, "We just have really, really, kind students," just as a group of seventh graders came barreling down the hall to give us a hug.

3. **Leverage professional learning communities (PLCs).** I also saw the magic of harnessing our collective professional wisdom through teacher relationships. Several of our partner schools had recently launched PLCs. In a PLC, small groups of teachers work together to advance student achievement.

They engage in common planning, collective support, and strengths pooling. Teachers meet, usually weekly, to plan, share, and problem-solve around teaching and learning. They consider all the work that goes into teaching and distribute it among themselves, leaning on each other's strengths to work smarter.

Richard DuFour and Robert J. Marzano are often regarded as our top experts on PLCs in schools and districts. Their work teaches us that effective PLCs operate on three guiding principles: (1) to ensure all students learn at high levels, educators must work together to clarify what we want students to know, how we will know if they have learned that, how we will respond if they don't learn it, and how we will enrich and extend the learning for students who have already mastered this skill or content; (2) to help all students learn, educators must work collaboratively; and (3) educators must be focused on student results (DuFour & Marzano, 2011). Our school communities who had cultivated this practice were thriving. It felt like they had discovered the secret to more effective and happier teaching, because in a way, they had.

Reflective Work for Continuous Learning

Relationships are the heart of great teaching, great leadership, and the greatest predictor of achievement. Research consistently points to positive teacher–student relationships as "one of the most powerful predictors of a student's development, learning and well-being" (Gregoriadis et al., 2022, p. 1). In their 2021 overview of interpersonal communication in the instructional context, Fei Xie and Ali Derakhshan write that "a positive instructor–student relationship is identified with empathy, caring, involvement, trust, and respect" (p. 2). They go on to share that across studies, positive teacher–student relationships are strong facilitators of positive student outcomes including engagement, learning, achievement, wellbeing, motivation, success, and hope.

Healthy relationships are built on care and learning. In our global and multicultural context, educators and school leaders have a lot to learn. As we learn about the cultures, values, backgrounds, and lived experiences of our students and their families, we also learn about ourselves (Warger, 2001). Learning across cultures and identities has the potential to be transformative. On Teacher2Teacher, I am quoted as saying, "Small moments matter. Every time we talk to a student, we have the chance to build positive school culture." The same is true in our interactions with faculty and staff.

Below are some reflective exercises to learn from the teachers in your own life.

1. **Name your most impactful teachers.** The previous sections focused on the lessons we learned in our early years in education and the continuous lessons we learn from our student leaders. As a school leader, it is important to remember that you were a teacher first. As we close this section, I invite you to think back further and remember that you were also once a student. At some point, almost all of us have been fortunate enough to learn from a great teacher. Personally, I continue to be indebted to the teachers who believed in me, encouraged me, and ultimately helped shape me into the educator and human being I am today. Reflect on the teachers who have been important to you and answer the following questions:

   - Who was the teacher?
   - How did they build a relationship with you?
   - What did you learn from them?
   - How have those lessons continued to shape you?

   If you share these memories with your faculty and leadership teams, it is not uncommon for voices to crack or tears to fall at the memories of a beloved first grade teacher, or the geometry teacher who turned you on to math, or the music teacher who taught you the value of practice, or the English teacher who helped you find your voice. Teachers matter. And in all my years of listening to these stories, I've yet to hear someone mention a particular curriculum company, state or national standards, or a high-stakes assessment. Instead, what I hear is how that teacher saw you, made you feel, and believed in you. I hear about educators who showed young people they are capable of more than they thought. I hear about caring adults who listened when children were sad or worried, even when those concerns didn't have anything specific to do with class.

2. **Honor that teacher.** After reflecting on this impactful educator from your own life, I invite you to take two more action steps.

   - First, if possible, reach out to that teacher and say thank you.
   - Second, consider how you can dedicate the remainder of this school year to the lessons you learned from that educator.[2] As we focus on becoming more wholehearted school leaders, let's do so in ways that honor the impact of the teachers who helped us get to where we are today.

Notes

1 Portuguese for "Great!"
2 I learned this dedication strategy from Dr. Tony Castro, who was a mentor teacher for me in graduate school.

References

Brod, G. (2021). Toward an understanding of when prior knowledge helps or hinders learning. *NPJ Science of Learning, 6*(1), 24.

DuFour, R., & Marzano, R. J. (2011). *Leaders of learning: How district, school, and classroom leaders improve student achievement.* Solution Tree Press.

Gregoriadis, A., Vatou, A., Tsigilis, N., & Grammatikopoulos, V. (2022, February). Examining the reciprocity in dyadic teacher–child relationships: One-with-many multilevel design. *Frontiers in Education, 6*, 811934.

Haykin, S., & Chen, Z. (2005). The cocktail party problem. *Neural Computation, 17*(9), 1875–1902.

Kumar, A., & Epley, N. (2023). A little good goes an unexpectedly long way: Underestimating the positive impact of kindness on recipients. *Journal of Experimental Psychology: General, 152*(1), 236–252. https://doi.org/10.1037/xge0001271

Warger, C. (2001). *Cultural reciprocity aids collaboration with families.* ERIC/OSEP Digest.

Xie, F., & Derakhshan, A. (2021). A conceptual review of positive teacher interpersonal communication behaviors in the instructional context. *Frontiers in Psychology, 12,* 708490.

5

Cultivate Gratitude

Many years ago, as a public school teacher, I started a "Thankful Thursday" tradition with my high school students. While the specifics have evolved over the years, I have kept this tradition alive in my ongoing work in school leadership. This chapter calls us to integrate gratitude into our daily and weekly routines.

> **Key Concept:** Integrate gratitude into your daily and weekly routines.

On that first Thursday I was met with the scrunched eyebrows and perplexed looks of teenagers. I wished my students a "Happy Thankful Thursday," handed them a construction paper leaf, and asked them to write down the people and things they were thankful for. We hung these appreciations on a tree in my classroom. Over the week, students stopped by to read them, and the next Thursday we repeated the activity. Within a few weeks they were hooked, and soon the practice grew beyond my expectations. Over the semesters, the tree improved as student artists built elaborate 3D trees out of cardboard. Ultimately, a talented student asked if she could paint a large-scale mural of a tree on our classroom wall. We wrote a small grant for whiteboard paint so the students could write their appreciations directly onto the wall. Students from other programs started participating, too, and collectively we all looked forward to Thursdays.

When I moved into school leadership for an online and blended school district, I brought this practice with me. For the first couple of months, I modeled it, delivering handwritten notes and personalized emails of appreciation on Thursday. I also had a chalkboard that hung outside my office door. Each Thursday, I adjusted the prompt to something related to gratitude (e.g. *A colleague I am thankful for is… A teacher I am thankful for is… Something wonderful that happened last week is…*). Admittedly, it took longer for the practice to take hold with adults, but gradually my chalkboard started filling up with responses, and soon I wasn't the only one sending Thankful Thursday notes.

Today, years later, Thankful Thursday is a vibrant tradition in our school system. As our team grew larger and more distributed, a WhatsApp thread replaced my chalkboard. Every Thursday, our chat is filled with student, personal, and family celebrations. Some posts are deeply personal, such as the recovery of a spouse; some are rooted in community projects such as finishing a big accreditation report; and many are about the ways our team supports each other. As soon as a teacher or staff member sends an appreciation message, it is affirmed with heart and celebration emojis from their colleagues.

In psychology, these Thankful Thursday practices are a form of Positive Activity Intervention (PAI). "PAIs are simple, low-cost cognitive behavioral strategies that involve mirroring the thoughts and behaviors… to enhance well-being" (Walsh et al., 2023, p. 83). PAIs are highly accessible for students, teachers, mentors, and school communities. While I moved to the digital practice out of necessity, research suggests that this move may have contributed to the overall effectiveness of our team practice. Walsh et al. (2023) conducted a study on the impact of various types of PAIs related to gratitude. With a diverse sample of 916 undergraduates, the researchers assigned groups to one of three interventions or a control group. The interventions included writing private gratitude letters, texting benefactors one-on-one, or sharing thanks publicly on social media. "All three types of gratitude activities... benefited participants. However, those assigned to text their benefactors directly reported the biggest boosts in feelings of social connection and support" (p. 89). Said differently, the public, direct, and social dimensions of our WhatsApp thread are important aspects of our practice.

Gratitude also has the potential to have a community-wide impact on the overall culture of your school community.

In addition to the personal affective benefits of integrating gratitude into your school routine, gratitude also has the potential to have a community-wide impact on the overall culture of your school community. McCullough et al. (2001) conducted a large-scale literature survey on the functions of gratitude. They identified three major moral functions for cultivating this practice. They found that gratitude serves as a moral barometer, a moral reinforcer, and a moral motive. Naming and celebrating specific prosocial actions and behaviors reinforces those actions and behaviors. For someone to be grateful for the actions of another they must perceive those actions as intentional. Gratitude is further multiplied when the actions are altruistic and not self-serving (Bono & Froh, 2009).

This practice also contributes to a culture of appreciation and celebration. In their research on gratitude in schools, Bono and Froh go on to report that PAIs promote "social cohesion, relational and job satisfaction, and even organizational functioning" (p. 77). This is what we have experienced in my classrooms and teams, as well. Practicing gratitude together reinforces prosocial behaviors and strengthens what I call a belief that "we are for each other."

Does Thankful Thursday seem kind of cheesy? It sure does. In fact, when I tried it with high school *students,* I was worried it might fall flat. While it took a little time to take hold, and then a little longer with faculty and staff, I believe it ultimately works because it is rooted in authenticity. In short, the cheese-factor doesn't matter when the intentions and sentiments are sincere, consistent, and clearly communicated.

Key Strategies

1. **Choose one day a week to bookend with thank you notes.** Send an appreciation note at the start of your day and another to close your workday. Keep track of who you send these notes to, and each week strive to appreciate someone new. These notes can reinforce actions you want to see and affirm great work happening in your building or district. Therefore, it helps to make them both specific and personalized. For example:

    Thank you for your work preparing for the principal workshop next week. I appreciate how you built in so much time for collaboration among schools. It will be great to get everyone talking together about summer learning opportunities. I know leading this workshop is a little outside your usual scope, but after talking through your plans, I also know you are the right leader for the task. I can't wait to hear how it goes!

2. **End your team meetings with appreciations.** The first school I taught at had a tradition of ending each meeting with a time for appreciations. The strategy is simple and powerful. Open the floor for five minutes at the end of the meeting for anyone to share an appreciation. Write time for appreciations into your meeting agenda. Lead by example; appreciate the efforts or perspective of someone in the room.

Reflective Work for Continuous Learning

Before I left for our district office one morning, I committed to starting the day by writing thank you notes to our support service leads. I arrived at the office and within moments I was called into a meeting. It can be challenging to schedule appreciation into the hurried pace of school and it would have been easy to let those notes go. However, I believe this practice is worth making the time for. After that first meeting, I sat down and wrote the notes. It was the first cool day of fall and I delivered the notes with mugs of hot chocolate. I hoped the gesture would warm the spirits of our team as they juggled phone calls about server issues, test proctoring, and course pacing.

One year I worked for a school where we started the school year with a rousing standing ovation for our lunch crew. Another year, Dr. Jen Ruckstad, a principal I worked for, led us in making a spirit tunnel for our custodial staff. We cheered with enthusiasm as each staff member's name was called out over a megaphone. These were memorable practices that highlight the essential and too-often overlooked work our support staff do to keep our schools and students safe, fed, and cared for.

All these practices contribute to a more positive and prosocial school culture. Recent research by Amit Kumar and Nicholas Epley (2023) suggests we often underestimate the positive impact acts of kindness have on both the recipient and those performing the act of kindness.

Individually or with your leadership team reflect on the following:

1. **Encourage purposeful appreciation.** In addition to big celebrations at the beginning or end of the school year, what are ways you can integrate regular and purposeful appreciation into your leadership practice?
2. **Create an admiration matrix.** Choose a cross section of your staff and faculty roster. Scan the names and jot down the skills and qualities you admire from specific people on your team. Set a schedule to write specific notes letting each person know what you admire about them and their work. Keep the practice going.
3. **Audit for capacity.** Consider the big projects happening in your school or district right now. Given these projects, who is currently working beyond the scope of their role? First, how can you recognize these efforts, and second, how can you create greater sustainability for their work?

References

Bono, G. & Froh, J. (2009). Gratitude in school: Benefits to students and schools. In R. Gilman, E. S. Huebner, & M. J. Furlong (Eds.), *Handbook of positive psychology in schools* (pp. 77–88). Routledge/Taylor & Francis Group.

Kumar, A., & Epley, N. (2023). A little good goes an unexpectedly long way: Underestimating the positive impact of kindness on recipients. *Journal of Experimental Psychology: General, 152*(1), 236.

McCullough, M. E., Kilpatrick, S. D., Emmons, R. A., & Larson, D. B. (2001). Is gratitude a moral affect? *Psychological Bulletin, 127*(2), 249.

Walsh, L. C., Regan, A., Twenge, J. M., & Lyubomirsky, S. (2023). What is the optimal way to give thanks? Comparing the effects of gratitude expressed privately, one-to-one via text, or publicly on social media. *Affective Science, 4*(1), 82–91.

II

Lead for Justice Overview

LEAD FOR JUSTICE

Wholehearted Leadership Framework Focus Areas: *Agency, Inclusion, Relationships*

Tethering Ideas:

- Commit to antiracism.
- Hold space for healing.
- Foster a sense of belonging.
- Practice inclusion.
- Advocate for inclusion.

 Key Vocabulary

- **Social Justice:** Actions that further the values of fairness, respect, and access to "human rights in all spheres of life" (United Nations, n.d.). Social justice propels equity and inclusion movements for currently and historically oppressed and marginalized populations (Duignan, 2024).
- **Advocacy:** Actions that support, work in favor of, and/or defend others. (See also: *self-advocacy*.)
- **Upstander:** Someone who speaks, acts, or intervenes to support others and stop bullying.

> **Trauma-Informed Schools:** Also called *trauma-sensitive schools*, are schools that cultivate practices to ensure all children experience belonging, safety, and the space to heal, grow in skills, and learn at high levels. This work requires continuous learning on the part of school leaders, teachers, and staff about trauma, vulnerabilities, adverse childhood experiences (ACEs), wellbeing, and the brain.

Lead for Justice Guiding Questions

1. How does your school or district further *social justice* both internally in your classrooms / school communities and externally in the broader community?
2. As a school leader, what are your top core values? Would your school community identify these as your core values? If not, what additional work do you need to do to bring your values and your practices into better alignment?
3. How are you working to safeguard belonging for all students and staff in your building? Especially consider community members from marginalized backgrounds.
4. What are specific ways that you and your leadership team teach and model upstander behaviors?
5. Are your advisory councils representative of your school communities? If needed, how will you expand your advisors to include more identities, cultures, and lived experiences?
6. How would your most underrepresented student groups describe your school culture as it relates to academic, social, and emotional wellbeing?
7. When making tough decisions about access, how do you keep your focus on *equity* and not just *equality*?
8. What professional learning goals could you set to grow in your knowledge of *trauma-informed leadership*? What is the first step you need to take to reach those goals?
9. As a result of the curriculum and instructional practices in your school, what do students learn about ethics, morality, and service?

10. Who are the advocates for social good in your school and district? How can you amplify and learn from their work?

References

Duignan, B. (2024, July 11). *Social justice | Definition, theories, examples, & facts*. Encyclopedia Britannica. www.britannica.com/topic/social-justice

United Nations. (n.d.). *Message on World Day of Social Justice | Department of Economic and Social Affairs*. https://sdgs.un.org/statements/message-world-day-social-justice-10379

 ## Concept Study: Trauma-Informed School Leadership

This concept study is a powerful companion to Chapter 7 on Holding Space for Healing.

In 2015 I taught a summer course for rising high school juniors. This course forever changed the way I think about student support. My opening lesson for the summer semester was on little "t" truths (personal truths) and big "T" truths (universal truths) in literature. My class had a good conversation and I dismissed them for the day feeling excited for the semester ahead. The next day the students returned with an idea. Instead of studying literature this summer as I had planned, they wanted to use action research (see p. 203) to study truth. After some back and forth, I agreed to the new plan and we dove into learning more about research methodology.

The main research prompt my students wanted to explore through their study was:

♦ *A truth that is difficult for me to share is…*

The class planned to survey the 300+ students in our summer program, but before doing so wanted to beta test these questions on themselves. They thought they would get more honest answers if they encouraged anonymous submissions. So on a sunny afternoon in June, I walked the group outside as they sprawled out in the courtyard writing their own answer to this question on index cards. To protect the anonymity of my students, I collected the cards and shuffled them.

Walking back into the school building is a moment I will never forget. There I stood several feet behind my students, all of whom had just met each other earlier this week. They were proud of their project and walked arm-in-arm in front of me. None knew yet what the others had written. To prepare myself for our upcoming conversation, I started skimming the cards. My stomach dropped:

- Card 1: When I was younger, my uncle sexually abused me.
- Card 2: I am struggling with an eating disorder but don't plan to tell anyone because I don't want to stop.
- Card 3: Last summer, I attempted suicide. I am glad I wasn't successful.
- Card 4: I am afraid to come out as gay because I think my parents will kick me out.
- Card 5: I was bullied at my old school and can't stop thinking about it.
- Card 6: I think I am depressed but don't know who to talk to.
- Card 7: I don't know why I am in gifted classes because I am not as smart as those kids.
- Card 8: My dad is incarcerated and I've never told anyone.

The cards continued, each difficult to process. I felt an aching as I thought about the students in my class who were living through and with these truths. The sentences were written in magic marker—red, purple, green. Some of the students had doodled around the edges in swirling loops and designs. I remember, the cards started feeling heavy in my hands. As a teacher leader and new school administrator, I wasn't sure what the next right step was, so I leaned into care and honesty.

I asked my students to circle up their desks and told them their work was so powerful we were going to have to find the best way forward together.

Then I read the cards aloud.

The room was silent and also connected. I passed out new index cards and asked students to write their names on these cards and answer a few questions about care and immediate safety concerns including planned next steps for meeting with me and our school psychologist. Next, I met with each student individually in the hallway. As I did, I could hear the class inside. Someone put on some music. I was surprised to hear laughter and students singing along.

At the end of class that day, a student said, "I know this is surprising, but I am so glad we are doing this research. I am so glad that like me, everyone will know they are not alone."

I was grateful to hear this as I was struggling physically and emotionally with all this information. One of my first thoughts was that maybe I shouldn't have allowed this project in the first place. The mental health professional we worked with for the rest of the term helped me normalize these feelings. "A common first reaction to learning of these traumatic events is to wish you had not asked, or that the student hadn't shared them," he told me. "That is a natural and understandable reaction, as now you are faced with the responsibility to respond. The fears and anxieties this brings up are real." He reminded me that just as our students were learning that they are not alone, educators don't have to do this work alone either.

With administrator approval and extra mental health support, my students carried out their research project. We heard many difficult stories that summer.

We also connected students to new resources, and all learned more about trauma. This was nearly a decade ago and I now count it as one of my most important learning experiences as an educator and human being. In fact, on my most difficult days in school leadership, I still remind myself that each of us is likely carrying a heavy index card; maybe we have tucked away somewhere, or maybe it's right there in our pocket ready to be shared. Our students, staff, each of us carry truths that are difficult to share. Sometimes school is the place where those stories come out. My rising juniors taught me about belonging, humanity, trauma, and care. Most importantly, as they told me, they taught each other that "sometimes it is okay to not be okay."

*****

Trauma-informed schools are schools where all children experience belonging, safety, and space to heal as they grow in skills and learn at high levels. Trauma-informed, also called *trauma-sensitive*, schools require continuous learning on the part of school leaders, teachers, and staff about trauma, vulnerabilities, well-being, and the brain. School leaders play an essential role in establishing and maintaining the policies, practice, and culture needed to foster trauma-informed schools and bring about crucial changes in wellness and achievement for children who have experienced trauma including adverse childhood experiences, or ACEs (National Center on Safe Supportive Learning Environments, 2021). ACEs are potentially traumatic events that occur in childhood (0–17 years). Examples include: violence, abuse (physical, emotional, and sexual), neglect, losing a family member to suicide, substance abuse in the home, and instability due to parents or others in the household being incarcerated.

In 2023, I had the responsibility of working on a state-wide course on caring for vulnerable children (Fishman-Weaver, 2023). In that course, I offered five building blocks childhood professionals can use to help prevent ACEs and the harm caused by these experiences. These building blocks, listed below, align with recommendations for establishing trauma-informed schools including those released by The National Child Traumatic Stress Network (2020) and the National Education Association (2023).

1. Partner directly with families.
2. Promote violence prevention.
3. Offer support for emotion regulation, resilience, and healing.
4. Provide stable relationships to children in your programs.
5. Report harm, including abuse and neglect.

As you work with students and staff who are navigating trauma it is important to remember that vulnerable students are vulnerable through no fault of their own. It is also important to remember that supporting someone through trauma is a team process. Even as a leader, you don't have to carry this work all on your own. Finally, it helps to remember that not only do trauma-informed schools help children right now, working as a community, these practices can also prevent future ACEs. In a 2024 report on trauma and children, the CDC writes that "ACEs and their associated harms are preventable. Creating and sustaining safe, stable, nurturing relationships and environments for all children and families can prevent ACEs."

As someone who views public education as a public health profession, trauma-informed care is a justice issue in our schools. All students, staff, and faculty deserve classrooms and school buildings where they experience safety, belonging, support, and space to connect and heal.

As someone who views public education as a public health profession, trauma-informed care is a justice issue in our schools. All students, staff, and faculty deserve classrooms and school buildings where they experience safety, belonging, support, and space to connect and heal.

Questions for Consideration

1. Review the five building blocks for supporting vulnerable students above. Which of these does your school excel at? Which of these do you or your team need more support and training with?
2. What is *an index card moment* you have had with your students? How did you find your way forward together?
3. Many of the truths shared in this class project weren't new. In fact, some were ACEs from early childhood. While I wouldn't recommend passing out note cards with the sentence starter "A truth that is difficult to share is…" I know that part of the power of this research project was the invitation to share. How will you invite students, teachers, and staff to share the stories they have been waiting to share with someone and then wrap care around them?

References

Centers for Disease Control (CDC). (2024, May 16). *Preventing adverse childhood experiences.* www.cdc.gov/aces/prevention/index.html#:~:text=Adverse%20childhood%20experiences%20(ACEs)%20and,full%20health%20and%20life%20potential.

Fishman-Weaver, K. (2023). *Caring for vulnerable children.* Produced by Mizzou Academy for the Missouri Department of Elementary and Secondary Education Office of Childhood.

National Center on Safe Supportive Learning Environments. (2021). *Leading trauma-sensitive schools action guide.* https://safesupportivelearning.ed.gov/sites/default/files/TSS_Training_Package_Action_Guide_0.pdf

The National Child Traumatic Stress Network. (2020, December 15). *Creating, supporting, and sustaining trauma-informed schools.* www.nctsn.org/resources/creating-supporting-and-sustaining-trauma-informed-schools-system-framework

National Education Association. (2023). *Trauma-informed practices.* www.nea.org/professional-excellence/student-engagement/tools-tips/trauma-informed-practices

6

Commit to Antiracism[1]

With a focus on critical reflection and equity, this chapter explores ways school leaders can commit to antiracism in their practice. Drawing on my work in secondary schools, the examples in this chapter build on research about the achievement and opportunity gaps in schools, the impact of implicit bias in discipline and teacher–student relationships, and the impacts historical and continuous racial discrimination including microaggressions and responses to minor infractions can have on student wellbeing, school climate, and achievement. This chapter calls on school leaders to commit unequivocally to antiracism and to maintain that commitment through policy, practice, and professional learning.

> **Key Concept:** Commit unequivocally to antiracism. Make this an ongoing commitment that is reflected in policy, practice, and professional learning.

> **Key Vocabulary**
>
> ♦ **Race:** A social and cultural construct. This term is culturally specific—meaning its definition and boundaries are fluid across borders—and used to differentiate/define

DOI: 10.4324/9781003517122-12

> groups of people who have similar physical and cultural characteristics.
> - **Racism:** A system of power that unfairly gives certain groups access and privilege over other groups.
> - **Antiracism:** The active and intentional process of identifying, resisting, and dismantling racism by changing systems, policies, practices, and attitudes so that communities are safe, people are affirmed and valued, and power is distributed equitably.

A lanky young man I had never met before tumbled into my gifted center. This was during our passing period between second and third block. He reached into the bookcase, grabbed a copy of James McBride's *The Color of Water* (2006) and said, "Hey, can I borrow this? I'll bring it back soon." Before I could answer, he was gone with the book.

He brought it back after class and stuck it back on the shelf. "Thanks!" he shouted, running off.

This pattern persisted for two weeks. After which, his English teacher appeared in my doorway. I later learned that she gave points to students for bringing a silent reading book to class each day and reading it for the first 15 minutes of the period. She didn't think Jayden "deserved" these points. In fact, she pointed a finger at me and accused me of "enabling" him.

"By lending him a book to read?" I asked, trying to steady both the confusion and annoyance in my voice.

"He's not reading it!" she said and then she stomped her foot. "He's using you to game the system."

This was several years ago. Today, I might have had the courage to ask her which system she meant. Did she mean our educational system or a broader system of power and privilege? At the moment, though, I was too stunned to be clever. I remember looking into her light-colored eyes and trying to decide what to say next.

While thinking this through, I thought of an essay I had recently taught in my teacher education class. In his 2016 piece for *Learning for Justice,* Chad Donohue writes that he always gives pencils to students who need them—no questions asked. He shares,

> Of course, there is the chance I will be taken advantage of. I welcome this chance. I resolve to remain a patient advocate for the child even if he is testing me... We should all be extended such grace... Students learn best in a psychologically safe, mistake-friendly environment. We all make mistakes. How teachers respond has everything to do with whether or not their students feel valued as human beings. We are responsible for creating a psychologically safe classroom. In all possible situations, we should seek to uphold the dignity of the student.

With this in mind, I told the English teacher that young people were always welcome to "use" my classroom and me to access books. The next day Jayden grabbed the book from *his spot* on the shelf and called out to me, "Did you read the part about him teaching his mom to drive? I did that, too. Teach my mom to drive."

I wish I could tell you that Jayden and I developed a close relationship, that we talked about books for the rest of the year exploring narratives and making connections. However, we didn't. I was simply a teacher leader with a full bookshelf and an open door. Jayden borrowed a few more books from me during the course of the school year. He tended toward books written by Black authors and especially appreciated my collection of titles by Jason Reynolds. During that semester, Jayden frequently shouted quick text-to-text, text-to-self, and text-to-world connections about the books he was borrowing.

*****

In her essay on bioethics in medicine, Rebecca Dresser (2011) proposes that small choices have significant impacts on patient treatment. In the words of one of her colleague interviews, "Doctors and nurses make constant small ethical decisions [in their] everyday clinical work, like whether to make eye contact with a patient or take seriously a patient's complaints about treatment side effects... Their choices have a major impact on patients and caregivers" (p. 15). The same is true in schools. Look at what happens when we trade the medical terms in this quote for school-based terms: "Principals and teachers make constant small ethical decisions [in] everyday school work, like whether to make eye contact with a student or take seriously a student's feelings about a lesson, teacher, or peer group... Their choices have a major impact on students and learning." Our microethics around antiracism have a tremendous impact on school culture and student learning.

I hadn't thought of Jayden in a long time. Again, our interactions had been brief and were several years ago. However, when working on antiracist teaching materials with my team I remembered him and another African American student we'll call Hank. Once identified as *struggling readers*, students were assigned to my literacy intervention program. I learned that often these students did not lack reading skills as much as they lacked an interest in engaging with books that had little to do with their own lived experiences.

This was the case with Hank, a bright-eyed football player. One day, Hank's English teacher cornered me. No, this was not the same teacher I talked with about Jayden, and yes, I have tremendous respect and adoration for English teachers in general. This teacher demanded to know why Hank was in her general education class "because" she continued, "he doesn't know how to read."

I had recently found a large book on the history of football strategy and Hank had been enjoying it in the back of the room. I asked if he would please bring the book to us and share the passage he was reading. "Sure," he said, reading happily and fluently and offering his own commentary and connections to the text.

These stories are not the most overt examples from my career, nor were they the most impactful for me. After some reflection, I realized that it wasn't Hank and Jayden that first drew their memories to my focus; instead, it was my interactions with their teachers, and what those interactions can teach us about teacher support, school leadership, and implicit bias. These two educators came to me, angry with preconceived beliefs about how students wouldn't or couldn't read. These accusations cut deep in my educator heart. As the mother of a Black son who was a highly proficient reader at home, this accusatory rhetoric felt all too familiar. In hindsight, it is easy to vilify this behavior. As we look at these examples, we can see that these teachers were wrong in their assumptions and actions. And yet, if we practice some critical reflection, can we also recognize ourselves in these scenarios? When have I, too, been that frustrated educator in the doorway, the one who acts before having all the information, the one who gives into her amygdala, the one who is so sure she sees things correctly only to learn that she didn't, in fact, have all the information?

At the moment, I was so anxious to prove these teachers wrong, that I failed to do the more important work that needed to follow. As Lori Gottlieb (2019) writes, anger is often sanctimonious. What should I have said and done differently in these critical conversations? Unfortunately, I have many opportunities to practice. As school leaders we navigate countless micro-ethical moments. Here is the protocol I now try to follow: (1) call out inequitable and unjust behavior; (2) address the systems that allow and encourage these beliefs and actions; and (3) act with empathy and high professional expectations recognizing that we are all works in progress.

> *What should I have said and done differently in these critical conversations? Unfortunately, I have many opportunities to practice. As school leaders we navigate countless micro-ethical moments. Here is the protocol I now try to follow: (1) call out inequitable and unjust behavior; (2) address the systems that allow and encourage these beliefs and actions; and (3) act with empathy and high professional expectations recognizing that we are all works in progress.*

Moments like those shared above have a significant impact on the self-efficacy and achievement of our children. Said differently, Hank and Jayden deserve better. While I can't be certain of the role race played in these interactions, I know that the historical and continuous patterns of both lower expectations and over-disciplining African American youth, and Black boys and young men in particular, is well-documented in schools. For example, in a 2023 Ballard Brief on *Racial Inequality in Public School Discipline for Black Students in the United States*, Emily Peterson reports that in the 2013–2014 school year, Black students were four times more likely to receive out-of-school suspension than their white peers and three times more likely than their Latine peers. Black students were also more than twice as likely to be referred to the principal's office. Peterson found that while some other countries also suspend Black students at a higher prevalence rate, the discrepancy is most significant in the United States (2023).

The scenarios above are also consistent with policies and practices that conflate grading with behavior, or worse, with access to resources. They are implicated in the ways we identify students for remedial classes, and by a curriculum that centers narrow and eurocentric narratives. Finally, these examples are also reinforced by implicit bias about what or whom a scholar looks like. In his bestselling memoir *How to Be an Antiracist*, Ibram X. Kendi (2019) challenges that decisions and policies are not race neutral. In fact, he says there is no such thing as "race neutral." Policies are either racist or antiracist; so are our behaviors. Throughout this book, I talk about the high professional standards wholehearted leaders hold themselves to, and among these are an unequivocal commitment to antiracism. Below are strategies and reflective exercises to aid us in this ongoing work.

Key Strategies for Practice

A couple years ago I attended a training by the Racial Equity Institute. The trainer showed us a photo of a dead fish and then asked us what conclusions we might draw if we came across that fish in a nearby lake. Participants offered varied hypotheses about how the fish might have become sick. The trainer then showed us a photo of two dead fish and again asked what conclusions we might draw. Again, most participants guessed that something was wrong with the two fish that had led to their death. Next the trainer showed us a photo with hundreds of dead fish. "Are you still wondering what is wrong with the fish," she asked, "or have you started to wonder about the water they're swimming in?" She then shared that racism is the water we are swimming in. This ecosystem metaphor is designed to help practitioners "internalize the reality that we live in a racially structured society, and that *that* is what causes racial inequity." In their terms, the Racial Equity Institute (2022) says that "groundwater" problems require "groundwater" solutions. The strategies in this section ask school leaders to consider ways they can address systemic racism in their schools.

1. **Address Systems of Oppression.** Systems of oppression refer to the ways injustice, discrimination, and unequal access are built into and across our institutions and structures, including schooling. The National Equity Project writes that these systems have interconnected and reinforcing historical antecedents. Systems of oppression intentionally disadvantage specific groups while advantaging others. In schools this is often evident in our achievement, discipline, and participation/attendance data. These data all tell a critical story about who is and who isn't experiencing belonging and success in our buildings.

    Systems of oppression intentionally disadvantage specific groups while advantaging others. In schools this is often evident in our achievement, discipline, and participation/attendance data. These data all tell a critical story about who is and who isn't experiencing belonging and success in our buildings.

Because systems of oppression have been learned, they can also be unlearned. School leaders can play a vital role in supporting this unlearning in their buildings and districts. "Systemic oppression and its effects can be undone through recognition of inequitable patterns and intentional action to interrupt inequity and create more democratic processes and systems supported by multi-ethnic, multi-cultural, multi-lingual alliances and partnerships" (The National Equity Project, n.d., para 4).

This unlearning also requires us to disrupt individual blaming and grit-based narratives that put the onus for achievement not on systemic changes but on marginalized students. What scholars have termed "the grit narratives" is a newer version of the meritocracy myth that the solution to success is simply hard work and perseverance (Gow, 2020; Mehta, 2015). While, of course, we want to teach hard work and perseverance in our schools, we cannot do so without also a deep understanding of the structural and systemic barriers that have contributed to achievement and opportunity gaps in schools. In her work with a group of 50 teachers, Katrina Schwartz (2015) found that grit narratives ignore many of the structural barriers that make it difficult for marginalized students to succeed in schools. The Stanford Center for Education and Policy Research has participated in longitudinal monitoring on educational opportunity gaps across racial lines. In addition to socioeconomic disparities, the Stanford Educational Opportunity Monitoring Project points to "the availability and quality of early childhood education, the quality of public schools, patterns of residential and school segregation, and state educational and social policies" as factors in "reducing or exacerbating racial achievement gaps" (n.d., Para 19). As school leaders, we have an obligation to address and remediate opportunity gaps and systems of oppression in our buildings and districts. Further, we have the responsibility to move beyond grit-based narratives and toward justice-based narratives based on equity, access, and belonging.

> As school leaders, we have an obligation to address and remediate opportunity gaps and systems of oppression in our buildings and districts. Further, we have the responsibility to move beyond grit-based narratives and toward justice-based narratives based on equity, access, and belonging.

2. **Get critical about your ABCs—<u>A</u>chievement data, <u>B</u>ias, and School <u>C</u>limate.** Achievement data, bias, and school climate are inextricably related. A recent three-year study by Dr. Ming-Te Wang and Juan Del Toro (2021) illustrates this relationship well. Wang and Del Toro analyzed school records for nearly 2,300 middle and high school students across 12 schools in the United States. Looking critically at both disciplinary data and grade point averages, they found that 26% of the Black students received at least one suspension for a minor infraction over the course of the three years, compared with just 2% of white students. These include things like dress code violations, inappropriate language, or cell phone use in class. Wang and Del Toro found that the students who were suspended for a minor infraction during the first year of the study had significantly lower grades both one and two years later than students who hadn't been suspended. They also found that the students who had been suspended for these small infractions were more likely to report unfavorable school climate one year later and that these perceptions were effective at predicting lower grades even one year after that.

Decisions about discipline are often subjective, leaving them more at risk for bias. Discipline decisions also have a lasting impact on students' self-efficacy, connection to school, and achievement. Therefore, school leaders need to exercise thoughtful microethics in making decisions about discipline. One of my favorite K-8 school principals used to help his students *keep small problems small*. This same advice applies to leaders. Keep small infractions in perspective. These small moments can have significant and lasting effects on achievement and belonging.

3. **Get Personal. Stay Vigilant.** Talking about race, racism, and systems of oppression is complex and charged. Navigating these conversations productively requires a willingness to practice courage and lean into "pedagogy of discomfort" (Boler, 1999).

Dr. Esther Ohito, an Associate Professor of English and Literacy at Rutgers University, has been an important voice in antiracist teaching for several years. Her research on teacher education has shed light on how educators form beliefs about antiracist teaching. In particular, she cites three interconnected factors that influence how educators understand antiracism in their classrooms: (1) race(ism) and family histories; (2) race(ism) and schooling experiences; and (3) race(ism) and embodiment (Ohito, 2019, p. 5). Exploring these beliefs asks educators to get personal about their experiences with race and racism, sometimes for the first time. Studies on the affective reactions that teachers, particularly white teachers, have to this work include "anger (e.g., Mazzei, 2008), discomfort (e.g., Aveling, 2006), fear (e.g., Case & Hemmings, 2005), and guilt (e.g., Nieto, 1998)" (as cited in Ohito, 2016).

In one study on her own preservice teacher education course, Ohito found that leaning into discomfort "punctured White supremacy by provoking both preservice teachers and [her] to individually and collectively make meaning of the contours of racial oppression by noticing and listening to the interactions between our bodies and emotions" (2016, p. 459). She also found that creating a climate where it was okay to feel discomfort contributed to greater "emotional openness to support each other in a learning community… [while] deepening critical consciousness" (p. 459).

As school leaders, we can also employ a "pedagogy of discomfort," an invitation to get personal with our personal racial histories, and a commitment to further antiracist work in partnership with our faculty, staff, and leadership teams. This is not one-time work or something that can be checked off at an annual training. Instead, this is ongoing work to revisit throughout the school year as an integral aspect of your professional learning and policy planning.

Reflective Work for Continued Learning

School leaders have immense power in creating a culture that values and supports ABAR [anti-bias, antiracist

> education]. I have often heard from hesitant principals and administrators that they're concerned certain staff members of the community are resistant and unwilling. I'd ask them to remember this phrase: *What you permit, you promote.*
>
> (Kleinrock, 2020)

Hope and anger are intentionally entangled across antiracism work. In a 2017 essay, I defined hope as "a universal form of resistant imagination." Black feminist scholars such as Audre Lorde have taught us that anger can also be a resistant imagination. Lorde's address at the NWSA Convention in 1981 reminds us that anger is not only useful but necessary in addressing racism. "Any discussion... about racism" said Lorde, "must include the recognition and the use of anger. It must be direct and creative, because it is crucial. We cannot allow our fear of anger to deflect us nor to seduce us into settling for anything less than the hard work of excavating honesty" (p. 8).

Hope and anger are not opposite positions in a philosophical debate. Instead they are partner drivers in antiracist teaching and school leadership. In Ohito's work, she often talks about the embodied experience of exploring race, racism, and antiracism. As I wrote about Hank and Jayden in this chapter's opening, I remembered these stories as embodied experiences. For me, I can feel anger as a knot in the back of my throat. As I was revisiting these experiences, I felt that tightening again. As a leader, when I experience that embodied reaction, I know it is important for me to name it and ask what my anger is telling me.

The final exercises in this chapter lean into that naming and noticing. They are intended to help you and your leadership teams find new ways forward through and with both anger and hope. May this work be a positive tipping point for your school. And certainly, if a long-legged teenager comes tumbling in from the crowded hallway seeking a book, pencil, or connection, may we make sure he knows these things are always available to him in our classrooms.

1. Assign accountability partners.
   - What feelings did the stories about Jayden and Hank bring up for you? When have you been the different characters in these stories? How so? What practical takeaways do you have from this chapter?
   - What biases are interfering with your ability to reach, teach, lead, and connect with all your students, particularly students from racial backgrounds that are different from yours? Answering this question requires deep critical reflection, courage, and honesty. What is your plan to address implicit bias in your own practice? Include specific actions and behaviors.
   - Who will you partner with to hold you accountable for this work around equity, ethics, and antiracism? (Assign partners.)
2. **Communicate your commitment to antiracism.** In a 2020 article for *Forbes*, Terina Allen urged leaders across sectors to have a conversation with their team/community about their stance on racism. Allen writes:

   Send a message—an unequivocal message—to indicate that you and the organization will not tolerate racism in any form. If you can't do this, start with asking yourself why, and assess your own values and beliefs. If the larger organization has put out a statement, use it as a starting point for your own, or just communicate your own stance in alignment with any organizational or corporate statement. However you do it, be certain to get your stance on the record.

   The timing of this article is relevant. In 2020, the United States witnessed powerful Black Lives Matter demonstrations and a renewed interest in addressing antiracism publicly. Many factors contributed to this climate, including the killing of George Floyd, racial disparities in health care that had been heightened during the COVID pandemic, and mounting racial tensions and inequities in our education and justice systems. Educators and school leaders played an important role in this essential conversation. I include this exercise here as a reminder that this is an ongoing conversation. It is important to revise the work your school did (or didn't do) during this time and to get clear on your own commitments to antiracism.

- Does your school or district have a clear stance on antiracism?
- If no, why not? This is an important question to explore. Begin a plan to start that work.
- If yes, when was your statement last revised? How often is it referenced/reviewed? Is it well known to students, staff, and families? Does your stance on antiracism guide school policies, curriculum, and decisions?

3. **Learn for antiracism.** In a school resource packet on antiracist teaching and reading, I wrote the following:

You can't read, love, or friend your way into fully understanding the lived experiences of another person or cultural group. This doesn't mean you should stop reading, loving, or practicing friendship. In fact, it is just the opposite. Teaching and leading for antiracism requires that we seek greater understanding of the history, conditions, systems, and structures that contribute to racism. Further, it acknowledges that we understand there are things some of us will never fully understand. Leading and teaching for antiracism requires us to center racially diverse voices in our curriculum, classrooms, and conversations; to celebrate, affirm, value, and learn from those who show us how to show up and be better.

- What are your professional learning goals related to antiracism?

- How will you commit to the learning and unlearning needed to build new kinds of ecosystems where equity, belonging, and antiracism are part of the groundwater of how we "do school" here? Systems change is longitudinal work. In addition to thinking big, set your first small goal now.
- Who are your advisors in this work? How will you practice humility and reciprocity in learning with and from them?

Note

1 An early version of some of the stories in this chapter appeared on my blog, *Wholehearted School Leadership*, under the title, "Everyday Ethics and School Equity Work."

References

Allen, T. (2020, December 3). 5 conversations credible leaders must have in this moment. *Forbes*. www.forbes.com/sites/terinaallen/2020/06/04/george-floyd-and-racism-5-conversations-credible-leaders-must-have-in-this-moment/

Aveling, N. (2006). "Hacking at our very roots": Rearticulating white racial identity within the context of teacher education. *Race Ethnicity and Education, 9*(3), 261–274.

Boler, M. (1999). *Feeling power: Emotions and education*. Routledge.

Case, K., & Hemmings, A. (2005). Distancing strategies: White women preservice teachers and antiracist curriculum. *Urban Education, 40*(6), 606–626.

Donohue, C. (2016) Give the kid a pencil. *Teaching Tolerance*. www.tolerance.org/magazine/give-the-kid-a-pencil

Dresser, R. (2011). Bioethics and cancer: When the professional becomes personal. *The Hastings Center Report, 41*(6), 14–18.

Fishman-Weaver, K. (2017). A call to praxis: Using gendered organizational theory to center radical hope in schools. *Journal of Organizational Theory in Education, 2*(1), 1–14.

Gottlieb, L. (2019). *Maybe you should talk to someone: A therapist, HER therapist, and our lives revealed*. Harper.

Gow, P. (2020, December 1). What's dangerous about the grit narrative, and how to fix it (Opinion). *Education Week.* www.edweek.org/education/opinion-whats-dangerous-about-the-grit-narrative-and-how-to-fix-it/2014/03

Kendi, I. X. (2019). *How to be an antiracist.* One World.

Kleinrock, E. (2020, June 30). Anti-racist work in schools: Are you in it for the long haul? *Learning for Justice.* www.learningforjustice.org/magazine/antiracist-work-in-schools-are-you-in-it-for-the-long-haul

Lorde, A. (1981). The uses of anger. *Women's Studies Quarterly.* https://academicworks.cuny.edu/wsq/509/

Mazzei, L. A. (2008). Silence speaks: Whiteness revealed in the absence of voice. *Teaching and Teacher Education, 24,* 1125–1136.

McBride, J. (2006). *The color of water: A Black man's tribute to his white mother.* Penguin.

Mehta, J. (2015, April 26). *The problem with grit.* The Harvard Graduate School of Education. www.gse.harvard.edu/ideas/news/15/04/problem-grit

Nieto, S. (1998). From claiming hegemony to sharing space: Creating community in multicultural education course. In R. Chavez, & J. O'Donnell (Eds.), *Speaking the unpleasant: The politics of (non)engagement in the multicultural education terrain* (pp. 16–31). State University of New York Press.

Ohito, E. O. (2016). Making the emperor's new clothes visible in anti-racist teacher education: Enacting a pedagogy of discomfort with white preservice teachers. *Equity & Excellence in Education, 49*(4), 454–467.

Ohito, E. O. (2019). Mapping women's knowledges of antiracist teaching in the United States: A feminist phenomenological study of three antiracist women teacher educators. *Teaching and Teacher Education, 86,* 102892.

Peterson, E. (2023, July 31). *Racial inequality in public school discipline for Black students in the United States.* Ballard Brief. https://ballardbrief.byu.edu/issue-briefs/racial-inequality-in-public-school-discipline-for-black-students-in-the-united-states

The Racial Equity Institute. (2022, October 19). *Groundwater approach.* Racial Equity Institute. https://racialequityinstitute.org/groundwater-approach/

Schwartz, K. (2015, May 5). *Does the grit narrative blame students for school's shortcomings?* KQED. www.kqed.org/mindshift

/39337/does-the-grit-narrative-blame-students-for-schools-shortcomings

The Stanford Educational Opportunity Monitoring Project. (n.d.). *Racial and ethnic achievement gaps.* https://cepa.stanford.edu/educational-opportunity-monitoring-project/achievement-gaps/race/

Wang, M., & Del Toro, J. (2021). The longitudinal inter-relations between school discipline and academic performance: Examining the role of school climate. *American Psychologist, 75,* 173–185.

7

Hold Space for Healing

Safe and stable relationships are essential for healing. Drawing on my work as a school leader and court appointed special advocate (CASA) for youth who are navigating foster care services, this chapter explores the ways leaders can cultivate healing environments in their school communities. This includes learning more about adverse childhood experiences (ACEs), trauma-informed practices, and ongoing commitments to safety, respect, inclusion, belonging, and teacher support.

> **Key Concept:** Safe and stable relationships are essential for healing.

The bright pinks and orange of a spectacular autumn sunset paint the sky over the Friday night lights at this high school stadium. I am rocking a baby on my hip and shouting encouragement to her "Buba," Jamal. Surprised to see me, a former colleague comes by and asks why I am at this rural school in a game outside my district. I am just about to stumble over a connection—*Well, I am a CASA but also a family friend and also I really love a good school football game*—when Jamal takes the ball and starts running full force for the end zone. Touch Down, Bears!!! We erupt with applause.

After years of supporting youth who are navigating foster services in my schools, I wanted a more direct way to support

DOI: 10.4324/9781003517122-13

this vulnerable population. Therefore, in 2021, I became a court appointed special advocate (CASA) for youth who are navigating the foster care system. As a result of this work, I have had the gift of learning directly with children from toddlerhood through high school. Research on the impact of CASAs aligns with many of the wholehearted leadership themes, particularly the power of relationships. For example, in a 2009 study on the CASA program in Houston, TX, Hersh Waxman, Robert Houston, Susan Profilet, and Betsi Sanchez reported that children who have a CASA achieved better academic and behavior outcomes in school. This finding has been replicated across the country and includes higher passing grades and fewer discipline referrals, including suspensions and expulsions (National CASA/GAL Association for Children, 2024).

A 2020 study by Colleen Cary, Peggy Grauwiler, Kerry Moles, and Sloan Post on the New York City CASA/GAL program reports that volunteers "play a critical role in supporting families by connecting parents with services aimed at securing safe and permanent housing and other support services that can aid in the reunification of their children." As Cary et al. share, there is limited empirical data on the close to 1,000 CASA advocates nationwide; however, similar findings have been reported in judicial circuits across the country.

Back at Jamal's game, I give his baby sister a high five and place her gently in her stroller. Her mama and I then jump around excited for Jamal and happy to be together. We are admittedly a loud group of foster parents, foster siblings, CASAs, biological siblings, Big Brothers, Big Sisters, mentors, neighbors, and friends. Tonight, I notice that the precipitating incident two years ago when Jamal and his siblings came into care feels long ago. Tonight, he is the home team football star and we are a family.

Every day in the United States nearly 370,000 children and youth, like Jamal, are navigating foster services (The Administration for Children and Families, 2024). As they go out for sports, sit for that algebra exam, and work up the courage to ask someone to go with them to the spring dance, they are also navigating past and current traumas including the ongoing effects of abuse and neglect, new placements, and court dates. It is no surprise that youth who are navigating foster care services often experience more difficulty in school compared to their peers. Research by McGuire et al. (2021) reports that these challenges exist across academic and behavioral domains in school. In their study they worked with 257 youth who were navigating care and asked these students to self-report on the factors that had the strongest positive difference on school outcomes. Teachers also participated in the study reporting on academic and behavior progress of the students. The two most important factors McGuire and colleagues identified were teacher support and social support. As a CASA myself, I have seen the ways stable consistent relationships, wrap-around services, and school-family-community partnerships can help fill in gaps in caring and supporting children as they journey from one day to the next. This work has also made me a better school leader.

In his bestselling book, *What Great Principals Do Differently*, Todd Whitaker (2020) writes that it is people not programs that bring change. It is our most human moments that define our relationships and set the culture of a school. In an interview with Education World, Whitaker said:

> The challenge for us as educators is to remember that we have chosen the most important profession; it is essential that we remind ourselves of this every day. The additional challenge for educational leaders is to help those we work with feel this level of importance each day. In education, we cannot afford to have a bad day—because the students we work with deserve never to have a bad day because of us.
>
> (Whitaker & Education World, n.d.)

In his book on great principals, Whitaker writes that unfortunately all of us can remember a time when we were treated poorly, often by a leader. This memory leaves a lasting mark on our confidence, efficacy, and trust. Whitaker argues that great principals, those who I would call *wholehearted leaders*, hold themselves to a high moral standard. It isn't that wholehearted leaders don't make mistakes. Of course they do, but they consistently place their priorities in people, are clear on their values, and practice thoughtful critical reflection to own and correct mistakes as quickly as possible.

I think of the principal who meets his students at the door each morning, the one who high fives kids as they jump off the bus, who calls each by name, and knows before 8:00 am who is walking into school in need of extra encouragement today. I think of the school leader who notices the eighth grader sitting alone in the cafeteria and leaves whatever she is working on to go share a peanut butter and jelly sandwich and make sure that young person sees a friendly face and laughs at lunch today. I think of all the football and soccer games, the art shows and science fairs. I think of these moments of connection and the school leaders who recognize that in the face of so much administrative work, emails, paperwork, and demands, it is these moments that matter most each day.

These moments also shape school culture—contributing to an environment where students are seen, known, safe, and when needed, can begin to heal. In their 2020 work, clinical psychologists Brandon Kohrt, Katherine Ottman, Catherine Panter-Brick, Melvin Konner, and Vikram Patel explored our human capacity to help one another to heal. Drawing on evolutionary theory, they cite empathy, emotional connection, self-regulation, and long periods of childhood as core drivers for the conditions that support our capacity to help each other heal. This process is inherently social and often nonlinear. Humans engage in emotional contagion. This means when we see another person, including a child, in a distressing situation we often engage in helping behaviors including perspective taking and compassion. When you can also draw on your relationship with the person, your knowledge of who they are and their context, you can personalize your support to console and provide compassion (Kohrt et al., 2020).

For some young people, the repeated impact of mistreatment through abuse and neglect contributes to chronic trauma. Again and again, I have seen how schools can be a safe haven, a place where young people are seen, known, and cared for—a place where healing can begin. I also know that it isn't only the young people in our buildings who find healing here. Teachers, staff, and administrators also come to our schools with their own traumas and griefs, and as the years stretch on, they too sometimes find healing here.

> ### Mandated Reporting
>
> As school leaders one of our most important roles is keeping children safe. This chapter has addressed some of the data around abuse and neglect; because of this, I want to include a reminder about our role as mandatory reporters.
>
> **All childhood professionals, including teachers, school counselors, and school leaders are mandatory reporters. A mandatory reporter is a person who is legally required to report any suspicion of child abuse or neglect.**
>
> The US Department of Health and Human Services defines child abuse and neglect as "any recent act or failure to act on the part of a parent or caregiver that results in death, serious physical or emotional harm, sexual abuse, or exploitation, or an act or failure to act that presents an imminent risk of serious harm" (2023).
>
> If you suspect child abuse or neglect, you are required to report it to the child abuse hotline immediately. Sometimes you may suspect abuse or neglect based on observation and other times children may disclose that they are being abused or neglected.
>
> If a young person shares this difficult information with you, listen actively. Your role as a responsive and trusted adult is critical in this situation. Thank the student for trusting you. Do not act shocked or ask lots of follow-up questions. You are not an investigator in this situation. Your job is to listen, to keep students safe in your care, and to connect families and students to resources as needed. Remind the young person that you care about them and their safety. Do not make promises about what the officials will or will not do after you report this. Focus on the things you can control within your office, classroom, or building. For example, reassure the student that you are committed to making school a safe place and to always act on behalf of their safety.

> While you will need to make the report, you can involve your school counseling team for support. You can also ask the student if they have another trusted adult in the building they would like to talk with, too.
>
> Reporting abuse and neglect is difficult work. Following a situation like this, check in with your own mental wellbeing. Consider professional resources for your own processing, too.
>
> You can read more about *trauma-informed leadership* in the concept study on Pgs. 67–73.

Learning and healing are interrelated processes. Caring professions like social work and education have the potential to promote what Loretta Pyles (2020) calls *healing justice*. She writes that doing so requires growing in intentional learning around self-care as a social justice issue, trauma-informed practices, compassion fatigue, organizational change, intersectionality, and collective care. Healing is one of the ways we get to practice belonging to each other. It is also how we learn a new way forward. Below are two strategies for safeguarding and promoting healing in your schools and districts.

Strategies for Practice

1. **Build responsive relationships.** School and outreach counselors provide responsive services or formative interventions to resolve and remediate immediate challenges or crises. During my career, I have worked with phenomenal school counselors, several of whom are referenced in this book. These professionals help students through difficult and sometimes unfair and unsafe situations. I have sat in on impromptu lessons on emotional regulation, safe relationships, and executive functioning. I have seen how the counselor's office can be a safe space during a hard day or exam. On my own tough days, I, too, have collapsed in a papasan chair in the back of a counselor's office only to find myself playing with a fidget toy from their desk and talking about my feelings.

In addition to responsive services, we want to also build *responsive relationships*. These critical relationships aren't just for counselors. Instead, school leaders, teachers, and support staff can all help fill these critical gaps for our students. In their 2018 research for the Swiss National Science Foundation, Luciano Gasser, Jeanine Grütter, Alois Buholzer, and Alexander Wettstein report that professionals like these "who consistently engage in building strong connections and are responsive to students' developmental needs provide students with an interaction context that is highly stimulating for the development of positive perceptions of student–teacher relationships" (p. 9). Their research showed that while relationships are essential for all students they have even greater significance for vulnerable children and youth. Responsive relationships are built on knowledge and the ongoing relationship work mentioned in this chapter such as sitting with students, meeting them at the door, attending sports and extracurriculars, and meeting with families. Responsive relationships are flexible enough to respond to immediate challenges and deep enough to build from a place of knowledge and care.

2. **Teach self-advocacy.** Cultivating self-advocacy in schools sends an important message to students that *you are the best expert on your experiences and needs. Your needs matter and when you speak for what you need, you deserve to be believed.* Self-advocacy teaches young people that they have agency in their learning and their healing.

    Cultivating self-advocacy in schools sends an important message to students that you are the best expert on your experiences and needs. Your needs matter and when you speak for what you need, you deserve to be believed. Self-advocacy teaches young people that they have agency in their learning and their healing.

To support students in growing as self-advocates, we need to (1) teach young people that their stories and identities are important, and (2) cultivate safe schools that celebrate differences and include a multiplicity of stories and identities. Bonnie Singer and Jennifer Mogensen (2021) write that self-advocacy is rooted in self-determination and self-value. To advocate on their own behalf, Stephen Shore (2004) writes that students must learn how to work toward mutual understanding, negotiate for necessary accommodations, and speak for their fulfillment. Just as advocacy and self-value are interrelated, so too are advocacy and disclosure. In order to speak on our behalf, we have to be able to articulate our needs.

Earlier this school year, I attended a conference on autism. The conference directors were intentional in including self-advocates as presenters in the sessions and panels. I found these voices among the most powerful teachers at the conference. Firsthand or lived experiences are knowledge-rich. When we learn with and from students from their own experiences we learn that "every student is... a layered human being with endless potential, brilliance, and access to community cultural wealth" (Safir & Dugan, 2021, p. 99). Superintendent student advisory councils, student-led IEPs, and open-door principal chats are all practices that I have seen help foster self-advocacy.

Reflective Work for Continuous Learning

Over the past decade, I have mentored new teacher leaders and teacher education students. These new and future educators often ask me what I wish I had known before entering the classroom. Sometimes it takes me a few moments to answer. It is not always because I am gathering my words; often it is because I am remembering specific students, young people like Jamal. There are a lot of stories I've come to know through my advocacy work with vulnerable children, including those navigating foster care services. While I can help carry those stories, most are not mine to share, and so I tell these future teachers that I wish I had had a better understanding of trauma, the way it presents in children, and the role safe schools and consistent relationships with adults can play in healing.

Holding space for healing is a hallmark of a supportive culture for all members of your school community. Below are reflective exercises to complete independently or with your leadership team to extend these practices further.

1. **Learn about ACEs.** "Adverse childhood experiences" (ACEs) are potentially traumatic events that occur in childhood (0–17 years). According to 2024 data by the CDC, approximately 61% of adults have experienced at least one ACE before age 18 and nearly 1 in 6 have experienced four or more types of ACEs. These include violence, abuse, neglect, losing a family member to suicide, substance abuse in the home, and instability due to parents or others in the household being incarcerated.

   ♦ What professional learning have you and your teams engaged in around ACEs?
   ♦ What supports do you have in place to help students who are navigating ACEs?
   ♦ What community partnerships and teachers can you leverage to support students who have experienced ACEs?
   ♦ Research by the National CASA/GAL Association for Children (2024) reports that "having a stable relationship with a supportive adult can help children do well; even when they have faced significant hardships." How can you support your team in building these kinds of stable relationships with students?

2. **Be for each other and for families.** At my current school, I often tell our team that *we are for each other*. Being for each other means that every member of our community is known and valued. It also means that the *family members* of our community are known and valued.

   ♦ How do you practice *being for each other* in your school community?
   ♦ What does this look like for students? What does this look like for staff?
   ♦ How well do you know the families of your students? How well do you know the families of your staff? Quiz yourself. What do you know about family compositions at your school? Do you know which students are navigating

foster care services including kinship placements? Do you know the students and partners of your staff?
- What additional work do you have to do in this area? How will you make sure families feel included and valued in your school traditions?

References

The Administration for Children and Families. (2024). *New data shows a consistent decrease of children in foster care.* www.acf.hhs.gov/media/press/2024/new-data-shows-consistent-decrease-children-foster-care#:~:text=%22ACF%20is%20focused%20on%20prevention,being%20and%20safe%20family%20reunification.%E2%80%9D

Cary, C., Grauwiler, P., Moles, K., & Post, S. S. (2020). *The context-specific service provision of CASA.* Child Welfare League of America.

Gasser, L., Grütter, J., Buholzer, A., & Wettstein, A. (2018). Emotionally supportive classroom interactions and students' perceptions of their teachers as caring and just. *Learning and Instruction, 54,* 82–92.

Kohrt, B. A., Ottman, K., Panter-Brick, C., Konner, M., & Patel, V. (2020). Why we heal: The evolution of psychological healing and implications for global mental health. *Clinical Psychology Review, 82,* 101920.

McGuire, A., Gabrielli, J., Hambrick, E., Abel, M. R., Guler, J., & Jackson, Y. (2021). Academic functioning of youth in foster care: The influence of unique sources of social support. *Children and Youth Services Review, 121,* 105867.

National CASA/GAL Association for Children. (2024, February 22). *Research and effectiveness.* https://nationalcasagal.org/our-impact/research-and-effectiveness/

Pyles, L. (2020). Healing justice, transformative justice, and holistic self-care for social workers. *Social Work, 65*(2), 178–187.

Safir, S., & Dugan, J. (2021). *Street data: A next-generation model for equity, pedagogy, and school transformation.* Corwin Press.

Shore, S. (2004). *Self-advocacy & autism.* Autism Research Institute. https://autism.org/self-advocacy/

Singer, B. D., & Mogensen, J. (2021). *Getting students to self-advocacy—step by step* [Dataset]. Leader Mag Digital Object Group. https://doi.org/10.1044/leader.ftr1.26082021.32

US Department of Health and Human Services. (2023, May 9). *What is child abuse or neglect? What is the definition of child abuse and neglect?* www.hhs.gov/answers/programs-for-families-and-children/what-is-child-abuse/index.html#:~:text=Child%20Abuse%20and%20Neglect%20Definition&text=%C2%A7%205106g)%2C%20as%20amended%20by,sexual%20abuse%20or%20exploitation%22%3B%20or

Waxman, H., Houston, R., Profilet, S., & Sanchez, B. (2009). The long-term effects of the Houston Child Advocates, Inc., program on children and family outcomes. *Child Welfare, 88*(6), 23–46.

Whitaker, T. (2020). *What great principals do differently: Twenty things that matter most.* Routledge.

Whitaker, T., & Education World. (n.d.). Motivating teachers: A wire side chat with Todd Whitaker. *Education World.* www.educationworld.com/a_issues/chat/chat042-5.shtml

8

Foster a Sense of Belonging

Belonging is well cited as an essential protective factor associated with both academic performance and wellness outcomes. This chapter explores strategies school leaders can use to foster a greater sense of belonging in their communities.

 Key Concept: Welcome people right where they are.

The students will arrive in a moment. For now we are organizing crayons and art materials, preparing ourselves for the chaos and excitement of 23 six-year-olds.

The first child to enter the classroom walks right up to me. In a few minutes, I will learn that she serves in dual appointments as class leader and class clown. For now, though, we are just meeting for the first time.

I lower myself to her eye level.

"Você fala português?" (Do you speak Portuguese?) she challenges me.

"Estou aprendendo, assim como você está aprendendo inglês." (I am learning, just like you are learning English.)

She looks at me seriously, and quizzes me to check if I am telling the truth. "Um dois três…"

DOI: 10.4324/9781003517122-14

When I answer, "quatro cinco seis!" she giggles and gives me a hug.

Now that we're friends, it is her responsibility to teach me their class handshake. It starts with a high five and ends with a fist bump. She has me practice twice.

****

I love this story of how a precocious six-year-old ensured I experienced a sense of belonging in her classroom. She knew that to belong in this space I would need some basic Portuguese, the class handshake, and a friend, and she was willing to provide all three. In recent years belonging has gained an important focus on research related to diversity, inclusion, and equity.

"Social belonging," write Carr et al. for the *Harvard Business Review*, "is a fundamental human need, hardwired into our DNA" (2019, para 1). It has long been cited as an essential protective factor for both academic and social-emotional outcomes (Arslan, 2021; Korpershoek et al., 2020). School climate, fairness, and safety are key indicators of a sense of belonging in schools (Evans, 2024).

When I stand by the door to greet students and staff in their home language, I am hoping to foster a brief moment of connection. I am hoping to send a quick message that in this school community, you are seen and valued. Belonging moments like these lead to a greater continuity between home and school (Bowen, 2021). Of course, multilingual greetings and special handshakes are not enough to shift school culture on their own. Instead strategies like this are one of many ways school leaders can foster belonging in their daily interactions with students and staff.

Research at BetterUp showed "that belonging is a close cousin to many related experiences: mattering, identification, and social connection. The unifying thread across these themes is that they all revolve around the sense of being accepted and included by those around you" (Carr et al., 2019, para 4). Researchers in the Netherlands and Norway conducted a meta-analysis on belonging outcomes and found that students' motivational, social-emotional, behavioral, and academic achievement outcomes were all positively correlated with a strong sense of belonging in schools. These findings held up in studies conducted across different school contexts (Korpershoek et al., 2020).

In his study of 244 high school students in Turkey, Dr. Gökmen Arslan found that *social exclusion* strongly predicted loneliness and mental health challenges. Conversely, *social inclusion* played an essential role in mediating these challenges. Consistent with other research on the topic, Arslan found that belonging-based interventions played a protective and proactive factor in promoting mental health and wellbeing in school settings (Arslan, 2021).

Strategies for Practice

As a school leader, you have the responsibility to ensure that all students and staff in your building(s) are seen and known. This includes fostering safe and supportive relationships with school staff and peers. While peer relationships are important in the classroom, often as students progress to secondary school, extracurricular activities become another essential opportunity to develop relationships, common interests, and new skills. A 2021 study by nine researchers in the US and Canada report that school-based extracurricular activities (ECAs) are "uniquely likely to sustain engagement" in school and life perseverance (Thouin et al., 2022, p. 2). Their paper for Applied Developmental Science cites that the academic and nonacademic skills and relationships developed within school-based ECAs can be readily leveraged to build perseverance. This outcome is most pronounced when activities are led by school staff (Thouin et al., 2022).

With these concepts in mind, below are three strategies to cultivate a greater sense of belonging in your schools.

1. **Make belonging visible.** A week or so before the new school year, Jessica Breyare, a preschool educator, found herself sitting *criss-cross applesauce* on the floor of an empty classroom, in a building where she didn't work. She thoughtfully strung W-E-L-C-O-M-E on a string and climbed up on blue plastic chairs to hang her brightly colored banner for the incoming

Grade 5 group. The elementary school was still looking for a Grade 5 teacher, and it didn't look like they would have a permanent hire before the school year started. Knowing that Jessica has a gift for classroom decorations and a heart for belonging, the principal asked if she would help ready the classroom for the incoming group.

Jesicca told me, "Even if they didn't have a teacher yet, we wanted those students to know we were excited for them to be there. We wanted them to know we had been thinking about them."

Once the students arrive, theirs is the next critical voice in setting up an inclusive learning space. Danish Kurani writes that "It's crucial school leaders consult students about the kind of school they want to attend. If students have a say, they're more likely to feel like the space belongs to them and that they belong there" (2024, para 1). Kurani goes on to share specific examples of student spaces including cafeterias and labs where students were instrumental members of the design team. When students see that their voice matters in how learning spaces are constructed those spaces become theirs. This ownership contributes to a powerful sense of belonging and translates to higher levels of learning.

In addition to involving students in design decisions, school and classroom leaders can also be thoughtful about including positive examples of student work and role models that represent their cultural and identity backgrounds (Terada, 2018). These design choices send a message to students that their work, their experiences, and their voice matters here. Peter Barrett, Fay Davies, Yufan Zhang, and Lucinda Barrett (2015) analyzed 153 classrooms and 27 schools and found that when students feel ownership of the classroom space, their responsibility, learning, and engagement all rise.

2. **Safeguard belonging as engagement.** On the first day of the new summer program, I was in the cafeteria for lunch. The nervous energy was almost palpable. Just across the way, a high school student stumbled, dropping his food and a very full glass of ice tea on the floor. A nearby student applauded in jest. Before I could say a word, a faculty member swiftly told

the jokester, "That's not how we do it here. If someone drops something, you help them pick it up." As he said this, he was already bending down to help gather up the plastic dishes. The jokester looked at him in surprise and then picked up a paper towel to help. I watched as the three cleaned things up and then finished lunch together.

For several summers now, I have had the opportunity to teach and support summer programming at the Missouri Scholars Academy. This residential program for gifted high school students is a masterclass in cultivating belonging. In addition to examples like the one above, if someone is sitting by themselves in the cafeteria, the school culture is to take notice and move to join them. Longtime faculty cite belonging as part of the magic of the program and know that one of their roles is to teach new scholars that in this space, belonging is how we engage with each other.

3. **Check your extracurricular activities for inclusion.** When she was in sixth grade, our daughter came home and announced she was going out for the middle school archery team. No one in our immediate family had ever shot an archery bow. "It's okay," she said, "I learned how in PE." This was precisely what Commissioner Tom Bennett of the Kentucky Department of Fish and Wildlife Resources hoped when he advocated with his state education department to make archery a school sport option for students. With his advocacy, the Kentucky Department of Education agreed to start the program, on the condition that archery also became a physical education class in middle school. The program grew rapidly. Since its inception in 2002, the National Archery in the Schools Program (NASP) has supported over 21 million students in grades 4–12 to learn archery basics and the program has grown to nearly 10,000 schools nationwide.

As a school leader, I was struck by the way this program intentionally fosters belonging. Their program page says, "NASP is an activity that doesn't discriminate based on popularity, athletic skill, gender, size, or academic ability. It's a different kind of team sport. It's open to any student. Its biggest supporters are professional educators. Teams come together around one thing: Archery" (NASP, n.d.). As parents of an archer, we saw firsthand what the NASP writes is the magic of archery—inclusion. "Archery… has proven to captivate students and leave educators awestruck by its uncanny ability to 'connect' students with their school. School connectedness is widely recognized as a major factor in dropout prevention." They go on to report that for many students, archery is the only extracurricular activity many of the athletes participate in and that until archery was added as a team sport, some of these same students displayed the risk-factors cited above for exclusion and loneliness.

The takeaway here isn't necessarily to start an archery program in your schools; instead it is to ensure that there are programs where inclusion is written into the ethos of involvement and where all students can experience belonging, challenge, and encouragement.

Reflective Work for Continuous Learning

Edutopia writer Sandra Castellanos tracks the origin of buddy benches to a second grade student leader named Christian Bucks. Christian envisioned a specially designated bench on the school playground where students could go if they needed a friend. If someone sat on the buddy bench, it would cue others to go sit beside them and invite them to play. Christian was on to something, as buddy benches are now a popular playground tool to promote belonging and friendship among early elementary students. Castellanos shares that "buddy benches create awareness, and with awareness comes the responsibility to act" (2023, para 4).

This reminds me of the faculty member who role models to others that in our cafeteria no one eats alone. It reminds me of the six-year-old leader who notices someone new in the classroom and welcomes her in by sharing the class handshake. There are countless ways we can show up for each other. When school leaders build belonging into how we do school, students and staff learn the most important lesson of all—you belong here.

Working alone or as a leadership team, consider these exercises and questions for ways to foster a greater sense of belonging in your school communities.

> *This reminds me of the faculty member who role models to others that in our cafeteria no one eats alone. It reminds me of the six-year-old leader who notices someone new in the classroom and welcomes her in by sharing the class handshake. There are countless ways we can show up for each other. When school leaders build belonging into how we do school, students and staff learn the most important lesson of all—you belong here.*

1. **Celebrate unsung heroes for belonging.** While school leaders set the tone and moral obligation for a culture of belonging in their buildings, it is often support staff who play vital roles in making sure students and families are seen and known. The first person I met when I started my career in public education was a parent leader who often helped families navigate our public systems, including health care. The second person I met was a school secretary who doubled as our school nurse and lead Spanish-English translator. At my current school, our front office specialist is often the first person to greet new families and students on the phone. These three people play a critical role in welcoming newcomers to our school communities and making sure they are supported and heard right away.
    - Who are the staff and unsung heroes in your schools that are engaged in this work?
    - How can you celebrate, support, and learn from them?
2. **Ensure that every student is well known by at least one adult in your building.** Several years ago one of our school goals was to *ensure that every student is well known by at least one adult in our school*. This goal came from our accreditation review process with the Cognia Global Commission. Achieving the goal required our faculty and staff to take a close look at

relationships across our school community. In auditing for these relationships, we were forced to ask important questions about opportunities and barriers for belonging. This exercise brought key strengths to light such as the way co-teachers collaborated to form more comprehensive support for students in one of our English Language Arts / Social Studies programs. It also brought key areas for improvement to light such as the need for more ECAs for our independent online students. I believe auditing whether every student is well known by at least one adult in the building is a useful exercise for all school leaders.

In smaller schools, I have heard of principals leading team workshops where they hang school photos of every student in the school and ask faculty and staff to write strengths and interests about the students on Post-It notes. This visual representation often brings new information to the surface both about specific student strengths and critical gaps in belonging for individual students or student groups. However you conduct your audit, take time to process the findings with your team and to plan intentionally for next steps to increase belonging.

3. **Cultivate belonging for your team.** Belonging isn't just for students. In a 2021 article for *Forbes*, Nicole Fernandes writes that even those workplaces that prioritize diversity, inclusion, and equity struggle to implement change in belonging outcomes. When individuals feel that they truly belong, they are more connected, committed, and engaged (Fernandes, 2021). Much like the student audit, thoughtfully review your staff and faculty rosters.

- How well do you know each of the people on your team? Consider strengths, family compositions, and challenges.
- How are you fostering a sense of belonging into your team processes? Consider mentorship, sponsorship, and allyship.
- Whose voices are amplified in team meetings and school decisions and whose are missing?
- What upcoming opportunities do you have to learn from each other and laugh together?

References

Arslan, G. (2021). Psychological maltreatment and spiritual wellbeing in Turkish college young adults: Exploring the mediating effect of college belonging and social support. *Journal of Religion and Health, 60*(2), 709–725.

Barrett, P., Davies, F., Zhang, Y., & Barrett, L. (2015). The impact of classroom design on pupils' learning: Final results of a holistic, multi-level analysis. *Building and environment, 89*, 118–133.

Bowen, J. (2021, October 21). Why is it important for students to feel a sense of belonging at school? "Students choose to be in environments that make them feel a sense of fit," says Associate Professor DeLeon Gray. *College of Education News.* https://ced.ncsu.edu/news/2021/10/21/why-is-it-important-for-students-to-feel-a-sense-of-belonging-at-school-students-choose-to-be-in-environments-that-make-them-feel-a-sense-of-fit-says-associate-professor-deleon-gra/

Carr, E., Reece, A., Kellerman, G., & Robichaux, A. (2019). The value of belonging at work. *Harvard Business Review.* https://hbr.org/2019/12/the-value-of-belonging-at-work

Castellanos, S. (2023, September 27). Kindergarten buddy benches. *Edutopia.* www.edutopia.org/article/kindergarten-buddy-benches/

Evans, M. (2024, May 8). *Nurturing a sense of belonging at school: What helps pupils feel connected?* National Children's Bureau. www.ncb.org.uk/about-us/media-centre/news-opinion/nurturing-sense-belonging-school-what-helps-pupils-feel

Fernandes, N. (2021, April 21). Belonging: The intersection of DEI and engagement. *Forbes.* www.forbes.com/councils/forbeshumanresourcescouncil/2021/12/22/belonging-the-intersection-of-dei-and-engagement/

Korpershoek, H., Canrinus, E. T., Fokkens-Bruinsma, M., & De Boer, H. (2020). The relationships between school belonging and students' motivational, social-emotional, behavioural, and academic outcomes in secondary education: A meta-analytic review. *Research Papers in Education, 35*(6), 641–680.

Kurani, D. (2024, May 7). *How to design a school for belonging.* Getting Smart. www.gettingsmart.com/2024/04/18/how-to-design-a-school-for-belonging/

National Archery in the Schools Program (NASP). (n.d.). *What is NASP®.* www.naspschools.org/what-is-nasp/

Terada, Y. (2018, October 24). Dos and don'ts of classroom decorations. *Edutopia.* www.edutopia.org/article/dos-and-donts-classroom-decorations?utm_source=Facebook&utm_medium=Social&utm_campaign=BTS+24&utm_id=BTS24&utm_term=classroom+decor&utm_content=research&fbclid=IwY2xjawEoiw9leHRuA2FlbQIxMQABHaRzKnnrg0GgbuW2spu5oJZCf8Sp-0qcNC_8yOd-0FszqGVViWa2kwFjXA_aem_uIKyUPFN0J7FrLFx2VJGew

Thouin, É., Dupéré, V., Dion, E., McCabe, J., Denault, A. S., Archambault, I., ... & Crosnoe, R. (2022). School-based extracurricular activity involvement and high school dropout among at-risk students: Consistency matters. *Applied Developmental Science, 26*(2), 303–316.

9

Practice Inclusion

With a focus on supporting students and staff from the disability community, this chapter offers school-based strategies for advancing inclusion and ongoing learning. With chapter contributor Kaci Conley, we argue that cultivating a culture of belonging doesn't happen by accident or inertia. Instead it happens through countless daily decisions, intentionality, and learning. Inclusion is an active practice.

> **Key Concept:** Cultivating a culture of belonging doesn't happen by accident or inertia. It is an active practice that happens through countless daily decisions, intentionality, and learning.

The World Health Organization (WHO) reports that "Disability is part of being human." According to the WHO, almost everyone will temporarily or permanently experience disability at some point in their life. In their 2023 report, the WHO estimates that 1.3 billion people—about 16% of the global population—currently experience a significant disability. Faculty, staff, and students in your school communities are among those represented in this report. The Individuals with Disabilities Education Act (IDEA) provides the legislative foundation for disability inclusion in US schools. Although this legislation affects us all, many

DOI: 10.4324/9781003517122-15

general educators have told me they have limited exposure to and knowledge about special education policy and best practices. Recently several confided that they were unsure about how to talk about disability and so they often avoided the conversation. While thinking through this, I remembered an advocacy training Kaci Conley and I worked on together in 2022. During that training, Kaci said, "I want people to know that disability isn't a bad word." Building on this idea, Kaci and I collaborated on the following chapter to help school leaders feel empowered to make inclusion an active practice in their classrooms.

When I first met Kaci, she was a high school junior. Even then she was already teaching our faculty, staff, and peers about the importance of service, leadership, and accessibility. Today, she is a psychological researcher. Her published work focuses on reducing ableism and exclusion for people with disabilities. Further, she shares her lived experiences in workshops teaching attendees how to be more inclusive of people with disabilities, and as a graduate student leader, she organizes and hosts events focused on disability advocacy, accessibility, and inclusion. As a person with complex medical and physical disabilities, Kaci proudly identifies with the disability community.

Our conversation began with the complementary ways educators can use both *people-first* and *identity-first* language to respect the personhood of students and staff in our school communities. Like other best practices, language evolves over time (NIH, 2023). As Kaci explains, "Disabled subgroups have differing preferences (e.g., the Deaf community typically prefers identity-first language like a Deaf adult, and the Down syndrome community typically prefers person-first language like a child with Down syndrome)." Knowing that practice shapes culture and language shapes perception, these decisions are more than just semantic choices (Fishman-Weaver, 2019).

Key Vocabulary

♦ **The Individuals with Disabilities Education Act (IDEA):** Enacted in 1975, IDEA provides the legislative foundation

for disability inclusion in US schools. The cornerstone pieces of this act include that all students are entitled to a *free and appropriate public education* in the *least restrictive environment*.
- **People-First Language:** A commitment to respecting personhood by putting a person before their disability. People-first language utilizes phrases such as "person with a disability," "individuals with disabilities," and "children with disabilities," as opposed to phrases that identify people based solely on their disability (Office of Disability Rights, n.d.).
- **Identity-First Language:** A commitment to respecting personhood by leading with the identities that a person values first. These identities may include disability or membership in a specific culture, including disability culture. The disAbility Law Center of Virginia (2024) writes that identity-first language "incorporates the disability into the description of the individual first, right off the bat. Not as a secondary item, but a clarifying one." Examples include "Autistic student," "Deaf artist," and "wheelchair user." Kaci shares, "Over the past few years, there has been a shift to reclaim the word disability."

Strategies for Practice

Below are three strategies to start the work of increasing inclusion and belonging, decreasing ableism, and opening up conversations about disability. These strategies are important for both your students and staff.

1. **Respect personhood. If you don't know, ask. If you can't ask, choose person-first approaches.** Each of us is the most important expert on our own lived experiences and identities. If you don't know the language a student or staff member prefers to use to talk about their disability—or any other

aspect of their identity—ask. Respect their answer and the person giving that answer.

As Kaci writes, "I typically explain that it is important to follow the preference of the person with the disability. When in doubt, I use person-first language. Either way, with person-first or identity-first language, both the disability identity and personhood are acknowledged. And I also mention to never just say *the disabled* because it is dehumanizing and fails to acknowledge personhood."

2. **Check your ableism. Ask yourself:** *Is (dis)ability relevant in this context?* Ableism is defined by Conley and Nadler (2022) as discrimination in favor of people without disabilities and against people with disability. "All forms of ableism are harmful and range broadly from well-meaning/benevolent to negative/hostile. Well-meaning ableism may stem from pity, and negative ableism may stem from negative attitudes towards people with disabilities" (Conley & Nadler, p. 21). Addressing abelsim requires vigilance, unlearning, and holding each other accountable.

Recently I worked with our team on a job posting for a school staff position. The posting used a standard HR form with a checklist of "required abilities" for the position. Among these were tasks like walking and lifting. The first draft I received had both of these checked. I couldn't see any reason why this desk position would require such abilities and so I asked for more information. This led to an important conversation about ableism, professional accessibility, and unchecking those boxes.

Likewise, ableism can cloud our expectations regarding what children with disabilities are capable of and what activities and classes they are or are not recommended for. As Kaci shared with me, "I always advocate for people to consider when it is appropriate to talk about someone's disability. If a situation requires mentioning a person's disability, I explain that using the appropriate language is important. However, if mentioning a disability is irrelevant to the situation, I explain that people don't have to mention it." Children with disabilities are children first. They are also athletes, scholars, leaders, artists, and valued members of our school community. Our language, practices, and expectations should reflect this.

3. **Be an active learner.** As school leaders and educators, we must commit to ongoing learning. Reading books like this one is a nice first step in learning. However, a more powerful practice is to commit to intentional listening and relationship building with students, families, and staff from the cultural groups you need to learn more about.

This chapter argues that inclusion is an active practice. As a school leader, you play an essential role in shaping the culture of belonging at your school. If your work is in public schools, you also have an essential, legal responsibility to ensure all students in your care receive a free and appropriate public education in the least restrictive environment possible. No matter where your work occurs, you have a moral responsibility that all students in your care feel seen and known, experience belonging, and are supported in achieving at high expectations. This lofty work requires continuous learning about the legal, personal, and academic needs of the students and staff in your schools.

As our schools work toward greater inclusion, the National Institutes of Health (2023) urge us to lean into creativity, flexibility, respect, and curiosity. "The disability community is such a diverse group," shares Kaci, who goes on to name "temporary and permanent disabilities, congenital disabilities, and disabilities that develop later in life" as examples. "Even individuals' relationships with their disabilities differ and may change over time. Some are less comfortable with identifying as a member of the disability community, which might be influenced by the ableism they face or have internalized, and some individuals take immense pride in their disability identity." As with so many things in education, "There is no one-size-fits-all approach. I believe an individualized approach is needed to ensure everyone is supported and included."

Often our most important learning happens through relationships. Our students' identities and personhood matters. These matter, because our students matter.

> *Often our most important learning happens through relationships. Our students' identities and personhood matters. These matter, because our students matter.*

✏️ Reflective Work for Continuous Learning

Dr. Temple Grandin is a prominent author and speaker on both autism and animal behavior. Half the cattle in the United States are handled in facilities she designed. Fifteen years ago, I taught my high school students about Dr. Grandin's work. For many of our students—especially our twice-exceptional students and students with agriculture backgrounds—they felt seen in ways they hadn't before in school. In 2024, I got to share this story with Dr. Grandin and say thank you.

She was 77 years old at the time we met and had just returned from a trip to Argentina to work with livestock handlers. Today, Dr. Grandin is a celebrated Professor of Animal Science at Colorado State University. However, as a young girl with autism, she writes that:

> she was considered weird and teased and bullied in high school. The only place she had friends was in activities where there was a shared interest, such as horses, electronics, or model rockets. Mr. Carlock, her science teacher, was an important mentor who encouraged her interest in science. When she had a new goal of becoming a scientist, she had a reason for studying.
>
> (Grandin, n.d.)

As educators and school leaders, we have the opportunity to be that pivotal person like Mr. Carlock. During her lecture, Dr. Grandin talked about the importance of practical approaches to inclusion and high expectations. She shared that high expectations means giving students opportunities to stretch beyond their comfort zones, to try something new, to make mistakes, and to work on interesting problems where finding the solution takes time. As I often remind my students, *wisdom is ubiquitous*. In her lecture, Dr. Grandin reminded me that genius is also ubiquitous, and that too often educators are missing the genius in their own communities. "Great minds," Grandin reminds us, "are not all the same."

Working alone or with your leadership team, consider these reflective exercises to apply the lessons from this chapter in your schools.

1. **Audit your school for inclusion and respond with intentionality.** Making inclusion an active practice in your school or district means knowing both the spaces to celebrate and the spaces where there is more work to do.
    ♦ Within your school communities, who are the individuals and groups that are still being educated in separate classrooms and programs?
    ♦ In addition to your physical spaces and programs, check your hiring practices and policies for barriers to accessibility and embedded ableism.
2. **Expand your advising circle. Representation matters.** Who are your advisors and mentors? This includes young people on your student advisory councils.
    ♦ Are members of the disability community represented in your advising groups? If so, what are you learning from these leaders about culture, accessibility, inclusion, and expectations?
    ♦ If not, what corrections can you make, so that these voices are better represented in your planning meetings?
    ♦ Are members of the disability community celebrated in your curriculum, assemblies, and guest lectures?
3. **Choose a starting place and keep going.** What steps will you take to expand opportunities for access, inclusion, friendship, and student leadership in your schools and districts? Consider both practical steps to inclusion such as attending to the material conditions of your buildings (e.g., fixing

flickering lights and installing additional ramps in high-traffic areas) and philosophical steps such as reworking your mainstreaming practices.
- ♦ What are the barriers to these opportunities and how will you begin to problem-solve for them?

References

Conley, K. T., & Nadler, D. R. (2022). Reducing ableism and the social exclusion of people with disabilities: Positive impacts of openness and education. *Psi Chi Journal of Psychological Research, 27*(1), 21–32. https://doi.org/10.24839/2325-7342.jn27.1.21

disAbility Law Center of Virginia. (2024, February 7). *Person first language and identity first language.* disAbility Law Center of Virginia. www.dlcv.org/language-blog

Fishman-Weaver, K. (2019). *When your child learns differently: A family approach for navigating special education services with love and high expectations.* Routledge Press.

Grandin, T. (n.d.). *Welcome to Temple Grandin's official autism website.* www.templegrandin.com

National Institutes of Health (NIH). (2023, April 19). *Writing respectfully: Person-first and identity-first language.* www.nih.gov/about-nih/what-we-do/science-health-public-trust/perspectives/writing-respectfully-person-first-identity-first-language

Office of Disability Rights. (n.d.). *People first language.* https://odr.dc.gov/page/people-first-language

World Health Organization (WHO). (2023, March 7). *Disability.* www.who.int/news-room/fact-sheets/detail/disability-and-health

 ## Concept Study: What Is an Upstander?

♦ **Upstander:** —Someone who speaks, acts, or intervenes to support others and stop bullying.

My school system's secondary programs include resources specifically designed to stand up to bullying. These resources were developed by school counselor Matt Miltenberg, who also partnered with me on this concept study. These upstander lessons are just one part of our holistic school approach to wellbeing, belonging, and student leadership. When implemented across policy, practice, and direct instruction, school leaders can help reduce bullying and build a climate of greater safety and inclusion.

Like racism, sexism, and homophobia, bullying is about power. School bullying includes bullies, victims, and often a large number of people who witness bullying (Eijigu & Teketel, 2021). Bullying is unwanted, aggressive behavior that attempts to exercise *power over* others. This can include physical, verbal, and social actions to harm another person. The wounds of bullying can be both physical and emotional. Bullying is repeated or has the potential to be repeated over time (ASPA, 2024). It can lead to ongoing and escalating harm to the victim's social-emotional wellbeing. Data from the Centers for Disease Control and Prevention (CDC) shows that students who experience bullying are "at increased risk for depression, anxiety, sleep difficulties, lower academic achievement, and dropping out of school" (National Bullying Prevention Center, 2020).

Most bullying situations include three roles:
- the person acting as a bully
- the person being bullied
- bystanders (active or passive).

Bystanders observe bullying but do not intervene. A passive bystander might walk by a bullying incident without engaging. An active bystander might participate in the situation by laughing or encouraging the bully. With cyber bullying, they might amplify the harm by sharing, commenting, or "liking" a hurtful attack.

While we often only see the three roles defined above in school bullying, there is a fourth role, too. When you make the choice to intervene in a bullying situation, you move from being a bystander to becoming an *upstander*. Upstanders can help change the outcomes of bullying by creating school environments where bullying behavior is less likely to occur. Being an upstander is powerful. It is also one the most difficult and courageous things we ask young people to do. This means it is something we must actively teach and support. As with all leadership skills, we want to teach upstander behaviors with compassion, reminding young people that they have agency in how to practice this skill.

In his school counseling work, Matt talks about the range of choices students have in practicing upstander behavior. These choices fall along a continuum of intensity depending on how they decide to intervene. The most intense choice is a direct approach during the escalating situation. In this approach the student speaks directly to the person engaged in bullying, telling them to stop. Somewhere in the middle of the intensity continuum might be coalition building with another peer nearby, causing a distraction that deescalates the situation, or otherwise makes it more difficult for the bullying to continue. The least intense choice might be speaking to the student who was bullied afterward. In this conversation, the upstander can let the student know that they saw what happened. This conversation says: *I see you and I care*. There are many ways upstanders can use their voice and their power for good. All of these help support healing, repair, and a safer school climate.

The power to be an upstander comes from within; it comes from doing the right thing and using your voice to speak up for inclusion even if it shakes as you do. It comes from telling bullies to stop and from calling out and reporting bullying, injustice, discrimination, and toxic gossip. There is documented power in being an upstander. Data by the National Bullying Prevention Center (2020) shows that more than half of bullying situations (57%) stop when a peer intervenes on behalf of the student being bullied. Instead of *power over* another, upstanders build toward *power with* to create more inclusive realities in their schools.

Solving bullying isn't just about student action, personal responsibility, or even courage alone. This is because bullying doesn't happen in isolation. It happens in social contexts, including the social context of our schools. As school leaders, it is essential that we build systems, policies, and practices that contribute to safe, inclusive environments. This means taking a hard look at our broader school climate and the roles each of us play in caring for our shared community. The Wholehearted Leadership Framework is based on relationships; so too, are inclusive school climates. As school leaders, one of the most protective factors we have is being intentional about building relationships and creating opportunities for students to do the same.

As Matt has found in his school counseling work, it is less likely that someone will be an upstander for a stranger. However, when we are intentional about creating positive relationships, we can create climates where students aren't strangers anymore. Now, the student who is being bullied might be a friend from Pokémon club or the kid I sat next to during that Algebra 2 Candy Cram after school. Relationships change our climate and our interpersonal dynamics—they also give us the courage to act.

As school leaders, we must be intentional about building relationships, modeling kindness and advocacy, and teaching upstander behaviors. Additionally, we can teach students and staff that they don't have to wait until a situation has escalated to bullying to intervene. As allies, advocates, and friends, we can all step in when situations begin to get uncomfortable or unkind. By establishing a culture of inclusion and belonging, each of us can use our power within to safeguard the wellbeing of every member of our school community and the inclusive climate we are building together.

Questions for Consideration

1. **Lead for Courage.** How will you affirm and support student leaders who practice care in both bold and quiet ways? Are agency and choice part of your upstander lessons? How will you collaborate with your school counselor(s) to teach students and staff about advocacy, safety, and becoming upstanders? Set specific goals for this collaboration.

2. **Lead for Justice.** Consider the ways your school climate is making bullying more or less likely. How will you build intentionality into relationships in your schools? What opportunities do students have to get to know each other and build new friendships particularly across student groups, cultures, and identities?
3. **Lead for Connection.** Early intervention can be an important safeguard for inclusive school climates. Which spaces in your school communities could use some early care regarding belonging and safety? What is the first step you will take to help shift the tides in these spaces?

References

Assistant Secretary for Public Affairs (ASPA). (2024, October 8). *What is bullying.* www.stopbullying.gov/bullying/what-is-bullying

Eijigu, T. D., & Teketel, S. Z. (2021). Bullying in schools: Prevalence, bystanders' reaction and associations with sex and relationships. *BMC Psychology, 9,* 1–10.

National Bullying Prevention Center. (2020). *Bullying statistics.* www.pacer.org/bullying/info/stats.asp

10
Advocate for Inclusion

This chapter explores strategies for advancing inclusion, ongoing learning, and a culture of belonging in your school communities. Drawing on examples from my own leadership practice as well as the research on the mental health experiences of LGBTQ+ students in schools, these examples call on school leaders to advocate for inclusion. This chapter is a powerful companion to the concept study on upstanders and affirms that educators can and do save lives every day (pp. 119–123).

> **Key Concept:** Through care and advocacy, educators can and do save lives.

In 2020, I was appointed the executive director of a large school system. When I stepped into that role, I pulled our team together to talk about values, advocacy, and inclusion. I shared how humbled I was to serve in this important role. I also shared that I expected all of us to stand up to bullying and other acts of exclusion. I told my team they could expect the same from me. I then asked that we hold each other accountable for creating an inclusive and safe school culture for all students, faculty, and staff. It was important to me that this was among the first messages the team heard from me. It wasn't that bullying was a growing problem in our school; instead, I wanted to establish right from the beginning the inclusive values that matter to me as a leader and the culture of belonging I wanted us to co-create. While my school wasn't seeing physical acts of bullying, I was aware of quieter moments of gossip. I also worried that not all students, faculty, and staff were receiving the message that they belonged. DoSomething.org (2019) reports that 70% of school staff have seen bullying. This means we all have work to do. My team got to work, and we haven't stopped since. Four years later, at our summer admin retreat, I asked our administrators to write down their top school-year celebrations. We went around the table and every administrator shared about our culture of inclusion, belonging, and support.

> *It wasn't that bullying was a growing problem in our school; instead, I wanted to establish right from the beginning the inclusive values that matter to me as a leader and the culture of belonging I wanted us to co-create... Inclusive school communities are made. They are built through intentionality, accountability, and ongoing learning.*

Inclusive school communities are made. They are built through intentionality, accountability, and ongoing learning. This work also requires context. For the remainder of this chapter, I want to share some of the work our team has done specifically to support LGBTQ+ students and staff in our school system.

*****

Around 2021, we started hearing from some of our LGBTQ+ students that they had transferred from their local schools to our online high school program because they felt safer in that school environment. This data is consistent with the most recent school climate survey by GLSEN (Kosciw et al., 2022). While I was glad to learn that students felt safer in our school, I felt an important responsibility to make sure our team was actively engaged in professional learning to address the alarming mental health and safety statistics released by leading organizations such as GLSEN and the Trevor Project. To start this work, we instituted mandatory Safe Space training for all faculty and staff in our school system (Safe Space Training, n.d.). The training was conducted by a local LGBTQ+ university resource center.

Safe space training and related professional learning is important because LGBTQ+ youth are at greater risk for mental health conditions including suicidal ideation (NAMI, n.d.). Below are some harrowing statistics on the experiences of LGBTQ+ students in schools:

- More than 70% of LGBTQ+ students reported feeling unsafe in school (GLSEN, 2021; Kosciw et al., 2022, xv).
- LGBTQ+ students are more than *twice as likely as their peers* to experience persistent feelings of sadness or hopelessness, with transgender youth facing even further disparities (NAMI, n.d.).
- 45% of LGBTQ+ students seriously considered attempting suicide in the past year (Paley, 2022).

Said more plainly, teachers and school leaders can (and do) save lives. In 2024, 78% of LGBTQ+ young people who attend school reported having at least one adult who is supportive and affirming of their LGBTQ+ identity at school (Nath et al., 2024). As a school leader, I wanted to make sure the teachers and staff in my school are equipped to be those caring adults.

Schools can play an essential role in changing this narrative. The Trevor Project reports that "LGBTQ+ young people who had access to LGBTQ+-affirming spaces, and transgender and nonbinary youth who had access to gender-affirming spaces, reported lower rates of attempting suicide compared to those who did not" (2020). Said more plainly, teachers and school leaders can (and do) save lives.

In 2024, 78% of LGBTQ+ young people who attend school reported having at least one adult who is supportive and affirming of their LGBTQ+ identity at school (Nath et al., 2024). As a school leader, I wanted to make sure the teachers and staff in my school are equipped to be those caring adults.

Strategies for Practice

To help with this, I partnered with Anthony Plogger, an educational coordinator on our staff. Together, we developed a series of professional learning resources for our team and later for future educators. I drew on this work in writing up the following strategies for practice.

1. **Be an upstander for belonging.** Being consistently safe, kind, and compassionate has a significant impact on student well-being. Encourage open communication with students. These regular check-in conversations and connections can set an affirming tone that can carry a young person throughout the school day or week. Those connecting moments—the high-fives at the door, the "Good to see you!" and "Way to go"—messages at the beginning and end of the school day matter, too.

At the start of the school year, revisit your expectations for inclusion, allyship, and upstander behavior. Ask your students and team what inclusion means and challenge them to name specific behaviors. In addition to establishing the behaviors that you will engage in, establishing a culture of belonging also requires a clear commitment to what is not okay, such as bullying, violence, and sarcasm or "humor" based on identities or culture. Students (and colleagues) should know unequivocally that these behaviors have no place in your classroom. Call out such behavior swiftly, "That's not okay." "That's not funny." "That's not how we treat each other here."

2. **Increase representation.** Audit your curriculum and classroom library for representation and inclusion (Nguyen, 2021). As you identify gaps in your curriculum in terms of content,

characters, or authors, work purposefully to fill those gaps. In a 2019 article for *Edutopia*, I wrote:

> As we read more broadly and talk about books more intentionally, we're able to shine light on more experiences. We can begin to increase representation in our classrooms in ways that tell young people that many experiences matter, representation matters, and most importantly, they matter.

Increasing representation doesn't end with the resources on your bookshelf. It also includes the heroes you study in history, the mathematicians and scientists you hold up as examples, the musicians and artists whose works you celebrate, and the special guests you invite into your classroom. Across your curriculum, ask yourself if all students are being positively represented by the examples you choose.

3. **Practice inclusive language.** Inclusive language matters. Trans and nonbinary youth who reported that their correct pronouns were used by most or all the people in their lives attempted suicide *at half the rate* of those who did not have their pronouns respected (The Trevor Project, 2020). Consistently use the pronouns students give you and consider including your personal pronouns in your teacher introductions, newsletters, and email signatures.

Several years ago, I moved our school to using the singular pronoun *they* across all curriculum and school communications material. Work with your team to trade gender-specific terms for more inclusive terms such as "explorers," "scholars," "authors," and "leaders." Many educators I work with have replaced "Good morning, boys and girls" with the more inclusive greeting "Good morning, Friends!" In the elementary space, this practice can also lead to purposeful conversations about what it means to be a friend.

Like all allyship, these strategies are rooted in action and require practice. As a leadership team, you may find it helpful to practice through role play by standing up to inappropriate teasing, navigating a coming out conversation with a young person, or increasing your collective fluency with pronouns such as they/them and ze/zir. In some school communities, a GSA sponsor or school counselor may be willing to support this kind of professional learning. Additionally, youth can be important teachers for new concepts. LGBTQ+-affirming community organizations, such as those cited in this chapter, can also be an important resource in your journey. Some even offer training or professional learning resources for teachers.

4. **Support inclusive student organizations.** There is a strong body of evidence that GSAs (originally known as gay-straight alliances and now known more often as gender sexuality alliances) offer improved wellbeing, a greater sense of belonging, and less risk for depression for LGBTQ+ students. GLSEN's 2021 report on GSAs points to administrator support as important in ensuring the success of their GSA (Truong et al., 2021). In countless small and intentional ways, educators and school leaders can help write a new narrative of inclusion and belonging in their schools.

Reflective Exercises for Continuous Learning

Youth identification with the LGBTQ+ community is growing. Data from the widely cited Youth Risk Behavior Surveillance System (YRBSS) by the CDC shows that in 2021, close to 1 in 4 high school students identified as LGBTQ+ (Lonas, 2023). The following reflective exercises build on the protective factors that contribute to a safe and affirming school. As you work through these exercises, consider the ways your leadership can set the tone for inclusion.

1. **Leverage knowledge as power.** How will you use this information to advocate for greater inclusion in your school community?

- Which of the strategies and statistics in this chapter most resonated with you?
- What professional learning do you need to engage in to grow in supporting the LGBTQ+ students and staff in your school and district? How will you reach these professional learning goals?
- How will you make similar professional learning available and encouraged for all members of your school community?

2. **Work toward a GSA.** Does your school have a GSA student organization?

- If so, what additional support does this organization need to experience more success?
- If not, what are the specific barriers to starting such an organization? How will you begin to address these challenges? (Even if addressing the challenges doesn't yet lead to a new GSA, this work will likely play a supportive role in advancing LGBTQ+ inclusion at your school.)

References

DoSomething.org. (2019). *11 facts about bullying.* https://dosomething.org/article/11-facts-about-bullying

Fishman-Weaver, K. (2019, December 3). How to audit your classroom library for diversity. *Edutopia.* www.edutopia.org/article/how-audit-your-classroom-library-diversity

GLSEN. (2021). *The 2021 national school climate survey.* www.glsen.org/research/2021-national-school-climate-survey

Kosciw, J. G., Clark, C. M., Menard, L., & GLSEN. (2022). *The 2021 national school climate survey: The experiences of LGBTQ+ youth in our nation's schools.* GLSEN. www.glsen.org/sites/default/files/2022-10/NSCS-2021-Full-Report.pdf

Lonas, L. (2023, April 27). 1 in 4 high school students identifies as LGBTQ. *The Hill.* https://thehill.com/homenews/education/3975959-one-in-four-high-school-students-identify-as-lgbtq/#:~:text=About%201%20in%204%20high,Surveillance%20System%20(YRBSS)%20found

NAMI. (n.d.). *LGBTQ+*. NAMI: National Alliance on Mental Illness. www.nami.org/your-journey/identity-and-cultural-dimensions/lgbtq/

Nath, R., Matthews, D. D., DeChants, J. P., Hobaica, S., Clark, C. M., Taylor, A. B., & Muñoz, G. (2024). *2024 US national survey on the mental health of LGBTQ+ young people*. The Trevor Project. www.thetrevorproject.org/survey-2024

Nguyen, H. P. (2021, August 4). 5 ways to audit your classroom library for inclusion. *Edutopia*. www.edutopia.org/article/5-ways-audit-your-classroom-library-inclusion

Paley, A. (2022). *2022 national survey on LGBTQ youth mental health*. The Trevor Project. www.thetrevorproject.org/survey-2022/#intro

Safe Space Training. (n.d.). *Creating safe spaces for LGBT+ people*. https://safespacetraining.org/

The Trevor Project. (2020). *The Trevor Project research brief: Gender-affirming care for youth*. www.thetrevorproject.org/wp-content/uploads/2021/08/Gender-Affirming-Care-January-2020.pdf

Truong, N. L., Clark, C. M., Rosenbach, S., & Kosciw, J. G. (2021). *The GSA study: Results of national surveys about students' and advisors' experiences in gender and sexuality alliance clubs*. GLSEN. www.glsen.org/sites/default/files/2021-11/GLSEN_ResearchInstitute_GSAStudy.pdf

Continuing to Lead for Courage and Justice

Leading with courage and justice requires us to act with a strong moral purpose. This work asks us to listen for understanding and learning. This deep listening often moves beyond the words being spoken and includes attending to context, nuance, and multiple perspectives. As we lead with and for courage and justice, we commit to compassion, resilience, and forward progress.

Social work scholar and author Brené Brown writes that "There is no courage without vulnerability. Courage requires a willingness to lean into uncertainty, risk, and emotional exposure" (2021). In the first part of this book, we explored what it means to lead with courage in schools. We read examples of leaders like Dr. Susan Deakins who used listening and showing up to help a team of frustrated teachers move forward during the COVID-19 pandemic. While the pandemic forced us all to find new strategies for teaching, leading, and living with uncertainty, these same skills can also help us lead through the everyday challenges in schools. As school leaders, we have a responsibility to model leading with courage and to show up not only as colleagues but also as human beings.

In the fall of 2021, I opened our weekly team newsletter with the following personal story.

> Last night marked the first night of Rosh Hashanah. Like many around the world, my multi-faith family has the tradition of dipping apple slices in honey. As we do, we share sweet memories from the past year. However, this time felt different. My dad was recently diagnosed with cancer. Because of the incredible heaviness, it was tempting to skip the tradition altogether. How can we focus on sweet things at a time like this? My dad begs to differ. "There's no better or more important time to focus on the good." As usual, he's right.

In Judaism, the shehecheyanu blessing is a prayer of gratitude; it marks the gift of arriving at something joyous and new (e.g. a new year, a reunion with an old friend, a birth, the start of a celebration, etc.). It's about giving thanks for the arrival and survival that brought you to this exact moment. We recited this blessing on Monday night, and then we dipped our fruit and counted our joys.

In Chapter 5, you learned about our school's Thankful Thursday tradition. This is one of the ways my team intentionally integrates gratitude into our weekly schedule. As my dad taught me, we keep the tradition going each week, even on the difficult ones—*especially* on the difficult ones. Wholehearted leadership is a commitment to care. It is a commitment to hold space for each other during difficult times and to celebrate successes. Sometimes we do this in loud ways like Dr. Ruckstad's spirit tunnel for our custodial team, and other times we do so more quietly, like the educators who showed up at my door with baskets of food and comfort when a few months later my dad passed away. These examples are located in specific spaces and places. As the leader of a global and blended school system, I spend a lot of time thinking about how space, place, courage, justice, learning, and connection all intersect.

 Key Vocabulary

Moral geography is the exploration of the ways ethical concepts intersect with space, place, and landscape.

Reflecting on Critical Moral Geography

In the introduction, I talked about the role of critical moral geography in school leadership (Aitken, 2001). In particular, wholehearted leaders explore the ways spaces and places act as sites for inclusion or exclusion. In her 2022 book *Mapping the Moral Geographies of Education*, Sarah Mills argues that youth and citizenship development is in conversation with geography. Over time formal and informal education have become increasingly blurred across space. In my school, I often tell my team that *teaching and learning are ubiquitous*. This work happens inside, outside, and beyond traditional classrooms. It happens in school yards, community organizations, and our neighborhoods. These spaces matter. They are also where relationships are built.

Questions for Consideration

- How do students and staff navigate and make meaning in our buildings and school yards?
- In what ways are school spaces responsive to community needs, values, and traditions?
- Can we map patterns of inclusion and belonging, and what work do we need to do to expand those boundaries?
- What does moral geography mean as online and blended learning environments continue to grow?

The stories in these opening chapters affirmed that relationships are the heart of great teaching, great leadership, and the greatest predictor of achievement. All relationships carry risk and uncertainty, which means all relationships require courage. Cultivating relationships often requires us to stretch toward a new understanding. This may mean listening or noticing beyond what is readily apparent.

In my own school system, Stephanie Walter, our Director of Teaching and Learning, has a gift for hearing not only what people are saying but the feelings behind those words. I first saw this skill in action early in my leadership tenure when she calmed a group of educators at a charged curriculum meeting. Our team was presenting a new curriculum. As we presented, the emotional temperature in the room kept rising. Stephanie sensed the tension and leaned in with courage, modeling deep listening. As she asked for questions, the teachers responded tersely with clarifications on a specific assignment or activity. This is when I noticed that Stephanie wasn't only listening for the questions, she was listening for meaning.

> *All relationships carry risk and uncertainty, which means all relationships require courage. Cultivating relationships often requires us to stretch toward a new understanding. This may mean listening or noticing beyond what is readily apparent.*

"I can hear that you are worried about losing your voice in your classroom," she might say. "I get that. Whenever my administrators gave me a new curriculum, I worried about that same thing. No one knows my students better than me and I know how to teach reading. I have been doing it for years. We feel the same about you all. Let's talk it through."

Maria Ross (2019) calls this the "empathy edge." Empathy, like courage, is layered. *Affective empathy* refers to absorbing or mirroring what another person is feeling. *Cognitive empathy* refers to perspective taking or using logic and knowledge to understand another's emotions (Greater Good, n.d.). Throughout this book, we explore the distinct and interrelated nature of the cognitive and affective domains. Responding to charged or crisis situations requires leaders to use both affective and cognitive empathy. This approach is what Paul Eckman and Daniel Goleman call *compassionate empathy* (Goleman, 2008). It asks leaders to build on both what we feel and what we know.

While these examples are interpersonal, the same applies to data and policy work. In many of the chapters in this section, I encouraged school leaders to explore their achievement, discipline, and participation data for the stories this data tells us about belonging and success. In a sophisticated analysis of large datasets by the Office of Civil Rights, the US Department of Education, the Stanford Educational Data Archive, and Common Core, Farkas et al. (2020) found that the overidentification of students of color in special education isn't static across contexts. Instead, it is district specific. District-level achievement discrepancies are the strongest predictors of racial-risk ratios for special education identification. George Farkas and his colleagues found the districts with the greatest racial achievement discrepancies were the most at-risk for overrepresentation, specifically for Black and Hispanic students.

This begs the question: what are the systemic causes of these achievement gaps? Dr. Richard Milner (2012) cautions educators that achievement gap explanations often do not tell the whole story and have been used to conceptualize marginalized students as deficit or lacking. Milner's work shows that often these gaps in achievement are rooted in gaps in opportunity. It is not our students who are lacking; it is the access they have to services, programs, educators, policies, and curricula rooted in justice, courage, connection, and learning. It is by expanding opportunity that we can begin to pay back what Gloria Ladson-Billings (1995) called the "education debt." We pay this back by the services and care we owe to students and families who have been poorly and unjustly served by problematic practices in and beyond school. We work to make this right by leading with courage and justice.

As school leaders, we have to ask these hard questions and look at feedback and data from many perspectives. How can we better see what is already there but isn't necessarily evident? In the spring of 2024, our students in Missouri had two opportunities to witness incredible celestial events. On April 8, a total solar eclipse was visible along a narrow track from Texas to Maine. Four weeks later, the Northern Lights could be seen across much of North America. At my school, Ericca Thornhill, our Division Chair for science, coached our community on eclipse safety and timing so that as many of us as possible could enjoy the rare alignment of the sun, moon, and earth. We donned special glasses and looked up at the sky in wonder. Likewise, when it came to the Northern Lights, our school community learned how to set longer exposure times on our cell phone cameras. We looked up at the sky through the lens in our pocket and unveiled a dazzling display of magenta, orange, and green.

In an earlier chapter, you read about my struggles to connect across languages. You read about charged times where I had to approximate what I wanted to say, and you read about the middle school leaders who helped translate for me. Their whispers with this word or that bit of culture were the eclipse glasses I needed to meet these multilingual moments with compassion. Much like the celestial events Ericca helped us enjoy, these moments showed me new perspectives. However, to see this, I had to learn to look in a new way. I had to take the time to see something I hadn't seen before, to notice something incredible and present right there on our campus.

References

Aitken, S. C. (2001). *Geographies of young people: The morally contested spaces of identity*. Routledge.
Brown, B. (2021). *Atlas of the heart: Mapping meaningful connection and the language of human experience*. Random House.
Farkas, G., Morgan, P. L., Hillemeier, M. M., Mitchell, C., & Woods, A. D. (2020). District-level achievement gaps explain Black and Hispanic overrepresentation in special education. *Exceptional Children, 86*(4), 374–392.
Goleman, D. (2008). Hot to help: When can empathy move us to action? Greater Good. https://greatergood.berkeley.edu/article/item/hot_to_help
Greater Good. (n.d.). Empathy definition | What is empathy. https://greatergood.berkeley.edu/topic/empathy/definition
Ladson-Billings, G. (1995). Toward a theory of culturally relevant pedagogy. *American Educational Research Journal, 32*(3), 465–491.
Mills, S. (2022). *Mapping the moral geographies of education: Character, citizenship and values*. Routledge.
Milner IV, H. R. (2012). Beyond a test score: Explaining opportunity gaps in educational practice. *Journal of Black Studies, 43*(6), 693–718.
Ross, M. (2019). *The empathy edge: Harnessing the value of compassion as an engine for success*. Page Two.

Part 2

Leading for Learning and Connection

In 2019, I challenged the future teachers in our preservice class to defend, refute, or qualify this prompt: *All learning is connection.* We received 15 essays from future teachers, and each defended that learning is indeed connection. The teachers in our class did not write about neuroscience or how connection happens in the brain. Instead, they wrote about connecting with students, families, and the community. They wrote about learning through service at youth centers, at after school programs focused on mitigating access gaps for low-income families, and in adaptive sports programs, such as therapeutic horseback riding for children with disabilities. They wrote about discovering that teaching and learning are ubiquitous and that, just as all learning is connection, all of us are connected, too. This section on Leading for Connection and Learning builds on these lessons.

*****

In my first year as the academic director for a large school system, our student population doubled. Within a month, my team pointed out that I had developed a catchphrase. The phrase was: *And so we grow...* While our school was growing in quantifiable ways, this phrase referred to things that were harder to measure, things like problem-solving, productive struggle, and courage.

And so we grow... became a way to call us to the fact that we, too, are learners. This was a powerful moment in our school history, and we were actively growing our way through it. The catchphrase has persisted. In fact, one of our academic leads has it tattooed on her wrist. To date, this is my all-time favorite citation of my work.

Wholehearted leaders are also wholehearted teachers and learners. What does leading for connection and learning look like in practice? "Good teachers," says Dr. Sarah Lawerence-Lightfoot, renowned educational researcher, "are lifelong learners who throughout their careers continue to be curious; who model for their students a love of, and a quest for, learning; who ask deep and probing questions of their students and also of themselves; who know their students well and get a kick out of being among them. I also think that good teachers are open to learning from their students—class discussions are encounters of mutual discovery. And good teachers are interested in their students' stories and are willing to reveal their own" (Walsh, 2024, para 19).

> *Wholehearted leaders are also wholehearted teachers and learners.*

This next section calls on school leaders to remediate barriers to participation and expand inclusion, access, and learning in our schools. It also calls us to model learner behaviors like grace, growing from our mistakes, and seeking out teachers and advisors ourselves. Supporting young people in stretching beyond their comfort zones and growing toward their full potential is noble and transformative work. However, at its best, it isn't just the students who learn in our schools. In fact, it isn't even just students, teachers, staff, and leaders. At their very best, our schools become dynamic learning communities. We learn together. We iterate. We enact change. We connect. To lead for learning and connection asks that our priorities, values, and practices support both individual and organizational learning.

Peter Senge is a systems scientist and lecturer at MIT. He created the term "learning organization" and has advanced our knowledge of systems thinking. In his seminal 1990 book, *The*

Fifth Discipline: The Art and Practice of the Learning Organization, Senge writes that continuous growth, sustainability, and innovation are the strategies and tools we need to transform organizations. Drawing on the work of physicists including Albert Einstein and Werner Heisenberg, Senge writes that the collective intelligence of well-functioning teams can be greater than the added intelligence of individual members. Critical to collective intelligence, Senge argues, is the generative power of *dialogue*. Dialogue is a vehicle for how individuals and systems can learn from each other. Dialogue is based on many of the principles that we explored in the first part of this book, including active learning, trust, and a commitment to keep showing up even when we don't yet have all the answers. This is in contrast with other patterns of communication and discourse such as *discussion* and *debate*. In discussion or debate individuals are usually focused on wanting to be heard and be right; this does little to move our collective intelligence or our schools forward. Instead, what moves an organization, like a school, forward is the ability to listen for understanding, to co-create solutions, and to learn from one another.

The concept of building a learning organization has gained popularity across business, management, health care, and education sectors. In a 2007 article for the *Sultan Qaboos University Medical Journal*, Rashid Al-Abri and Intisar Al-Hashmi write that learning organizations consist of five key components: team learning, shared vision, mental models, personal mastery, and systems thinking. Just like the Wholehearted Leadership Framework (see p. 8), these components are dynamic and interactive. In fact, it is in the interactions that the most powerful learning occurs. Leaders play a critical role in facilitating learning cycles and creating opportunities for sharing, dialogue, and learning from one another and toward a common vision (Al-Abri & Al-Hashmi, 2007).

The following chapters remind us that *the world is small and that we are all connected*. This is yet another phrase I tell my team all the time. Writing this book reminded me that the world of education is even smaller. I am indebted to the mentors, advisors, and colleague friends named throughout this book. As I continue into the third decade of my career, I am struck by the staying power of educator relationships. I am fortunate to still be able to call colleagues from my first year in the classroom. These colleagues remain some of my favorite people to talk about school with. Likewise, there are leaders I have collaborated with on projects ten years ago who still reach out when something surprising, or wonderful, or terrible happens at their school. We have been through a lot together, and we get it and each other in ways that are hard to explain outside of education circles. Much like the research I have cited throughout this book, these relationships now span the globe.

Dr. Jill Brown is a more recent colleague-friend of mine; however, because we worked together through COVID school leadership, we rapidly experienced the trials much longer partnerships have and then some. For those of you who led schools during this season, I suspect you and some of those colleagues also share personal and professional histories that pulled you together in ways that are difficult to explain outside of education circles. Jill and I met in the spring of 2020, when we were partnered together to develop an online learning solution for elementary students in a large public school district. As either of us will tell you, any successes we experienced with this project—and there were many—were due to the collective intelligence and determination of our phenomenal team of educators, specialists, and school leaders. Within three months we opened the largest elementary school in the state and ran a completely virtual program for one school year. The work was hard. The conditions, unprecedented. And the only way through was together. The partnership we developed in that challenging year continues to have ripples through the school projects we work on today both separately and together.

Just like my teacher education students argued, all learning is connection. The leaders, families, and students we meet along the way often become our most important advisors. In addition to these professional relationships, in this next section you will meet student leaders who are also doing transformative work in education. You will meet early elementary students like Luiza, whose parents were told by doctors that she would likely never achieve functional literacy. One year later she led a large-scale community-project in our K-8 school and ten years after that she graduated high school, reading, writing, and thriving. You will meet a middle school leader named Amari who is using her voice to teach teachers about inclusion and racial equity. And you'll meet Nala, a gifted high school student who taught our school about humanity.

Today, Jill and I can look back at that huge elementary school project with wonder. How did we do that? In a later chapter on "progress as a team process," you will meet educational leader Karen Scales who reminds us that teachers and school leaders "make magical things happen out of an idea... all the time." Leading for learning and connection sometimes calls on us to do the impossible. When this happens, it helps to reach out to a colleague-friend. It helps to pull your team together and to remind one another that collectively we are not only more than the sum of our limitations, we are also, to use Karen's word, "magically" greater than the sum of our individual strengths.

References

Al-Abri, R. K., & Al-Hashmi, I. S. (2007). The learning organisation and health care education. *Sultan Qaboos University Medical Journal*, 7(3), 207–214.

Senge, P. M. (1990). *The fifth discipline: The art and practice of the learning organization*. Doubleday.

Walsh, C. (2024, February 20). "I have always been temperamentally wired to carry on." *Harvard Gazette*. https://news.harvard.edu/gazette/story/2014/04/i-have-always-been-temperamentally-wired-to-carry-on/#:~:text=Good%20teachers%20are%20lifelong%20learners,out%20of%20being%20among%20them

III

Lead for Learning Overview

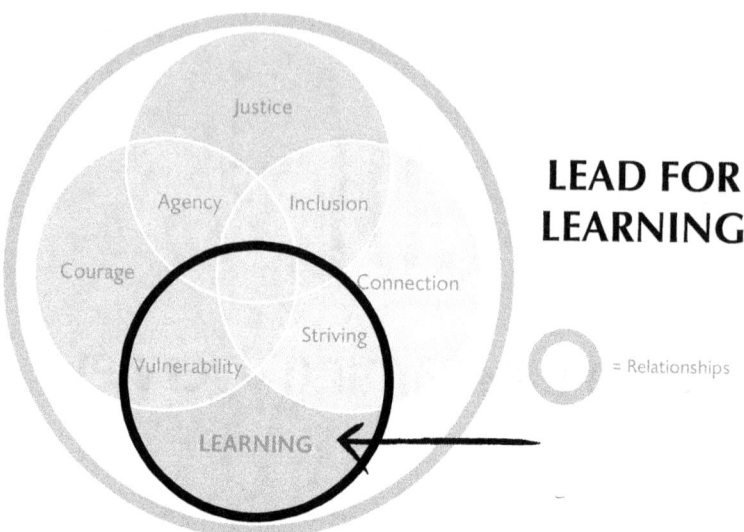

LEAD FOR LEARNING

> **Wholehearted Leadership Framework Focus Areas:** *Striving, Relationships, Vulnerability*
>
> **Tethering Ideas:**
>
> - Advance Agency and Opportunity
> - Support Learner-Led Projects
> - Leverage Emerging Technologies
> - Lean into Brain-Based Leadership
> - Diversify Your Professional Learning

> **Key Vocabulary**
>
> - **Productive Struggle:** Persisting and problem-solving through challenges, often those that require the learner to stretch just beyond what they already know how to do.
> - **Inquiry-Based Learning:** A learner-centered model that leverages curiosity and discovery.
> - **Collective Wisdom:** Intelligence gained through collaboration and leveraging the experiences, perspectives, and ideas of a group to make good decisions.

Lead for Learning Guiding Questions

1. What are the conditions needed to support high-level learning for *students* in your school communities?
2. What are the conditions needed to support high-level learning for *staff* in your school communities?
3. What are *you* currently learning? What are your personal, professional, and leadership learning goals for this school year?
4. Where do students have choice and agency to take ownership of their learning?
5. How are you building capacity for action research in your schools or districts?
6. Consider the last quarter or semester. What are the most powerful examples you have experienced of leveraging *collective wisdom* in your school community?
7. What do your school processes and learning philosophies teach others about productive struggle?
8. How do you advocate for equity to ensure all students in your care have access to high-level learning opportunities?
9. What emerging technologies have captured your attention? How are you growing in your learning about them?
10. How do your responsive services connect learning with psychological safety?

11

Advance Agency and Opportunity

Agency, trust, and opportunity can transform mindset and achievement. Yet, too often leaders miss the barriers that prevent students and staff from having access to these opportunities, particularly the opportunity to lead. Drawing on my experiences as both a teacher and administrator, this chapter offers examples for how school leaders can build leadership opportunities and powerful learning into their practice.

> **Key Concept:** Actively expand agency for students and staff by believing in the inherent talents of everyone in your school community.

"I am looking for young people for a new leadership program," I told the Grade 7 teachers. "Send me your challenging students," I encouraged. The only criteria I gave was not to send me students they already thought of as leaders. What happened next has had a lasting impact on my work as an educator and administrator.

A few days later, four middle school students showed up at my classroom door not quite sure why they were there. I welcomed them to the art table in the back of my classroom. The table was a comfortable height for second graders, but admittedly awkward for anyone over four feet tall. We sat there and looked at each other. I smiled and congratulated the students on being part of this leadership team. "I am glad you are here," I said, "because I need some help." This was true. As a new teacher starting a new special education program for elementary learners, I had a lot to learn. Our classroom was in the middle school wing, and while my second graders needed academic support, they also needed the safety of finding some friendly faces in that hallway of so many "big students." I hoped this program would help us make some new friends.

The students who joined the leadership program included Jax, Luciana, Mari, and Chass. Jax was a class clown, an athlete, and an African American student in a predominantly Latine school. He had also received more office referrals that year than any other student in our building. Luciana and Mari were both newcomers from Mexico. They rarely spoke a word aloud in English or Spanish. Although they were not related, they stuck close together. Our faculty couldn't seem to draw them out. And then there was Chass, a bilingual and multiracial child. Chass was gender nonconforming and a gifted student in a school without gifted programming. He was looking for belonging and not quite sure where to find it. On their most recent standardized tests, all four students had scored "far below basic" in mathematics proficiency.

I asked them to tutor my students in elementary math. The students fell into quick and lasting patterns. Jax coached a small group of boys on multiplication facts. Chass gave the class interesting challenge questions and then supported students in finding the answers. Mari connected with a student with profound disabilities. She was especially patient coaching her on counting and adding single digit numbers, and the two adored each other. Luciana worked with a group of Spanish-speaking girls on adding and subtracting two-digit numbers. I can still hear their giggling in my memory. Tutoring time quickly became my second graders' favorite part of the day. Over a couple of weeks, I watched my second graders go from feeling nervous in the hallway to eagerly scanning for *their* middle school friends. When they saw each other, there were hugs and high fives.

Initially, I thought this program would benefit the students being tutored, and it did. However, I was moved by the impact this program had on my leadership students. Originally I asked them to join us twice a week. It didn't take long before they were coming every day. Then they started joining me for lunch. Almost every day for two years, we ate together at that art table, while they prepped materials for *their* lessons. By second semester, Jax was rarely in the office. Mari and Luciana couldn't stop talking, sometimes in Spanish, sometimes in English, often in song. Chass started coming by my classroom at the end of the day, too. He helped me organize our read aloud library and translate poems, vocabulary words, and positive notes from English to Spanish.

This leadership program became the basis of my master's thesis on tutoring as an intervention for the tutor. These middle school students taught me about agency, opportunity, and the power of having someone look up to you. In their chapter on the pedagogy of voice (2021), Shane Safir and Jamila Dugan write that "agency is the idea that people have the capacity to take action, craft and carry out plans, and make informed decisions based on a growing base of knowledge" (p. 102). Working as tutors and leaders, Jax, Luciana, Mari, and Chass did all of this and more. At the end of the school year, they took another round of required standardized math assessments. All four had skyrocketed from "far below basic" to "proficient" or "advanced."

******

As research shows us, expectations have a direct and positive effect on confidence and achievement. In this chapter, we explore how transformative the opportunity to lead and be asked to lead can be. In his 2023 book *Hidden Potential*, organizational psychologist Adam Grant writes about the *tutor effect* or how teaching others improves our own learning. "Teaching others can build our competence," Grant writes, "but it's coaching others that elevates our confidence. When we encourage others to overcome obstacles, it can help us find our own motivation" (p. 137).

Leadership opportunities like these often map against broader systems of opportunity gaps in schools. In their 2023 book *Closing the Opportunity Gap for Young Children*, Rebekah Hutton and LaRue Allen write that the opportunity gap is

> the unequal and inequitable distribution of resources and experiences on the basis of race, ethnicity, socioeconomic status, English proficiency, disability, immigration status, community wealth, familial situations, geography, or other factors that contribute to or perpetuate inequities in well-being across groups of young children in health, social-emotional development, and education.
>
> (2023, para 4)

This opportunity gap has a direct and profound impact on achievement. In fact, many scholars in learning and justice work write that we do not have an *achievement gap*—we have an *opportunity gap*, of which achievement differences are a product (Milner, 2012).

When students and staff have opportunities to lead, this communicates trust, belief, and expectations about their abilities and talents. All of these positive expectations can be self-fulfilling and important for learning. The American Psychological Association defines self-fulfilling prophecy as:

> a belief or expectation that helps to bring about its own fulfillment, as, for example, when a person expects nervousness to impair their performance in a job interview or when a teacher's preconceptions about a student's ability influence the child's achievement for better or worse.
>
> (2023)

Research on self-fulfilling prophecies in schools cites four behavioral dimensions of teacher expectations. These include how expectations are communicated through *input* (teaching and questioning), *output* (opportunities to stretch), *feedback* (interest and goals for future work), and *climate* (quality of teacher–student interactions). Teachers and leaders communicate their expectations through action. Giving students opportunities to lead crosses all four dimensions.

In his literature review on self-fulfilling prophecy in K-12 settings, Abderrahim Bouderbane (2020) writes that teacher behaviors have a significant effect on student learning.

These include teacher efficacy, pedagogical beliefs, and opportunity to learn. *Arguably, opportunity to learn has the most effect on student learning since students will learn what they are given the opportunity to learn.* They are likely to learn more in classrooms where learning experiences are challenging and exciting and where higher order thinking skills are fostered.

(p. 21, my emphasis)

In 2019, Lauren Eskreis-Winkler, Katherine Milkman, Dena Gromet, and Angela Duckworth conducted a large-scale study showing how giving advice improves academic outcomes for the advisor. In their study, they compared report card grades in two classes. The focus group of nearly 2,000 high school students were asked to give motivational advice on how to stop procrastinating to young students. The students who were asked to act as advisors consistently earned higher report card grades on their final report cards. The authors write that these findings "highlight the underappreciated motivational power of placing people in a position to give, not just receive" (p. 14809).

In 2020, Sarah Gentrup, Georg Lorenz, Cornelia Kristen, and Irena Kogan conducted a review of longitudinal data from 64 classrooms and 1,026 first-grade students in Germany. They found that "teacher expectations significantly predicted students' end-of-year achievement, even after prior achievement, general cognitive abilities, motivation, and student background characteristics were considered" (p. 1). They also cite that these expectations are not random but instead align with specific patterns of historical and continuous marginalization. The New Teacher Project found that even when they controlled for prior academic achievement, classrooms with more low-income students and students of color had fewer academic opportunities, including grade-appropriate academic work and experiences than their more affluent and white peers (2018). In terms of the Wholehearted Leadership Framework, student access to challenging opportunities and the encouragement to practice leadership are issues in both how we *lead for learning* and how we *lead for justice*.

The following strategies will help you think critically about opportunity, agency, and the power of shared leadership and high expectations in your school.

In terms of the Wholehearted Leadership Framework, student access to challenging opportunities and the encouragement to practice leadership are issues in both how we lead for learning and how we lead for justice.

Key Strategies for Practice

1. **Nurture leadership and celebrate new leaders.** Giving others the opportunity to lead can transform mindset and achievement. Yet, as cited above, too often our marginalized students and staff are given the least access to leadership opportunities. School leaders play an important role in disrupting who has these opportunities in your buildings and districts. As an administrator, I often think of Chass, Mari, Jax, and Luciana. These middle school students taught me the power of believing in someone enough to trust them with important projects. Being a leader means seeking out hidden potential, nurturing leadership, and developing the talents that might otherwise have been missed in our school communities.

Being a leader also means trusting people to make their own good choices. Sometimes this means that projects take turns I hadn't expected. These turns may impact processes and products. As our school finds more spokespeople and advocates, our messages and learning take on new layers. As a leader, it is my responsibility to both learn from these new leaders and amplify their successes. A visual strategy I used to hold myself accountable for representation was bolding the names of every student and staff member mentioned in our weekly school newsletter. This served as an audit for me on representation, authorship, and who we were celebrating. I could quickly scan the newsletter for bolded names each week to notice patterns and set opportunity goals for the following week. I did this for 18 months, and it helped us transform shared leadership at school. Today, our newsletter is filled with features written by and celebrating our diverse student and staff populations.

2. **Explain less. Discover more.** "As an instructional designer, I am always thinking about how we can get away from explaining and, instead, focus on how we can guide a student to discover information, which feels a lot more powerful," noted Jacquelyn Kay, who oversees instructional design for the extensive co-teach program at my school. Over the last several years, she has played an essential role in helping our school transition to a more learner-directed curriculum model.

Prior to leading our team in instructional design, Jacquelyn taught and coordinated world language courses at the college level. While working on this chapter, I reached out to her for ideas. Jacquelyn told me, "One thing I always told the language teachers I supervised was, *If your throat is starting to get dry, you are explaining too much. Step back and find a way for students to arrive at the same conclusions through carefully-planned activities.*"

This is great advice in the classroom. It is also the advice I needed when I first started leading school meetings. In my first meetings, I did too much of the planning and way too much of the talking. Yes, the team needs to hear from me on strategic priorities and specific celebrations, but if they only hear from me it's not a team meeting, it's a *me meeting*. Today, when planning team meetings, I intentionally audit for voice and participation. Now our meetings are team-led meetings with reports from faculty, staff, and student leaders. I personally invite these people to present on special projects, lead key topics, and facilitate activities. This practice helps ensure that leadership is shared and that we all have the opportunity to listen and learn from each other.

> *Yes, the team needs to hear from me on strategic priorities and specific celebrations, but if they only hear from me it's not a team meeting, it's a* me meeting. *Today, when planning team*

meetings, I intentionally audit for voice and participation. Now our meetings are team-led meetings with reports from faculty, staff, and student leaders. I personally invite these people to present on special projects, lead key topics, and facilitate activities. This practice helps ensure that leadership is shared and that we all have the opportunity to listen and learn from each other.

3. **Be mindful about ownership.** Throughout this chapter, we have talked about how leadership opportunities are an exercise in trust and expectations. As students and staff step into lead projects in my school system, I trust them to make good choices and support them when and if they make mistakes. Recognizing that there is a power and privilege imbalance between me and those leading these projects, when mistakes are made and need to be reported on externally, I take ownership for these. I specifically use ownership language in these cases: "I am sorry this happened. I want to own that mistake and then I want to work together to fix it." There is seldom any need to say more. When a mistake is made, we own it, we apologize, we focus on next steps, and then as a team we think through how not to make that mistake again. There is no need to place blame or make excuses. The quickest way to undo learning and trust is to throw a new leader under the bus. When, instead, I apologize and take ownership for the mistake, it can deescalate a tense situation and get us back to focusing on solutions. It's also true. As a leader I have a responsibility for the actions, mistakes, and opportunities happening in my school. Following this kind of meeting, the project leads and I can then work together to find the best way forward.

Alternatively, when successes happen, I take as a little ownership as possible. One of the best ways to grow trust and capacity is to give credit, celebrate authentic successes, and build on celebrations to help fuel future projects.

The quickest way to undo learning and trust is to throw a new leader under the bus. When, instead, I apologize and take ownership for the mistake, it can deescalate a tense situation and get us back to focusing on solutions. It's also true. As a leader I have a responsibility for the actions, mistakes, and opportunities happening in my school... One of the best ways to grow trust and capacity is to give credit, celebrate authentic successes, and build on celebrations to help fuel future projects.

Reflective Work for Continued Learning

In August 2024, I met with high school students in the northeastern part of Brazil. We discussed how community-based impact projects often start by noticing an injustice and then having the courage to act. "Action research," I explained to the high schoolers, "is conducted through cycles of observation, action, and reflection. Observation is the art of noticing. Action is the science of change. Reflection is the power of iteration." The students then told me about issues that mattered to them, and we started brainstorming how they might enact change.

In a 1968 speech at Ebenezer Baptist Church, Dr. Martin Luther King famously said, "Everyone can be great, because everybody can serve." Leadership is service, leadership is learning, and with the right opportunities and support, we can all be leaders.

Below are reflective exercises to support you and your teams in advancing agency and opportunities in your school communities.

1. **Leverage the tutor effect.** Have you seen examples of the *tutor effect* in your school? If so, what can you learn from those? How will you leverage the tutor effect to build agency, opportunity, and achievement?
2. **Identify barriers.** What are barriers for advancing student leadership opportunities in your school/district? What are

barriers for advancing staff leadership opportunities in your school/district?
3. **Engage in personal work.** What work do you need to do to give others authentic opportunities to lead? Recognizing that leadership is an exercise in trust, how will you resist micromanaging while still giving support? How will you communicate expectations in a way that gives people space to grow? Write down specific practices and phrases you can use to support others in growing in their leadership.
4. **Audit your practice for ownership.** Consider the section on ownership (see p. 156). Are you comfortable owning mistakes and giving credit to others? What strategies will you use to celebrate student and staff leadership in your school?

References

American Psychological Association. (2023). *Dictionary of Psychology.* https://dictionary.apa.org/self-fulfilling-prophecy

Bouderbane, A. (2020). Student social background and teacher expectations: The self-fulfilling prophecy. *Cross-Cultural Communication, 16*(1), 17–22.

Eskreis-Winkler, L., Milkman, K. L., Gromet, D. M., & Duckworth, A. L. (2019). A large-scale field experiment shows giving advice improves academic outcomes for the advisor. *Proceedings of the National Academy of Sciences, 116*(30), 14808–14810.

Gentrup, S., Lorenz, G., Kristen, C., & Kogan, I. (2020). Self-fulfilling prophecies in the classroom: Teacher expectations, teacher feedback and student achievement. *Learning and Instruction, 66*, 101296.

Grant, A. (2023). *Hidden potential: The science of achieving greater things.* Penguin.

Hutton, R., & Allen, L. (2023, October 2). *Summary: Closing the opportunity gap for young children.* NCBI bookshelf. www.ncbi.nlm.nih.gov/books/NBK596378/

King, M. L. Jr. (1968). *The drum major instinct sermon.* Transcript. www.africanamericanreports.com/2018/01/transcript-martin-luther-king-jr-drum.html

Milner IV, H. R. (2012). Beyond a test score: Explaining opportunity gaps in educational practice. *Journal of Black Studies*, 43(6), 693–718.

The New Teacher Project (TNTP). (2018, September 24). *Choosing the opportunity gap*. The New Teacher Project. https://opportunitymyth.tntp.org/choosing-the-opportunity-gap

Safir, S., & Dugan, J. (2021). *Street data: A next-generation model for equity, pedagogy, and school transformation*. Corwin.

12

Support Learner-Led Projects

Learner-led projects have the capacity to advance critical thinking, collaboration, and impact in schools and communities. With a focus on action research and inquiry-based learning, this chapter offers strategies for school leaders to expand these types of learning opportunities. Written with contributors Lisa DeCastro and Angie Hammons this chapter argues that impactful learning is community-based and must be supported by school leaders.

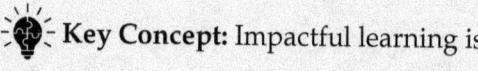

Key Concept: Impactful learning is community-based.

Did you know that Brazil is the only country named for a tree?

Two Grade 5 students taught me this during a recent visit to São Paulo. The *paubrasilia echinate*, known more commonly as brazilwood, is the namesake tree of Brazil. The tree has a rich history, and these young scholars thought it was important that their guest teachers knew this history, as well.

They began their surprise presentation with tactile facts. "Did you know, the brazilwood can reach 15 meters high?!" one student asked, pointing high above her. "It grows leaves, flowers, and seedpods." The second added, "The flowers smell great!"

Next they shared about the artistic significance of the tree for making red and orange dyes and also its utility for violin and cello bows.

Then they turned to more nuanced and interdisciplinary connections, including the tree's role during Portuguese colonization and the effects of overharvesting this great natural resource.

These important turns often happen in student-directed research. A project about a tree is rarely just about a tree.

As the children talked, their eyes lit up with emotions describing how their country got its name and how today this namesake tree is endangered.

"Today many people are working to replant the brazilwood trees!" one presenter shared, and then she shook her head, saying that it was "slow work."

At the end of their presentation, the two students proudly presented us with a potted brazilwood tree that they are tending to in their school garden. They placed it carefully on the table in front of us, "Study it," one student said. "Take all the time you need."

These important turns often happen in student-directed research. A project about a tree is rarely just about a tree.

*****

Lisa DeCastro, the elementary coordinator for my school system, met these student arborists with me in the Spring of 2024. We were on a work trip to learn with partner schools in Brazil. These surprise student presentations were a highlight of my visit and reminded me of my early work, 20 years ago, at an expeditionary learning school in East Oakland, California. Coincidentally, this is also the school where I first met Lisa.

Expeditionary learning is an interdisciplinary educational approach that focuses on learning by doing and encourages students to integrate classroom learning with community and global experiences. The learning expeditions my students and I created shaped my beliefs about research, leadership, and community in and beyond the classroom. These projects included large mural installations educating our communities on ecology and nonviolence, recording and producing bilingual CDs and books of poetry, and creating a documentary on the importance of caring. These projects were led by early elementary learners, many of whom received IEP services for disabilities. Their projects continue to have a lasting impact on the school and neighborhood community where we worked together.

Learner-led models including action research and inquiry-based learning are hallmarks of the curriculum at my current school system. Therefore, I reached out to Angie Hammons, our Director of Curriculum and Technology, and Lisa DeCastro as thought partners on this chapter. When we met up to talk through these ideas, Lisa and Angie were working on leadership lessons for elementary students.

"When you tell students they can do something, and then help them see that they can, the whole world opens up," Angie shared. To help make worlds open up for students in your schools, below are three leadership strategies for practice.

Strategies for Practice

1. **Make both learning and assessment active processes.** As a new secondary social studies teacher, Angie remembers being struck by how often social studies was taught passively. She recalls that much of the emphasis was on memorizing facts, dates, and names. She found this teacher- and fact-directed model did little to engage her students or make lessons relevant to their lives. Angie longed for what Pitchford et al. (2021) called "authentic learning." In their handbook on authentic learning, these authors write:

   > Authentic learning... reflects those episodes where complex, "higher" knowledge comes to life through application. It's where learning is planned and structured with the intention of enabling students, and staff, to deploy their understanding and capabilities for the benefit of others. To achieve this, learning experiences

and journeys need to be organised in new and different ways.

(2021, p. vii)

In Angie's words, "The goal of social studies classrooms is to understand cause and effect and how history impacts the world we live in today." As a newer teacher, she found that inquiry-based learning gave her a pathway to move away from memorization and toward learner-led and authentic models. She's never looked back. As Angie's classroom became more active and more connected to the community, she saw important critical thinking and leadership changes in her students. They "began to question what they've been told and how they viewed world events" and they started taking on leadership beyond her classroom. By studying social studies thematically and asking students to connect classroom concepts to their communities, her lessons gained both relevance and engagement.

"It isn't enough to just make learning active," adds Lisa. School leaders and educators can also make assessment structures more active, too. One of the strengths of student-led research projects is that they lend themselves to choice and flexibility. As an example, Lisa tells me about a K-1 learning expedition where she and partner teachers built choice into the assessment structure. In this project, students could choose to show their mastery through dance, cooking, or art. Lisa goes on to share that just as there isn't one way of knowing, there also isn't just one way of demonstrating your knowledge. She encourages teachers and school leaders to "gather data in multiple ways such as writing, drawing, interviewing, and taking photos and videos." Using multiple data sources is a best practice in student research and assessment.

At the secondary level, Angie shares an example of a student-led project where the project was the assessment. In a rural high school, Angie worked with a group of seniors to build an outdoor seating area for students. Before the project could get off the ground, students had to write a proposal and present it to the school board for approval. As a cross-curricular project, Angie remembers students were tasked with budgeting, outreach for resources, managing and motivating volunteers, and construction work. Angie beams when talking about this project and shares that the outdoor seating area "is still used today and all the students who worked on it are incredibly proud of what they contributed."

2. **Protect common planning time.** Planning, executing, and processing inquiry-based projects takes time and collaboration. Lisa shares that one of the most important ways school leaders can support inquiry-based learning and student-led research is to protect time for collaborative planning. As a teacher, Lisa remembers that "it helped immensely to collaborate with co-teachers, share lessons learned, and reflect on the teaching and learning." Today, Lisa supports teachers and coordinators in finding this time in their own master schedules. Research and inquiry projects are almost always cross-disciplinary. This means that teachers need time to collaborate not just with their subject- or grade-level peers, but across departments and electives. "Planning time gives teachers time to think outside the box," says Lisa, which is exactly what we want students doing, too. When school leaders create this kind of collaboration, educators can brainstorm projects, plan field and service trips, and learn from other subject-area experts.

3. **Join the learning conversation.** Today, when Angie helps school leaders and coordinators implement inquiry-based learning in their K-12 programs, she often reminds them that inquiry-based classrooms look, sound, and feel different from libraries or testing centers. "The room might be really loud with lots of conversations going on," she says. "There might even be arguments happening as students debate ideas. Or the classroom may move outside or to another location to foster discussion and learning."

From Angie's perspective, one of the best things school leaders can do to support student-led research is join the conversation. She encourages school leaders to "jump into a class session and listen to what the students are saying," review work in progress, and ask what students are working on or thinking about. In her own career, Angie has seen how a *pedagogy of voice* (Safir & Dugan, 2021) can lead to impactful projects. When I asked for examples she listed student-led recycling, tutoring, and inclusion projects that had grown from student interest and leadership in her schools. Angie adds, "There are so many opportunities for learning to become bigger than the classroom and school leaders can facilitate that by listening and being present."

Reflective Work for Continuous Learning

The following reflective exercises and questions invite you and your leadership teams to consider ways to expand learner-led research and practices in your school communities.

1. **Celebrate student work as data.** Through my work, I have had the privilege of launching several inquiry-based learning programs internationally. Particularly in more teacher-centered cultures, an important step in program implementation is making learning visible. Projects offer different types of data than a standardized test, and a presentation shows mastery differently than quiz statistics. As Lisa says, "Inquiry-based learning is often different from how teachers and families learned themselves. Therefore, school leaders play an important role in helping to explain inquiry-based learning to families."

Recently, she and I helped lead a family meeting on some of these differences at a new partner school in Rio de Janeiro. At the meeting we shared photos from the classrooms we had been working with. These photos illustrated learner engagement, excitement, and collaboration. We also shared student work such as written products and videos of student performances. In a similar family meeting the week before in São Paulo, student leaders presented to their families on their own learning from our programs. When families saw the work and heard from students about what and how they were learning, everyone was on board. In learner-led programs, the most compelling data about transformation and growth is often student work and student voice.

- What do families know about the instructional and curricular models at your school?
- Where can you add more student voices to explain what learning looks like in your school? (Consider student-led IEP meetings, student presenters at PTA events, and student presentations to school boards.)
- What formats would work best for your school community to teach families and teachers about inquiry-based learning and learner-led research?

When families saw the work and heard from students about what and how they were learning, everyone was on board. In learner-led programs, the most compelling data about transformation and growth is often student work and student voice.

2. **Model productive struggle.** Supporting learner-led research means making space for productive struggle. Productive struggle, sometimes called *effortful practice*, is the act of problem-solving and pushing through a concept or task to learn and improve. Lisa shares, "It's hard to not jump in and help problem-solve for your students… but teachers can teach students to look to themselves and each other for solutions and feedback." This advice isn't just for students. In my own school leadership practice, I have seen how giving space and support for teachers to work through challenges and projects often leads to better results than me jumping in too quickly with my own ideas. Creating a culture that supports productive struggle hinges on teachers and leaders modeling this themselves.

- Do your students and team know about the challenges you haven't solved yet?
- What are others learning from you about the ways you model problem-solving and collaboration?

3. **Analyze your master schedule for cross-departmental learning and collaboration.** The master schedule is a logistical challenge. From lunch and bell schedules to passing periods to space needs in the arts and sciences, the master schedule is an exercise in leveraging finite human, material, and fiscal resources, space and instructional access, and organizational flow. As the "structural foundation on which a school builds high-quality instruction and sustains a culture that reinforces it" (Hibbeln, 2020, para 9), the master schedule plays an essential role in how traditional schools run. For this chapter, I encourage you to analyze your master schedule for cross-departmental learning and collaborative opportunities.

- What opportunities do teachers have for common planning time, including time to learn together across departments?
- Check for equity. Are there specific populations of students or teachers who have less access to collaborative time? If so, how can you creatively solve these access challenges? (For example, you might consider students who receive special education or English language services, teachers working in the arts or elective courses, and teachers traveling between buildings.)
- How can you expand collaboration in your school and protect it through the master schedule?

References

Hibbeln, C. (2020). *Mastering the master schedule.* ASCD. https://ascd.org/el/articles/mastering-the-master-schedule

Pitchford, A., Owen, D., & Stevens, E. (2021). *A handbook for authentic learning in higher education: Transformational learning through real world experiences.* Routledge.

Safir, S., & Dugan, J. (2021). *Street data: A next-generation model for equity, pedagogy, and school transformation.* Corwin.

13

Leverage Emerging Technologies

Emerging technologies offer schools new opportunities for access, learning, and connection. This chapter explores the role emerging technologies have played across my career in education. The following stories and reflective exercises ask us to consider how we can leverage technology to advance learning and inclusion, particularly in the age of artificial intelligence.

> 💡 **Key Concept:** School leaders have a responsibility to cultivate digital literacy, foster problem-solving and critical thinking, and safeguard authenticity and integrity.

My first classroom had one computer. We held our breath as we turned the machine on and waited with hope as it shook itself to life. On more than one occasion the machine's start-up seizures knocked pencils to the floor. In those days, our cell phones were just phones, meaning I took a camera with me on field trips. I printed out our class newsletter and sent it home in physical "Friday Folders."

As a new special education teacher in the early 2000s, I was aware of emerging technologies. In the classroom next door to mine, a colleague and community volunteer were building a Linux lab with refurbished computers. Google Docs, Wikipedia, and Facebook were new platforms and popular topics for graduate school conversation. While the connection in our K-8 building was intermittent at best, occasionally we were able to gather around a computer and "find information on the web."

The access challenges to these technologies were significant. In my early years I never considered writing technology accommodations into my Individualized Education Plans (IEPs). I also wasn't writing digital citizenship objectives into my lesson plans and graphic design wasn't part of any rubric our class completed. Over the next two decades all of this changed.

*****

I was directing a large school system when the artificial intelligence (AI) ChatGPT was released for public use in late 2022. Within five days of its November launch, it had over 1 million users. Within two months, it had over 100 million users. This made ChatGPT the fastest-growing consumer technology adoption in history. At my school, Stephanie Walter, our Director of Teaching and Learning, quickly formed a thought group with teachers and staff to organize professional learning around AI.

At its release, ChatGPT was unique from other AI programs that are part of our daily lives (e.g., Alexa, Amazon Echo System; Google searching, suggestive advertising on social media or Amazon; voice assistants including map navigation). Soon other similar Large Language Models (LLM) entered the public access arena, and even as I write this, more AI tools are being integrated into platforms we already use including Google and Microsoft. Openly accessible LLMs do not require technical training to program. Instead, they are programmed through language queries and are responsive to conversational commands, similar to text messages or email queries you might send your friend or advisor. What does—and will—this new tool mean for teaching, learning, and high expectations?

Access to AI tools is expanding at a pace I could have never imagined as a new teacher. Instead of holding our breath as a refurbished computer tries to power on, the sixth-grade students in my school community are showing me new video editing tools they are using on their phones as they produce content to share with friends across the world.

Strategies for Practice

How can we leverage emerging technologies to advance equity and inclusion? In the first school newsletter I sent about ChatGPT, I wrote that our essential question for this new technology is *How can we teach students to use this tool in ways that support (and do not undermine) their learning?* In that newsletter, I offered three strategies for practice. These strategies continue to help me think through processes, policies, and approaches for emerging technologies in schools.

> *How can we leverage emerging technologies to advance equity and inclusion?*

1. **Teach students about process thinking and technology.** The abacus dates back to 2500 BC. While I don't know what mathematics education looked like in ancient Sumeria, I certainly remember when Texas Instruments released the TI-Nspire handhelds in 2011. Like its recent predecessors, these new graphing calculators had an integrated Computer Algebra System. With these tools, students could import images and graphs in 3D. This allowed them to interact with math and visualize data dynamically (Texas Instruments, n.d.). As a math teacher, my colleagues and I were worried. We had meetings and training sessions. I remember clumsily trying to grasp how to use these new tools while also figuring out what they meant for my teaching. Despite our worries, tools like this were not the end of mathematics education. Our students continued to learn advanced math, and we learned right alongside them.

The recent accessibility of AI tools has led to a similar focus on process learning and digital citizenship and literacy in schools

(Jones & Vanderpool, 2024). *Edutopia* writer Rachelle Dené Poth shares,

> The rapid evolution of technology, especially with generative AI, means that we need to consistently help students learn how to evaluate online sources, identify fake news, and develop skills in analyzing multimedia content carefully and critically. In some cases, students may overly rely on technology, which is why it's important to provide opportunities for students to find balance in the use of tech and to learn how to use it responsibly and effectively.
> (2023, para 8)

When ChatGPT was released, I had a memorable conversation with our Mathematics Division Chair, Brennan Ransdell. He shared that, as a mathematics educator, he felt like he had been through much of this before. Together, we recounted how graphing calculators, computer applications, and Wolfram Alpha had shifted mathematics instruction. Brennan shared that as technology has developed during his career, so have his conversations with students about mathematical thinking. Brennan is thoughtful about writing problem sets that focus on process. He asks his students to demonstrate their thinking and talk him through their steps in finding a solution. He gives them work with process errors and challenges them to find and correct the mistakes. Brennan wants his students to know how to use the technology available and to develop the problem-solving tools they need to grow as mathematical thinkers. This approach, which privileges process, technology, and critical thinking, has utility across and between all the subjects we teach.

2. **Teach students about authenticity and academic integrity.** As educators, we have a responsibility to learn with our students and to teach them the best ways to use technology while still protecting their voice, integrity, learning, ethics, and safety.

While working on this chapter, I met with a high school student who had misused AI on an assignment. Rather than using it as a tool, she asked the LLM to write a complete paper for her. As a school leader, I knew my approach needed to match my values. I explained that misusing AI tools robs her of her authenticity and learning. "Your voice and learning are too important to me for that!" I told her. Next, we talked through how to use AI tools in ways that support and do not undermine her learning. I gave the opportunity to try again, and she rose to the occasion.

AI tools have become an important part of our teaching about writing, research, and academic integrity. Through our lessons, conversations, and school academic integrity policies, our team teaches students that they should never present AI-generated text as their original work. Our teachers also strive to write assignments that are more resilient to AI misuse, including those that require multiple drafts, multimedia elements such as video and oral presentations, those that draw directly on students' personal lived experiences, and those that include showing process instead of just product.

3. **Commit to critical thinking.** LLMs are programmed with large data sets created from written works, including written works that present different opinions. As such, the outcomes they produce are imperfect. They sometimes get information wrong. They can miss nuance. They can even fill in gaps with false information, known as hallucinations or confabulations. This can include false citations, references, and wrong information presented as facts. This is such a pressing issue that Dictionary.com named "hallucination" as the 2023 word of the year. In an article on the announcement, Nick Norlen and Grant Barrett shared that 2023 was "the year we all began to witness, wonder at, and worry about how many aspects of life are impacted by AI" (para 6).

As LLMs and open-access encyclopedias amplify human knowledge, they also amplify bias. Simply put, not all of the information being fed to LLMs is good information. We want to equip students with the skills to suss this out. In my own school community, our teachers often remind students that in our fast-paced, computer-driven world, information is readily accessible and that their power as a learner lies in what they do with this information. We want our students to see themselves not only as consumers of information, but also as producers of knowledge.

By actively teaching about AI and giving practice opportunities, our students can learn how to use these tools as an aid and not as a substitute for the writing process. We show students how they can use AI for support with grammar, punctuation, organization, and translation. Critical thinking is the thread that connects these lessons. Our students know that they are responsible for the work they submit including taking accountability for the accuracy and bias of content generated by AI tools. Most importantly, they know that their voice, learning, and ideas matter.

> *Critical thinking is the thread that connects these lessons. Our students know that they are responsible for the work they submit including taking accountability for the accuracy and bias of content generated by AI tools. Most importantly, they know that their voice, learning, and ideas matter.*

Reflective Learning for Continuous Improvement

School leaders have the responsibility to build safe and supportive learning environments for young people. Teaching students about technology also means teaching caution. In addition to reading for bias or misinformation, we want to teach students to be protective of the information they share, particularly personal information about themselves or others. Within these environments, we want to give students tools that will expand their access to information and support their learning at high levels. I am hopeful that we will find creative and personalized ways to leverage these tools in schools.

Reid Hoffman (n.d.), co-founder of LinkedIn and the author of the first book co-authored with ChatGPT, refers to AI not as "Artificial Intelligence" but "Amplified Intelligence." He posits that LLMs don't create new information; instead they replicate existing information, sometimes in new ways. This sounds a lot like what I know about teaching and learning. Just as I clumsily experimented with graphing on the latest TI instruments decades ago, educators have a continued responsibility to learn alongside their students.

The following reflective questions and exercises give you the opportunity to think deeply about your relationship with technology, the alignment between your technology policies and your school values, and opportunities for deeper learning. As always, you can work on these questions individually or in dialogue with your leadership teams.

1. **Remember where you have been with tech.** Take a moment to reflect on the technologies available in your early days in the classroom. How has your relationship with technology changed during your career in schools?
2. **Check your practices for leveraging technology.** What practices do you have in place to support students in using technology *as a tool for learning*? Who are the professionals in your building who excel at this, and what can you learn from them?
3. **Be honest about challenges.** What are the biggest challenges to responsible technology use in your school or district and how are you working to mitigate those challenges? (Examples might include student/family access and the technology gap, responsible use, distractions, and information quality.)
4. **Align your policies to your values.** Do your technology policies and practices align with your school values? If not, how can you bring these into greater alignment?

References

Hoffman, R. (n.d.). *Impromptu: Amplifying our humanity through AI.* Impromptu. www.impromptubook.com/

Jones, W., & Vanderpool, J. (2024, April 16). Why teaching students how to use artificial intelligence could make them employable adults. *Technology Solutions That Drive Education.* https://edtechmagazine.com/k12/article/2024/04/why-teaching-students-how-use-artificial-intelligence-could-make-them-employable-adults

Norlen, N., & Barrett, G. (2023). *Dictionary.com's 2023 word of the year is...* https://content.dictionary.com/word-of-the-year-2023/

Poth, R. D. (2023, November 16). Developing students' digital citizenship skills. *Edutopia.* www.edutopia.org/article/teaching-digital-citizenship-skills/

Texas Instruments. (n.d.). Timeline. https://education.ti.com/en/snapapp/timeline

 Concept Study: Strengths-Based Perspectives in a Digital World

In the spring of 2024, I attended a support team meeting for a middle school student we'll call Amari. She is a talented performer, a confident presenter, and a natural leader. She also has recent disability diagnoses and profound learning gaps from chronic absenteeism due to childhood trauma. As a team, I wanted to make sure we were considering a range of accommodations and supports that built on Amari's strengths, supported her in experiencing success, and held her to the high expectations I knew she could achieve.

To make sure the meeting was framed around high expectations and care, we began the conversation by talking about Amari's strengths and the great relationships she has with her teachers. Recognizing her specific history and current needs, I asked us to commit to equity, inclusion, and access as non-negotiables in our support planning.

The team shared that their primary academic concern was Amari's writing skills. Continuing with our strengths-based approach, I asked her teachers to identify Amari's strengths and areas for growth. Below is the list we generated.

Strengths	Growth Areas
• Critical thinking • Analysis • Voice	• Spelling • Grammar • Handwriting • Organization

When laid out like this, it is clear that Amari's strengths represent higher-level thinking skills and are far more important for argumentation than her areas of concern. That isn't to say we want to ignore her areas of concern. Just the opposite. We want to build from her strengths and support her in building more skills. In short, we want Amari's bright voice to shine through as she grows as a writer.

This list of skills lends itself to potential AI tool support such as ChatGPT and Grammarly. Below are some suggestions we proposed for her formal support plan.

A. Give Amari permission to type a first draft on her own without concern for spelling or grammar. Remind her that she has great ideas and that getting those ideas across is the most important thing.
   ♦ If needed, allow for chat-to-text for this first draft.

B. Give Amari permission to run her paper through Grammarly or ChatGPT. If using ChatGPT, give her a prompt so that ChatGPT only corrects for grammar and spelling.

C. Have Amari bring both drafts to her language arts teacher. These drafts will guide their writing conference with specific and personalized skills to work on together.
   ♦ Select one focus skill per session.

Questions for Consideration

1. How are you building high expectations into your support practices and plans?

2. How are you leveraging technology as a support for learning, including personalized accommodations?
3. This concept study includes references to childhood trauma as a critical factor in the student's academic experiences to date. What practices do you and your support teams have in place to learn about adverse childhood experiences (see pp. 70–71) as part of understanding academic, behavior, or social concerns?

14

Lean into Brain-Based Leadership

Learning, processing, and feeling are essential activities for growth and wellness—they are also brain-based activities. This chapter builds on recent advancements in neuroscience including plasticity, neurodiversity, and emotional regulation. This chapter offers strategies that school leaders can use to cultivate brain-healthy classrooms and communities. In these spaces students and staff can find productive challenge, belonging, and wellness.

> **Key Concept:** Cultivate brain-healthy classrooms and communities where students and staff experience productive challenge, belonging, and wellness.

> **On Cauli(flower): A Science Lesson**
>
> The middle school scientists are stirring. Craning their necks, curious and unbridled. "Doc," they demand, "what are you getting at with all this cauliflower? This must be another lesson on neuroanatomy."
>
> Careful, I caution about jumping to conclusions. Notice the flower within the cauliflower, the connections to cabbage

and kale. And now, tell me about the gyri, the sulci,[1] the fact that perched on this vegetable stalk you are holding a whole cerebrum.

When you walk through a garden or city street, pay attention to the patterns that keep repeating. To learn about the brain is to learn about the walnut and the cauliflower, our ancestors, and their stories sprouting forth from the earth.

Make two fists and press them together at the knuckles. There you have a corpus callosum. And there, hemispheres and lobes. Listen to this secret: within your palm is a complete model of a limbic system. This ancient structure both keeps you alive and gets you in trouble. In other words, it helps you survive.

"Tell us its story," asks a wide-eyed girl in the front row. She craves the narrative arc of evolution. Like all adolescents, she wants to know where she is from. I tell the class about mitochondrial DNA. I tell them if you steam the cauliflower just so, you can still taste the Mediterranean Sea. Our origin stories shape us.

Science needs patterns and precision, but it also needs our faith. I want my students to know that in so many ways, if they crack open the universe, it is really a geode.

And by paying attention, I want them to find those sweet moments of certainty, when they don't have to break a thing open, just to know it's there—sparkling, surprising, and ancient.

*****

I wrote this prose poem after leading a neuroscience lab with 100 middle grade learners. I've found that teaching K-12 students about neuroscience is a powerful strategy for teaching students about themselves. This was the basis for my book on brain-based learning (2020), which explored how teaching and learning about neuroscience can help us better support student learning and wellness. These lessons also impact our work in school leadership. In fact, there is a growing interest in exploring how neuroscience can inform education and educational leadership (Stiliadi, 2024).

Recent advancements in neuroscience research have propelled what we know about the brain. This research has direct implications for learning, classroom practice, and school leadership, leading some scholars to start referencing a new field of collaborative study called *neuroeducation* (Gkintoni et al., 2021; Goldberg, 2022). However, there is still some disagreement about whether this is a new field of study or a new application for research. For example, psychologist Hagar Goldberg of the University of British Columbia says rather than developing a new field, educators can just focus on *teaching for and about the brain*, developing what Jelle Jolles and Dietsje Jolles (2021) call *neuroscientific literacy*. "The promise of neuroscience research for the field of education may lie more in the use of insights related to the interaction between learning and development" write Jolles and Jolles "and in the internal and contextual factors that impact learning, including the application of pedagogical principles."

Regardless of what it is called, there is compelling evidence that neuroscience research can help educators better understand behaviors, thoughts, feelings, and learning processes. Among some of the most transformative work of neuroscience and teaching is the disrupting of persistent neuromyths.

Disrupting Neuromyths

A neuromyth is a false and persistent assumption about the brain that is not backed by empirical research or science. Two examples of these neuromyths are the right/brain left brain myth and the learning styles myth. Both have been debunked by science (Grant, 2023; Jolles & Jolles, 2021).

1. **Truth: We have one coordinated brain.** The two hemispheres of the brain work together to perform both logical and creative tasks. As Drs. Kelly-Ann Allen and Rick van der Zwanb write, while "a simple model of hemispheric specialisation for learning is attractive as a heuristic, the notion is a fallacy" (p. 192). There is no empirical evidence

to suggest that people use one hemisphere more than another or more for certain thinking tasks than others (Allen & van der Zwan, 2019; Fishman-Weaver, 2020).
2. **Truth: Multiple modalities + productive challenge = learning.** While learners may *prefer* certain modalities (e.g. visual learning), teaching to those preferences does not lead to improved educational outcomes (Brown, 2023; Grant, 2023). In fact, exploring a concept through multiple modalities, even when this requires learners to work through productive struggle, is important in supporting learning.

In their work for the University of Patras in Greece, Evgenia Gkintoni, Paraskevi Meintani, and Ioannis Dimakos write that neuroscientific literacy (or neuroeducation) can support improved practices for specific academic skills such as reading, mathematics, and problem-solving, affective skills such as emotional regulation, and learning processes such as attention, perception, concentration, comprehension, and memory (Gkintoni et al., 2021). The following strategies build on this research to advance learning and wellness in our schools.

Key Strategies for Practice

1. **Incorporate neuroscience in your emotional regulation lessons.** Emotional regulation refers to a person's ability to effectively manage and respond to a range of feelings and experiences. Emotional regulation strategies can be both taught and learned in schools. Research by Abigail Rolston and Elizabeth Lloyd-Richardson at Cornell University cites walking, connecting with friends, exercise, journaling, noticing when you need a break, and meditation as examples of healthy emotion regulation strategies. These are all strategies we can model and utilize in our work with students. Further, Rolston and Lloyd-Richardson stress the importance of "paying attention to negative thoughts that occur before or

after strong emotions" (n.d., p. 1).² While some feelings are certainly more pleasant than others, it is important to teach students that emotions aren't good or bad. Incorporating neuroscience into your social-emotional lessons can help us step back and see their emotions for what they are—a coordinated response to stimuli. Once we understand why we are having big feelings, we can then pay attention to the information they give us. This process is the root of emotional regulation.

When teaching about the neuroscience of emotion, I start with the limbic system. This set of brain structures (hippocampus, thalamus, hypothalamus, amygdala, and olfactory bulb) plays a significant role in the formation of memories, emotional processing, and behaviors (Fishman-Weaver, 2022). Even with young children, I teach them the scientific names for each of these structures. Understanding your neuroanatomy is empowering. As we introduce this language in our classrooms, students can then use it to aid in their emotional processing and regulation. When having a conversation with a sixth grader about an outburst in math, he might tell me, "Well, doc. That was a major amygdala trigger for me!" Teaching students the neuroscience of emotions helps normalize the full range of our emotional responses and gives us a place to move forward together.

2. **Leverage the lessons of neuroplasticity.** In 2014, the school I worked for engaged in a year-long study of Carol Dweck's (2006) famous book, *Mindset: The New Psychology of Success*. Dweck's work around growth mindset introduced many to the concept of neuroplasticity. Neuroplasticity is the ability of the brain to reorganize, grow, and adapt based on experience and environmental factors (Fishman-Weaver, 2022). Said differently, just like us, our brains are a continued work in progress. Most plasticity occurs in the synapses of brain circuits, or the space between cells. It is also an ongoing process, meaning our brains continue to shift, grow, and adapt over time. In my brain-based learning book I write:

> Although plasticity occurs throughout our lifetimes, in young children—particularly very young children—brains are almost continuously engaged in plasticity processes. (Mishra, Merzenich, and Sagar, 2013). Neuroscience studies suggest that these early experiences play a significant role. However, rather than thinking of these times as the only times people can learn, it's more accurate to think of these early years as *sensitive periods* for brain development (Tibke, 2019, pg. 20).
>
> (Fishman-Weaver, 2020, p. 121)

Neuroscience research has shown us that plasticity persists throughout our lifetimes. That is the brain neural circuitry continues to evolve through experience and learning. By building on the power of productive struggle and our understanding of plasticity, educators can write lessons that focus on process over product, practice strategies that encourage students to lean into problem-solving, and message and role model how with effort we can all improve and persist through challenge. Just as wholehearted leaders strive to rewire their schools for courage, justice, learning, and connection, we can also build on neuroplasticity to help rewire brain circuitry for challenge and learning.

> *Just as wholehearted leaders strive to rewire their schools for courage, justice, learning, and connection, we can also build on neuroplasticity to help rewire brain circuitry for challenge and learning.*

3. **Celebrate neurodiversity.** Neuroplasticity can help us reframe our learning expectations. Because the brain continues to build new connections and adapt based on new experiences across our lifetimes, we cannot predict the limits of potential. Therefore, we want to teach and lead from a place of hope and high expectations. We also want to respond with reverence to the diversity of strengths and perspectives that different kinds of brains bring to our school communities. Neurodiversity offers a *strengths or asset-based approach* to

cognitive differences or disabilities. This term was originally used in relation to autism spectrum disorder (ASD) but now includes a wide range of cognitive diversities.

Recognizing that our students and staff experience and interact with the world around them in many different ways and that this range of processing has value is the foundation for neurodiversity; there is no "right" way of thinking, learning, and behaving. Scholars in neurodiversity teach us that differences and disabilities represent important and even necessary variance in the human genome. We need different kinds of brains to solve different kinds of problems and to bring new perspectives to our communities. And we need schools and school leaders who help us reframe deficit-based models to teach and lead in ways that celebrate the inherent strengths every student brings to our classrooms. (For more information on leading for inclusion, see Chapter 9 on pgs. 11–118.)

> *We need different kinds of brains to solve different kinds of problems and to bring new perspectives to our communities. And we need schools and school leaders who help us reframe deficit-based models to teach and lead in ways that celebrate the inherent strengths every student brings to our classrooms.*

 ## Reflective Work for Continued Learning

Neuroscience Learning Targets for School Leaders

The field of neuroscience is exciting and vast. As a school leader, there is a lot to learn. So where can you start? Jolles and Jolles (2021) propose four key themes of study for teachers and school leaders to improve their neuroscientific literacy. These are based on Neuroscience Core Concepts formulated by the Society for Neuroscience. I adapted these as learning targets for your own professional growth.

Educators and school leaders should develop a basic understanding of:

1. **Neuroanatomy**—the nervous system and its functions, including its role in emotional regulation and behavior.
2. **Neuroplasticity**—how environments impact learning and what constitutes a brain-healthy environment.
3. **Cognitive Neuroscience**—how learning happens in the brain and environmental or pedagogical factors that can impede or support learning.
4. **Neurodiversity**—the different ways students and staff process, perceive, and problem-solve. This understanding should be matched by a commitment to high expectations and inclusion.

Offering bright white swim caps and markers, I directed a room full of teachers and curriculum coordinators to diagram the human brain. We were at a state conference for new educators and school leaders. Working in small groups, I asked the professionals to include the following structures: forebrain, midbrain, hindbrain, brain stem, spinal cord, right hemisphere, left hemisphere, gyri and sulci, corpus callosum, frontal lobe, parietal lobe, temporal lobe, and occipital lobe. The educators had various levels of prior knowledge on this topic. As a support, I did some pre-teaching on these structures and offered some curated resources for continued learning. Much like when I teach this activity to fourth graders, the room buzzed with play and learning. Each group assigned a brain model who pulled the swim cap over their hair so their teammates had a clean drawing surface. At the end of the activity, we held a brain fashion show. Teachers modeled the *eyes in the back of their head that their students always knew they had* (occipital lobe), their rainbow diagrams, and some "neuroscience swagger" (their term). Our conversation was informed by the next generation science standards; we covered patterns, cause and effect, structure and function, stability and change, and interdependence. For some teachers, this was their first lesson on neuroanatomy. Three years later, I still receive emails from teachers who participated in this workshop and are now teaching neuroscience in their classrooms.

While the brain fashion show is optional, below are some reflective exercises for your own continued learning.

1. **Scaffold higher-order thinking.** The brain develops from bottom to top and back to the front. This makes the Prefrontal Cortex (PFC) the last region to fully develop. For most people, the PFC is not fully developed until their mid to late 20s. Although important activity and development is happening within the PFC, this later development helps explain why children process information, including emotional information, differently than adults. It also explains why young people need additional scaffolding, practice, and patience when working through complex decisions, setting long-term goals, and completing multistep projects. As school leaders, when a problem emerges, in our best moments, we rely on the higher order thinking skills available through our developed PFCs. Alternatively, our students often begin this processing in their amygdala, meaning their first response is more emotional than cognitive.

As we all know, even adults can find that their first reaction to stress is based more on emotion than reason. However, we have the ability to recognize when our thought and feeling processes are discoordinated, what psychologist Dan Siegel calls "flipping our lids." These moments are powerful opportunities for modeling how to use higher-order thinking skills to reframe.

- ◆ What are strategies you use and model when you notice that you have flipped your lid?
- ◆ How does this information about brain development inform your work on student support?
- ◆ How are you helping teachers to build in additional scaffolding, practice, and patience for higher-order thinking and planning skills in their classrooms? Give specific examples.

2. **Lead for neuroplasticity.** Brain function and wellness play an essential role in learning, processing, and leadership (Akşahin et al., 2023). Therefore, as educators and school leaders, the processes, structures, functions, and overall health for brain development deserve our attention and continued learning. Earlier in this chapter, we read about Dr. Evgenia Gkintoni's work to advance neuroeducation. Gkintoni, a clinical psychologist at the University General Hospital of Patras, is also working with a team to explore the dimensions of *neuroleadership.* Neuroleadership attempts to leverage brain-based science, including our knowledge of neuroplasticity, to improve leadership practices. Said differently, this emerging field asks, *How is leadership learned and developed in the brain?* Gkintonki and colleagues point to decision-making, issue resolution, emotional regulation, and communication as key skills leaders can continue to refine and develop through targeted practice and reflection (Gkintoni et al., 2022).

   ♦ What leadership skills are you actively developing right now? How are you building in practice opportunities to build stronger neural connections with these skills? Recognizing that learning is a social practice, share the skill(s) you are working on developing with your team or another accountability partner.

3. **Cultivate brain-healthy schools.** The World Health Organization (2020) writes that "Brain health is the state of brain functioning across cognitive, sensory, social-emotional, behavioral and motor domains, allowing a person to realize their full potential over the life course, irrespective of the presence or absence of disorders." Many factors impact the quality of brain-healthy schools. This includes the access students and staff have to proper nutrition, hydration, sleep, and fitness. Through nutrition and physical education services, bathroom policies, community partnerships, and keeping clean pillows and blankets in the nurse's or principal's office, school leaders play an important role in expanding access to all these factors. Brain health is also strengthened when

people have access to challenging, safe, and supportive learning environments.

- ◆ Consider your school environment, including your wraparound services and community partnerships. What are you and your team getting right in terms of cultivating a brain-healthy school? What are your key areas for improvement? Set two tangible goals for the next month of ways you can improve brain health in your school.

Note

1 *Gyri* and *sulci* are the ridges and fissures on the surface of the human brain.
2 For more information on helping students respond to and reframe negative thoughts see the concept study on "The Cognitive Triangle" on pgs. 253–256.

References

Akşahin, H., Dagli, G., Altinay, F., Altinay, Z., Altinay, M., Soykurt, M., … & Adedoyin, O. B. (2023). Contributions of neuroleadership to the school administrator and teachers for the development of organizational behavior. *Sustainability, 15*(21), 15443.

Allen, K. A., & van der Zwan, R. (2019). The myth of the left-vs right-brain learning. *International Journal of Innovation, Creativity and Change, 5*(1), 189–200.

Brown, S. B. (2023, April). The persistence of matching teaching and learning styles: A review of the ubiquity of this neuromyth, predictors of its endorsement, and recommendations to end it. *Frontiers in Education, 8*, 1147498.

Dweck, C. (2006). *Mindset: The new psychology of success*. Ballantine Books.

Fishman-Weaver, K. (2020). *Brain-based learning with gifted students: Lessons from neuroscience on cultivating curiosity, metacognition, empathy, and brain plasticity: Grades 3–6*. Routledge.

Fishman-Weaver, K. (2022, March 17). Fostering emotional literacy begins with the brain. *Edutopia*. www.edutopia.org/article/fostering-emotional-literacy-begins-brain/

Gkintoni, E., Halkiopoulos, C., & Antonopoulou, H. (2022). Neuroleadership an asset in educational settings: An overview. *Emerging Science Journal, 6*(4), 893–904.

Gkintoni, E., Meintani, P. M., & Dimakos, I. (2021). Neurocognitive and emotional parameters in learning and educational process. In *ICERI2021 Proceedings* (pp. 2588–2599). IATED.

Goldberg, H. (2022). Growing brains, nurturing minds—neuroscience as an educational tool to support students' development as life-long learners. *Brain Sciences, 12*(12), 1622.

Grant, A. (2023). *Hidden potential: The science of achieving greater things.* Penguin.

Jolles, J., & Jolles, D. D. (2021). On neuroeducation: Why and how to improve neuroscientific literacy in educational professionals. *Frontiers in Psychology, 12*, 752151. https://doi.org/10.3389/fpsyg.2021.752151

Rolston, A., & Lloyd-Richardson, E. (n.d.). *Breaking the cycle: Emotion dysregulation, reducing high emotional arousal, and self-injury.* www.selfinjury.bctr.cornell.edu/perch/resources/what-is-emotion-regulationsinfo-brief.pdf

Stiliadi, S. (2024). Neuroscience contribution in educational leadership: Challenges and perspectives. *Technium Education and Humanities, 7*, 42–53.

World Health Organization (WHO). (2020, June 3). *Brain health.* www.who.int/health-topics/brain-health#:~:text=Overview,neurological%20disorders%20across%20the%20life.

15

Diversify Your Professional Learning

Teaching and learning are ubiquitous. This chapter explores the importance of learning with and from your students. Building on examples from an elementary capoeira lesson and teaching a high school fantasy novel, school leaders will consider why learning with their students is an important component of instructional leadership and professional learning.[1]

> **Key Concept:** Teaching and learning are ubiquitous. Wholehearted leaders actively learn with and from their students.

I find myself in the middle of a capoeira circle (a roda) in a school gymnasium in São Paulo, SP. I am twisting, poorly, into unique inversions, as my teacher, an eight-year-old, tells me to "feel the rhythm." I tell him I am still trying to "find the rhythm." My teacher, whom we will call Davi, giggles, brushing a thick swash of dark curls across his forehead. He is bright-eyed, patient, and clearly has bones made of rubber.

Capoeira is an Afro-Brazilian form of dancing martial arts. Two opponents play each other inside the roda while others form a circle around them singing, clapping, and playing instruments. Capoeira was developed by enslaved Africans living in Brazil. The art form served as both a cultural tool passed down through generations and as an important form of self-protection when it was used to resist capture. Like samba—which also originates from the cultural wisdom and traditions of enslaved Africans living in Brazil—capoeira was forcibly banned for several years in the 19th century.

Before I started working with partner schools in Brazil, I knew very little about Afro-Brazilian history. While I knew there was a significant history of slavery in Brazil, I didn't know the extent. In her overview on slavery in Rio, Sarah Brown, a correspondent for the BBC, quotes Ynaê Lopes dos Santos, a history professor at the Federal Fluminense University in Rio who states, "We deliberately aren't told about Black history and the significance of slavery in [Brazil]" (Brown, 2024).

Of the 12 million enslaved Africans brought to the western hemisphere, almost half—5.5 million people—were forcibly taken to Brazil. Slavery persisted legally in Brazil for over 300 years from 1540 until the 1880s (Brazil Lab, Princeton University, n.d.). The practice was legally abolished on May 13, 1888. However, instead of May 13, today Brazilians, especially Afro-Brazilians, celebrate the National Day of Zumbi and Black Consciousness on November 20 (Nunes, 2015). This holiday honors Zumbi dos Palmares, an important abolitionist and leader in the resistance movement against slavery and racism in Brazil. November 20 is considered a celebration of progress and resistance to injustice.

This celebratory spirit can also be seen in the way capoeira has spread. In 1932, a teacher, Mestre Bimba, opened a formal capoeira school called Luta Regional. Five years later, the school received official recognition by the government (Goncalves-Borrega, 2017). Today, the Capoeira Arts Center (ABADÁ-CAPOEIRA San Francisco, 2024) writes that capoeira is often taught to students to help them learn to "translate struggles into celebrations, to believe in their abilities, and to understand the richness of sharing with others." The benefits of teaching capoeira in schools have been linked to improved physical, social, and emotional skills, including hand-eye coordination, executive functioning, and cooperation (Fernandes et al., 2022). A 2023 study by Evelyn Ríos-Valdés, Susanna Soler, and Mercè Mateu reports that capoeira has the potential to serve as a "critical pedagogy through movement."

Key Strategies for Practice

After watching my students perform capoeira in the school yard, I started asking questions. I asked my colleagues about the history of this martial art at lunch. Sometimes they presented me with differing accounts and perspectives, which I then had to sort out. This led to reading, sometimes slow reading with translation checks, which led to more reading and more questions. As an educator, I know this is how learning happens and I know this kind of inquiry is important to understanding. As school leaders set goals around professional and continuous learning, this chapter asks us to diversify the subjects and teachers from whom we are learning. Below are some strategies to advance learning with your students.

> *In every school there is excellence you probably haven't discovered yet. Seek it out. Pay special attention to the skills and areas you know less about. Among others, ask your learning specialists, your art, digital media, family and consumer sciences, and industrial technology teachers for examples of impressive work. Celebrate these exemplars and ask the student leaders to teach you about their craft.*

1. **Seek out excellence.** Last semester, several of our faculty and I journeyed to a nearby ice skating rink to cheer on two of our student athletes. These students compete independently in figure skating, a sport those of us in attendance knew very little about. At the competition, we learned more about the sport, but we also learned more about our students. In addition to their individual routines, we watched as our

high school leaders lit up when coaching their adaptive classes. Months later, our team still builds on this experience both in our work with these students and as a treasured team memory. The two students even got us out on the ice to learn some skills from them. In every school there is excellence you probably haven't discovered yet. Seek it out. Pay special attention to the skills and areas you know less about. . Among others, ask your learning specialists, your art, digital media, family and consumer sciences, and industrial technology teachers for examples of impressive work. Celebrate these exemplars and ask the student leaders to teach you about their craft.

2. **Reading as learning.** Winona, one of my high school students, parted her hair at a sharp angle so that it hung dramatically across her face. She wore oversized black sweatshirts and couldn't stand for anyone to look at her for too long and yet she also desperately craved attention. Winona had profound visual impairments and refused to use any of her assistive technology in class.

That is, until she discovered Stephenie Meyer's *Twilight* series.

I will never forget the day Winona showed up to class with a large print edition of the first *Twilight* book that our media specialist had found her. She plopped down in the front row, pulled out her magnifier, and kept her nose in the book even after the bell rang. "Hush!" she shouted, tucking her hair behind her ear. "I am reading!" Within a week, Winona had the whole class and me hooked on the book. Some of my favorite memories of that school year are of sitting around with students talking about power, fantasy, legend, love, and adventure. *Twilight* was the first book Winona had ever read for fun. It was the first vampire book I had ever read and the most important professional reading I did that school year. It turns out vampires, werewolves, and a precocious teenage protagonist with a propensity for danger had a lot to teach me about connecting with a harder to reach student. If you aren't sure if that last reference is to Meyer's Bella or Winona herself, you're not alone.

As Winona reminded me, we often connect with the characters we see ourselves in. This is one of the reasons it is so important to ask your students what they are reading. Ten years ago, when I moved into school administration, I was anxious to learn as much as possible. I read everything I could find about school leadership. A few years later I thought of Winona, and I took an audit of the books on my desk and nightstand. To my alarm, not a single book in my stack was one my students were reading. I wrote about this audit in a 2020 article for *Edutopia* (Fishman-Weaver, 2020). Following this discovery, I started asking my students for their reading recommendations. They introduced me to new young adult and middle grade authors who were instrumental in my growth as a school leader and human being. Seek out the titles your students can't put down and read alongside them. The same is true for music and media. Meeting students where they are also means reading and listening where they are, too.

> *I started asking my students for their reading recommendations. They introduced me to new young adult and middle grade authors who were instrumental in my growth as a school leader and human being. Seek out the titles your students can't put down and read alongside them. The same is true for music and media. Meeting students where they are also means reading and listening where they are, too.*

Reflective Work for Continuous Learning

This chapter opened in a roda. My first time learning with students about capoeira was not only a mental stretch, but a physical one, as well. My memory of that early lesson is all socio-physical: How is that child kicking his leg so high? How many beats are in this rhythm (called *toques* in Portuguese) and how can I move to them? What does he mean when he tells me to "find the power in my lower body"? Surely, I am going to fall into a pretzel heap on this gymnasium floor and all the children are going to have to help me up!

The cultural and scholarly extensions of my learning came later. As I continued to engage with students in their passion area, new dimensions of learning opened up for me. Further, being willing to fall on my face, get shown up by an eight-year-old, and be a complete novice in a new skill also sent an important message to my students and my team about how we are all learners in our community. To start this reflective conversation about diversifying your professional learning, consider a new skill you have recently learned from one of your students. After sharing these skills as a group, you and your leadership teams can continue with the exercises and questions below.

1. **Practice active learning.** What activities have captured your students' attention? Of these, which activities do you know the least about? Develop a plan to learn more about these from and with your students.
2. **Think critically about your leadership bookshelf.** Audit the books on your recently read list. What patterns do you notice? What patterns do you want to change? Are student recommendations part of your regular reading habits and professional learning?
3. **Write a personal learning philosophy.** What do your personal learning practices demonstrate about your commitments to lifelong learning, curiosity, and the lives of your students?

Note

1 Thank you to Ana Cristina Nikolaou for your friendship and care in checking the Brazilian history and culture referenced in this chapter.

References

ABADÁ-CAPOEIRA San Francisco. (2024, December 28). *Capoeira History—Abadá-Capoeira San Francisco.* www.abada.org/capoeira-history/

Brazil Lab, Princeton University. (n.d.). *Racialized frontiers: slaves and settlers in modernizing Brazil*. Brazil Lab. https://brazillab.princeton.edu/research/racialized_frontiers

Brown, S. (2024, February 15). Brazil's heart-breaking site of two million enslaved Africans. *BBC*. www.bbc.com/travel/article/20240214-brazils-heart-breaking-site-of-two-million-enslaved-africans

Fernandes, V. R., Ribeiro, M. L. S., Araújo, N. B., Mota, N. B., Ribeiro, S., Diamond, A., & Deslandes, A. C. (2022). Effects of capoeira on children's executive functions: A randomized controlled trial. *Mental Health and Physical Activity, 22*, 100451.

Fishman-Weaver, K. (2020, September 21). Building a better bookshelf for school leaders. *Edutopia*. www.edutopia.org/article/building-better-bookshelf-school-leaders/

Goncalves-Borrega, J. (2017, September 18). How Brazilian capoeira evolved from a martial art to an international dance craze. *Smithsonian Magazine*. www.smithsonianmag.com/smithsonian-institution/capoeira-occult-martial-art-international-dance-180964924/

Nunes, D. (2015, November 20). National day of Zumbi. Awakening Black consciousness in Brazil. *teleSUR*. www.telesurenglish.net/opinion/National-Day-of-Zumbi-Awakening-Black-Consciousness-in-Brazil-20151120-0006.html

Ríos-Valdés, E., Soler, S., & Mateu, M. (2023). Capoeira as a critical pedagogy tool in physical education: From a continuing professional development program to the classroom. *Physical Education and Sport Pedagogy*, 1–13. https://doi.org/10.1080/17408989.2023.2260409

IV

Lead for Connection Overview

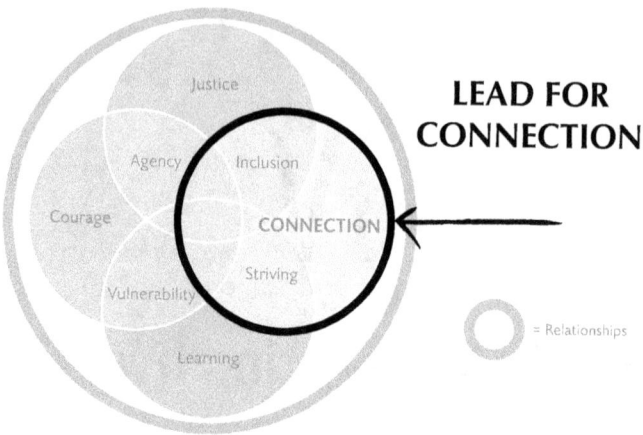

LEAD FOR CONNECTION

Wholehearted Leadership Framework Focus Areas: *Inclusion, Striving, Relationships*

Tethering Ideas:

- Practice cultural learning and reciprocity.
- Build accountability through grace.
- Communicate care across cultures.
- Progress is a team process.
- Expand learning, reduce barriers.

 Key Vocabulary

- **Intercultural Competencies:** Intercultural competencies refer to the abilities, skills, and attitudes that foster communication across cultural boundaries. These include:
  1. a recognition that all students and cultures in our school community have inherent value
  2. an awareness of one's own cultural identity
  3. the ability to learn and build on the varying cultural and community norms and wisdom of students, staff, and families.
- **Border-Crossing Theory:** Border crossing theory explores the physical and ideological borders that separate human

experience (Douglas, 2016; Giroux, 2005; Lopez et al., 2006). This theoretical framework explores the ways place, space, and boundaries are constructed, negotiated, and reconstructed both physically and metaphorically. Wholehearted leaders must be border crossers in building new connections and new kinds of spaces for learning and belonging.

- **Dialogue vs. Discussion:** Both dialogue and discussion are forms of discourse meaning they are ways to exchange or express information. However, they have different goals. Dialogue is a cooperative, two-way conversation where participants seek to build relationships and collective knowledge. Discussion is a one-way conversation where participants seek to be heard and prove their perspective correct. We want to increase meaningful dialogue in our schools.

Lead for Connection Guiding Questions

1. How do you build reciprocity into your partnerships with families and community organizations?
2. What do your school discipline practices teach students about grace?
3. What do your school leadership practices teach students about grace?
4. What norms have you set to encourage dialogue (as opposed to discussion) in your schools?
5. How has technology changed what *connected learning* means in your school community?
6. What action research projects do your students and teachers want to explore, and how can you support those?
7. What can you learn from your coaches and counselors about connection?
8. Who are the cultural advisors and gatekeepers you need to connect with to learn more about your students' cultures?
9. How is youth leadership celebrated in your school community?
10. What actionable ways do you commit to strengths- or asset-based approaches in your student support practices?

References

Douglas, T. M. O. (2016). *Border crossing brothas: Black males navigating race, place, and complex space*. Peter Lang.

Giroux, H. A. (2005). *Border crossings: Cultural Workers and the Politics of Education*. Psychology Press.

Lopez, G. R., Gonzalez, M. L., & Fierro, E. (2006). Educational leadership along the US-Mexico border: Crossing borders/embracing hybridity/building bridges. In C. Marshall & M. Oliva (Eds.), *Leadership for social justice: Making revolutions in education* (pp. 279–306). Pearson.

 ## Concept Study: Youth Participatory Action Research (YPAR)

Mariah, Sam, and Lacie were high-achieving students in my high school gifted program. One morning they came to me very upset. They were angry because they had received feedback from judges at an out-of-district debate tournament that pointed to a clear gender bias. Mariah shared that she and the other young women debaters were consistently marked down and told they were being "too aggressive," whereas their young men counterparts received higher scores and praise for being "assertive and confident." Lacie continued that young women were also the only ones to receive feedback on their dress during competition. Sam said that she and her friends were fired up and wanted to do something about this issue.

I taught them about YPAR and we used it as a framework to lead change on this issue. YPAR is a qualitative methodology for conducting research with student communities (McIntyre, 2008; Morrell, 2004).

Y	**YOUTH** *Engage in research with student communities.* Guiding principle: Young people are able to ask and answer the questions that matter most to their communities. In YPAR projects, youth serve as co-researchers, taking an active role in all aspects of the research process.
P	**PARTICIPATORY** *Research is a participatory process.* Guiding principle: Our communities serve as both classroom and teacher. Through collaborative inquiry we can gain a deeper understanding of issues and solutions.
A	**ACTION** *Focus on projects that benefit the community.* Guiding principle: Work gains meaning and purpose when it is of service to others. YPAR projects aim to make a positive difference. They typically culminate in outreach, knowledge-sharing, and service-oriented activities.
R	**RESEARCH** *Our lived experiences are data.* Guiding principle: The narratives, conditions, and experiences of our communities are knowledge-rich. Asking questions, gathering data, synthesizing, creative works, and disseminating information all happen in the context of community.

Often the only exposure students have to research is through the scientific method. Action research, such as YPAR, offers another alternative for sense and difference making (Maguire, 1987; McIntyre, 2008; Heron & Reason, 2002). YPAR operates on the assumption that young people are ready and able to both research and enact change in their communities. YPAR projects follow iterative cycles of reflection, action, and planning. As young people notice challenges or injustices in their community, they seek out ways to learn more, enact change, and continue to build toward projects that matter.

Together Mariah, Sam, and Lacie researched gendered judging in speech and debate competitions. They met with their debate coach, who was sympathetic to the cause and became an ally and advocate for their work. They published articles in our school paper. At the next speech and debate competition, the students made gender justice the focus for all events that allowed for student choice. This time they were praised for their work and noticed fairer scoring.

Following that tournament, Lacie told me they still had more work to do. Soon student groups branched off to lead additional research projects related to gender justice. One group presented their findings at a university symposium and another organized an inaugural student-led conference on this topic for the spring. The strategies these student leaders used to both call out and educate others on this important issue increased awareness among teachers and students. By engaging in this work, the student researchers also grew as learners and leaders.

Questions for Consideration

- What are other ways school leaders might have responded to the high school students?
- What skills do students learn through YPAR projects? What do they learn about research, data, and outreach?
- What issues have students brought to you recently that could be seeds for YPAR work?
- What role do school leaders play in growing the capacity for YPAR in their schools/districts?

References

Heron, J., & Reason, P. (2002). The practice of co-operative inquiry: Research "with" rather than "on" people. In P. Reason & H. Bradbury (Eds.), *Handbook of action research: Participative inquiry & practice* (pp. 179–188). Sage.

Maguire, P. (1987). *Doing participatory research: A feminist approach.* UMass Center for International Education/School.

McIntyre, A. (2008). *Participatory action research.* Qualitative Research Methods Series 52. Sage.

Morrell, E. (2004). *Becoming critical researchers: Literacy and empowerment for urban youth.* Peter Lang.

16

Practice Cultural Learning and Reciprocity

Wholehearted leaders use authenticity, vulnerability, and care to create a school culture where all students, teachers, and support staff are included, affirmed, and recognized as important members of the school community. Drawing on my time spent teaching and learning in South America, this chapter explores culture, culturally responsive teaching, reciprocity, and relationships.

> **Key Concept:** Effective school culture is one where all students, teachers, and support staff are included, affirmed, and recognized as important members of the school community.

Our global school district works with many schools in Brazil and I have had the opportunity to spend extended time in-country working with our students and partner schools there. On one visit, I co-led an international education conference. By this time I had spent several months learning with our students in Brazil and wanted to give my opening address in Portuguese. This first speech, although practiced, was clumsy, at best; yet it was met with warm applause. My friend and fellow educational leader, Cristiano Carvalho, was on the stage with me. He hadn't known about the speech and was touched by my language learning. "Learning Portuguese is an act of compassion. We all know that you can't separate language from culture. When you learn our language, you learn our culture."

There are several Portuguese words I've learned that express different ways people are connected to and/or care for each other (e.g. *cariño, saudades, apaixonar, xará*.) There isn't a direct English translation for any of these words. As Cristiano suggested, these words translate to cultural patterns of behavior and ways of being. I get to experience this in action in the enveloping embraces that accompany *bom dia / good morning* or *boa noite / good night*. I think about the playful arguments I've had regarding how many people can fit comfortably into an elevator or around a table. My Brazilian students and colleagues frequently double my answer. Scrolling the messages on my phone, I notice the affectionate emojis decorating almost every text.

Through my relationships, travel, and language studies, I've experienced an acculturation process of learning new ways of being, conceptions of time, and definitions of personal space. There is a pattern of care and generosity that I have learned from my school visits. When it comes to laughing, weeping, or being forthcoming with how much they care, the students and educators I work with in our schools in Brazil tend not to hold back.

This cultural learning has made me a more effective school leader in this specific context and a more effective human being in our global world. I am reminded of school lunches, singing at assemblies, and countless Portuguese lessons led by middle schoolers in the back of their classrooms.

I am also reminded of more difficult moments when I didn't have the language or cultural knowledge to navigate in the ways I wished I could. One afternoon, a school group took me to a community organization where families could stay while their children received treatment for cancer. A seven-year-old boy gave us a tour of the home. Following the tour, his mother came out to meet us. We embraced, and there were a hundred things I wanted to say and didn't know how. Another day, walking back from a school meeting, I met an unhoused family whose children called out to me for help. I had nothing in my pockets to give, but wanted to meet the children with compassion and presence. Again I didn't have the right words to respond in the ways I wanted. I held their gaze in mine and tried to communicate warmth. Another afternoon I met with the resident of a children's home that provides services similar to foster care for close to a hundred children and youth. I had a few moments with the director of the organization and wanted to thank her for her work. I also had questions about how foster services in Brazil compare with those in the United States. While I had been studying the language, I quickly lost my words when a small child grabbed my hand and started singing nursery rhymes in Portuguese. In each of these situations, eventually someone rescued me, and taught me a way forward. Often this person was a middle schooler, who would wrap an arm around my shoulder and whisper back and forth translations to me so that I could begin to approximate what I truly wanted to say.

Cultural learning is an exercise in authenticity, vulnerability, and care. In her work around cultural reciprocity, Cynthia Warger (2001) writes that:

> service providers must take the initiative in building a bridge between the cultures of diverse families and the culture of schools. A premise of the... process is that service providers must develop their own cultural self-awareness in order to recognize the cultural underpinnings of their professional practice.
>
> (p. 2)

Reciprocity is a cycle of learning and responding. Teachers and school leaders play an important role in practicing reciprocity and building bridges; however, often that role begins by being receptive enough to learn that a bridge needs to be built at all. Great initiatives can begin in humility. Wholehearted leaders are humble enough to learn from students and families who teach us a better way forward. The following strategies ask us to learn from these lessons and apply them to our leadership.

Great initiatives can begin in humility. Wholehearted leaders are humble enough to learn from students and families who teach us a better way forward.

⚙️ Strategies for Practice

1. **Become a world language learner.** According to data from the National Center for Educational Statistics, in 2020 over 9% or 4.5 million public school children in the United States were English learners. The most commonly reported home languages of this group include (in order of frequency) Spanish/Castilian, Arabic, English,[1] Chinese, Vietnamese, Portuguese, Russian, Haitian/Creole, Hmong, and Urdu (NCES, 2020). In the past few years, my own school district has welcomed students from 60 different countries. Language learning is cited throughout this book as an important skill in connecting. Find a place to start learning. What are the home languages of your students, faculty, and staff? Choose one. Learn to say good morning, thank you, please, and great work. From there, keep learning. Don't stop.
2. **Commit to culturally responsive leadership.** In her seminal work, Gloria Ladson-Billings (2006) developed "Culturally Responsive Teaching," a pedagogy to recognize and affirm the importance of students' culture(s) across all aspects of learning. In our global and interconnected world, culturally responsive practices are necessary in classrooms, schools, and student, family, and teacher communication. My classroom and leadership experiences have taught me that we need both culturally responsive teaching and culturally responsive school leadership.

While this section has focused on the intersections between language and culture, culture goes beyond language. It includes shared beliefs, customs, rituals, and traditions. In the text above, I shared that culture also includes ways of being, patterns of interacting, conceptions of time, and definitions of personal space.

Individuals are the best experts on what their culture means to them. The time we spend learning in relationship with our school stakeholders is always time well spent.

It is also important to remember that culture is nuanced. While a culture is shared among groups, individuals each belong to different and intersecting communities and microcultures that contribute to distinct cultural practices, beliefs, and rituals. As school leaders, we have an obligation to learn about the cultures of our students, families, and faculty and staff.

Reflective Work for Continuous Learning

Wholehearted leadership means creating a school culture where all students, teachers, and support staff are included, affirmed, and recognized as important members of the school community. Like all worthwhile practices in education, this requires intentionality and humility. Wholehearted leaders are eager to learn from and with their teachers, support staff, and students. As my friend and fellow educator Valerie Smallman says, they are humble enough to be: *teachable*.

As you engage with the content from this section, consider the following questions. To better track your own learning over time, you might choose to process these and other questions in this book in a reflective journal. I have included some notes on this strategy below.

1. **Something that might surprise you...** In writing on building culturally inclusive classrooms, Janice Wyatt-Ross (2018) shares that

    > When we talk about the dynamics of creating a culturally inclusive classroom community, the typical focus is on the diversity of the students in the room or school building. All too often the culture and diversity of the adults are on the periphery. But in order to navigate the intersection of student and adult cultural

> *diversity, we must first acknowledge and understand our adult beliefs and practices.*
>
> (para 4)

If this work is new for your school community, starting with your teachers and leadership team may be a powerful first step in community-building and better understanding the cultural wisdom and experiences of your team. You might start with these questions:

- Do you celebrate birthdays at home? If so, what do those celebrations look like?
- How does your family bring in the new year?
- What is an important lesson you learned from an elder in your family?
- Complete this sentence: Something that might surprise you about me is…
- Complete this sentence: Something I am still learning is…

With all of these questions, your modeling as a leader matters as does your commitment to making the space both safe and brave for people to share as much (or as little) as they are comfortable with.

2. **Keep a reflective journal.** Maintaining a regular writing and reflective practice has made me a more thoughtful and effective school leader. While I prefer to keep a digital journal on Google Drive, I know other leaders who like the pen and paper version. I label my leadership journal *autoethnography* to emphasize that the purpose is as a self-study on becoming a more effective school leader. I don't write in it every day or even every week. I turn to my journal when I have something big to work out—an idea or an experience I don't want to forget. It is unusual for more than two weeks to go by without an entry. This organic rhythm works for me. That said, I also know leaders who schedule reflective journaling once a week, often on Fridays. I use my journaling as space

to chronicle lessons learned, questions explored, and to safeguard moments I don't want to lose. I turn to this journal as a safe personal processing space. This journal is one of the places I turn to work out questions I don't have the answer to yet. It is also where I draft letters to my team and test out ideas for my school leadership blog. While many of my entries feel like they are just for me, I am reminded that writing is never "a solitary activity… it involves engaging other perspectives—those you read and those of your peers—as well as giving and getting feedback" (Clevinger & Rust, 2022, p. 4). For this reason, writing is one of my most important tools for continuous learning.

Note

1 English learners bring multicultural and multilingual strengths to our classrooms. English is heavily reported as one of the languages used at home in multilingual families.

References

Clevinger, K., & Rust, S. (2022). *Writing as inquiry: A guide to WR 121 at the University of Oregon*. University of Oregon Libraries.

Ladson-Billings, G. (2006). From the achievement gap to the education debt: Understanding achievement in US schools. *Educational Researcher, 35*(7), 3–12.

National Center for Educational Statistics (NCES). (2020). *English learners in public schools*. https://nces.ed.gov/programs/coe/indicator/cgf/english-learners

Warger, C. (2001). *Cultural reciprocity aids collaboration with families*. ERIC/OSEP Digest.

Wyatt-Ross, J. (2018, June 28). A classroom where everyone feels welcome. *Edutopia*. www.edutopia.org/article/classroom-where-everyone-feels-welcome

17

Build Accountability Through Grace

This chapter builds the case that grace and forgiveness are core leadership competencies for educational administrators to develop. With an emphasis on productive focus, this chapter asks school leaders to build capacities to foster relationships, forgiveness, and repair.

> **Key Concept:** A culture of accountability through grace guides leaders in strengthening relationships and maintaining a productive focus on people first.

As I learned many years ago, grace is about gratitude, and to lead with grace is to lead grateful for the opportunity and with thanks to those around you. To lead is a privilege, partially earned and partially due to all sorts of luck, and to lead well is necessarily to rely on others. Those who have entrusted you to lead and those on whom you depend deserve your gratitude, and you shouldn't hesitate to show it every chance you can.

(Ryan, 2017)

We need grace because sometimes we fall short. We need forgiveness because sometimes we make mistakes. We need accountability because when we count on each other, we can do great things. These three foundational lessons inform my work around navigating challenges.

In 2010, I launched a wellness retreat for high school students. I asked Jake Giessman, my supervisor at the time, to speak to the group. He gave a lecture called "Cheat Codes for Life." I am pretty sure Jake has never played a video game, so I enjoyed the irony. His "cheat codes" included general wellness and prosocial advice, including the importance of forgiveness. At the time, his focus on forgiveness caught me by surprise. I asked Jake about it later, and he shrugged and told me life was too short to spend it holding grudges. "Learn to forgive," he said, "and move on."[1]

I started paying attention to my own interactions with Jake to see how he cultivated a culture of accountability through grace. I forgot to turn in a professional development form two weeks ahead of the training date. I lost the receipt for a Thanksgiving charity dinner. I didn't copy all the right people on a planning email. These mistakes caused Jake more work, yet he never belabored the errors, instead just as he had advised at the retreat, he helped us both move on quickly. In the grand scheme of the important work I was doing to support student achievement, wellbeing, and culture, these mistakes were *small potatoes* and by spending his energy on solving the problem, Jake and I both kept them small. "Let's just see if we can get another receipt."

Later that school year, there was a death in our school community. I was blindsided with grief when Jake found me in the workroom. When I couldn't get myself together, he was there with tissues, and when my breathing slowed, he had a plan. Together, we met with our students to share the very difficult news. We connected our students and staff with the counseling team, held space for each other, and wrote cards of comfort to the family. This, too, is grace.

****

We need forgiveness because sometimes we all make mistakes. Often as leaders move into roles with increasing responsibilities, the challenges they're tasked with solving become more complex and charged. Some also require restorative processes for individual and organizational healing (see pgs. 18–19). All acts of forgiveness, from small to more significant, build from emotional regulation and relationships. In their 2023 paper for the *Journal of Organizational Behavior*, Daniel Brady, Maria Francisca Saldanha, and Laurie Barclay write that "At its core, forgiveness involves a process of intraindividual change in which an individual improves their emotions toward a transgressor. Forgiveness is therefore not a singular act (e.g., "I forgive you") but rather involves setting emotion goals and then regulating the trajectory of… reaching these goals over time" (p. 284).

There is a growing body of research on the positive impacts forgiveness has on individual and organizational culture (Cao et al., 2021; Erwin & DeVoll, 2021; Brady et al., 2023). In their paper for the American Psychological Association, Wenrui Cao, Reine C. van der Wal, and Toon W. Taris (2021) cite evidence that "forgiveness is an essential aspect of well functioning and lasting social relationships" (p. 2). They go on to name forgiveness as a condition of pro-relationship, organizational citizenship, and interpersonal citizenship behaviors (Cao et al., 2021).

As I started paying attention to how forgiveness functioned in my own leader practice, I learned several important lessons. First, I found that most of the time when someone in our school made a mistake, they rarely needed help identifying that they had made a mistake. Sometimes, they needed help apologizing. Apologizing with authenticity and ownership is another powerful skill leaders can teach, practice, and model. When I noticed a student or staff member was struggling with apologizing, I learned that they were often worried about forgiveness. This became a culture signal to me. How was I modeling forgiveness? How were we talking about mistakes in our school buildings? Other times, I found people needed help moving past the mistake. This, also, meant I had work to do. I needed to think through how to help reframe the situation through grace and productive focus. The more I paid attention, the more I found that forgiveness is the vehicle that gives us permission to make things right and move forward.

In their book *Leadership Is a Relationship*, authors Michael Erwin and Willys DeVoll (2022) include forgiveness as one of seven essential leadership traits for putting people first in the digital world. They write that forgiveness is "the hard, uncomfortable work of leading through relationships. Accountability doesn't prevent failure… When people let us down… great leaders choose to sit with discomfort and meet it with humble love…" They make the "decision to acknowledge each other's failing with unflinching clarity, recommit to each other's lives, and walk together" (pp. 26–27). That sounds like wholehearted leadership to me.

Below are three strategies for building a culture of accountability through grace.

Strategies for Practice

1. **Stay forward facing.** In the heat of the moment, the best path forward is almost always… forward. As school leaders, we set that focus.

Recently, I was working with a curriculum coordinator through some significant mistakes. After thoughtful review, it was clear that we had to make some tough calls, including a new plan and different support. This was a hard conversation. I did my best to present it with care and acknowledged that the news was difficult. The coordinator was rightly upset and his emotions escalated quickly.

As he became more agitated, a member of our HR team offered me data, records of his mistakes, and justifications for our decision. I told him no thank you. I did not need any of this information. The coordinator was aware of everything that had happened, and so was I. We weren't here to rehash it. Instead, I needed us to focus on where we were going together.

This productive focus guided my response. Yes, the school leader had made some mistakes, and yes, he cared for students and wanted to do better. These latter points gave us somewhere to grow from and the plan pointed a way forward together. If he was willing to keep the focus on student learning and wellbeing, I assured him we would implement this plan with respect and care. Ultimately, he agreed and we got to work. In situations like these, it is easy to get sucked back into the past. Wholehearted leaders resist this urge to dwell on the past; instead, they commit to moving their schools and teams forward with grace.

2. **Model the courage to make it right.** "A culture of forgiveness often yields a culture of bravery," write Ervin and Devoll. "When forgiveness spreads from person to person, it creates a culture where people can acknowledge and learn from failure rather than hide it out of fear of punishment or exclusion" (2022, p. 41). Operationalizing forgiveness can create a proactive measure against higher level mistakes like those referenced above. It also contributes to the culture of support and making it right that we need to navigate the everyday errors that come from working across systems and groups.

As school leaders, we have plenty of opportunities to practice. Each week, there are countless small ways we mess up: someone is short-tempered with a colleague; someone forgets to attach the right file; someone verbally attacks the person instead of critiquing the idea; a parent blames a support person for an error actually made by their child; we run out of time in the meeting for a teacher to share the information they had thoughtfully prepared. Feelings are hurt. Projects are stalled.

I have seen three main approaches to these sorts of situations. The first is that leaders ignore them altogether. If this becomes the norm, it can degrade trust and culture. The second and third strategies build on accountability—one does so through fear and the other through grace. Below is a chart for what that might look like.

In a culture of accountability **through fear**, leaders...	In a culture of accountability **through grace**, leaders...
• Lecture • Patronize • Keep a score of mistakes and hold grudges • Belabor the error • Tell others what to do	• Listen • Communicate with kindness • Keep a score of successes • Focus on moving forward • Offer help and support

Creating accountability through grace moves us forward and builds bridges between people even in tense times. This is the kind of culture that sees the best in people, gives permission to make mistakes, and offers us all a softer place to land. This means that when I, too, fall short of these best practices, which I inevitably do, we have established a culture of being for each other and the courage to make it right together.

> *Creating accountability through grace moves us forward and builds bridges between people even in tense times. This is the kind of culture that sees the best in people, gives permission to make mistakes, and offers us all a softer place to land.*

3. **Put the person before the behavior.** Very shortly after taking the position as academic director, I had my first big discipline case. A student had made some significant integrity mistakes. She had been dishonest with her parents, her teachers, and herself. It was my job to figure out our next steps. I met with the student and asked how she was doing. I learned that she had been stressed. Up to this point, she had been an outstanding student, and her classwork had come easily to her. This semester felt different. Her classes were suddenly a challenge. Meanwhile, her older brother had continued as an academic superstar. Tearfully, she told me her parents were getting a divorce. She wanted me to know that she wasn't making excuses. She knew her choices were wrong. She also shared that talking to me about all this was "helpful."

We talked through the next steps. There were some apologies to deliver, a reflection prompt I wanted her to work through, and then the chance to try again. She couldn't believe this last one. When I met with her dad later that day he told me something that has stayed with me ever since: "There are many decisions you could have made in this case and we would have respected them all, because our daughter made a mistake. Your decision, though, taught her two important lessons that I know she will always remember. You taught her that there is a way forward even after you have messed up and that leaders can lead with grace."

A few years later, we celebrated this student's high school graduation. We never had another discipline issue with her and she graduated as an honor role student. In an article for *Forbes*, Shelia Murty (2020) writes, "When people feel psychologically safe, valued and cared for… they will bring their best selves forward and give you their discretionary effort. But make no mistake, grace is an inside job—it's our role as leaders to model it, invest in it and commit to it" (para 10).

> "There are many decisions you could have made in this case and we would have respected them all, because our daughter made a mistake. Your decision, though, taught her two important lessons that I know she will always remember. You taught her that there is a way forward even after you have messed up and that leaders can lead with grace."

Reflective Work for Continuous Learning

We need accountability because when we count on each other, we can do great things. Building accountability through grace has the power to transform schools. Below are a few reflective exercises for you and your leadership team to use in considering how these lessons can help your school communities level up.

We need accountability because when we count on each other, we can do great things. Building accountability through grace has the power to transform schools.

1. **Practice everyday grace.** This chapter offered several examples of everyday opportunities to extend grace. Consider the last few times you have seen these kinds of situations.
   - Which approach did you use? Did you ignore, did you tighten up accountability through fear, or did you extend grace?
   - Knowing that there are countless opportunities for this work, what will you do differently next time?
2. **Maintain a productive focus.** When mistakes are made, what support do you need to keep your focus on solutions, students, staff, and families?
3. **Create space to repair.** Reflect on the past semester or school year. What are some of the more difficult challenges that have happened in your school community?
   - What aspects of these situations are yours to own? As a school leader, often the answer is: Quite a bit!
   - Have you taken time to reflect and process these situations? If so, how? (If not, give it a try.)
   - Have you created the space to build healing and repair? If so, what additional work needs to happen to prevent a similar situation and to keep your school community moving forward?
4. **Give yourself grace.** This chapter can sometimes bring up more difficult feelings. What does it look like to give yourself grace, too?

Note

1 I reflected on some of these lessons from Jake's talk in an earlier article printed by the professional journal of the New York Academy of Public Education in May 2016.

References

Brady, D. L., Saldanha, M. F., & Barclay, L. J. (2023). Conceptualizing forgiveness: A review and path forward. *Journal of Organizational Behavior, 44*(2), 261–296.

Cao, W., van der Wal, R. C., & Taris, T. W. (2021). When work relationships matter: Interpersonal forgiveness and work outcomes. *International Journal of Stress Management, 28*(4), 266.

Erwin, M. S., & DeVoll, W. (2021). *Leadership is a relationship: How to put people first in the digital world.* John Wiley & Sons.

Murty, S. (2020, July 7). What it means to lead with grace. *Forbes.* www.forbes.com/sites/forbeshumanresourcescouncil/2020/07/07/what-it-means-to-lead-with-grace/

Ryan, J. (2017, May 25). *Lead with grace the prepared remarks of Dean James Ryan for the 2017 HGSE presentation of diplomas and certificates.* Harvard Graduate School of Education. www.gse.harvard.edu/ideas/news/17/05/lead-grace

18
Communicate Care Across Cultures

Wholehearted leadership asks us to grow in intercultural competencies, recognizing that all cultures in our school communities have wisdom and value. Building on Dr. Milton Bennett's work with the Developmental Model of Intercultural Sensitivity, this chapter explores communication and care practices across cultures. Many of these practices were sharpened during my time visiting international schools in the Red River Delta (Vietnam) in 2020.

> 💡 **Key Concept:** All cultures in our school communities have wisdom and value.

Connection isn't only technology; it's communication. Communication isn't only language; it's care and curiosity about another human being.

I arrived in Hanoi just as the sun was setting. A school coordinator met my teaching director and me at the airport. As she drove us to the hotel, she told us stories about the city. Using magical realism in a way I had never before heard in everyday conversation, she told us about dragons and fairies alongside project plans for the construction of a new bridge to streamline airport traffic. She pointed to the river and told us this is where Hanoi, which means *inside of the river*, gets its name. We drove by

DOI: 10.4324/9781003517122-31

the famous miles-long mural, an art installation to celebrate the 100-year anniversary of the city. It sparkled even in the dark.

I woke up early the next morning, still foggy from travel. I stepped outside with a cup of coffee and watched the city wake up. Motorbikes whizzed past as I thought about the students and teachers we get to work and learn with here. Many of these young people had visited our campus in the United States, and today we would get to visit their campuses, schools, and neighborhoods.

International school visits like these have been transformative in my personal growth as a school leader and human being. The 5th century philosopher Heraclitus said that one never steps into the same river twice. The same is true in schools. Each class, experience, and family who joins our community changes our communities. As a school leader, I know that I am forever changed by my experiences teaching and learning abroad.

******

I slide off my dress shoes and add them to the pile at the front of the bright-colored kindergarten building. Looking down the hallway, I notice dozens of irregular snowflakes cut with safety scissors and hung with a teacher's care. Although this is my first visit to Vietnam and this school, I feel immediately at home.

My work in global education has shown me the shared humanity that courses through our school hallways. Whether I am at a Catholic school in Brazil, a private school in Vietnam, or a public school in the United States, all students and teachers want to connect. My time in Hanoi sharpened my understanding about the power and universality of classroom connection. Below is a list of observations I made in my journal during these school visits. In hindsight, this list feels simple and obvious. However, as I revisit it, it is also a reminder about human relationships and interaction. In my current school system, over 90% of our students speak a home language other than English. The multilingual talents and cultural experiences these young people bring to our classrooms are among our school's greatest strengths. As we teach and lead across languages, geographical borders, and experience, simple reminders are sometimes the most profound.

> **Even if you don't speak the same language as your students, you can still appreciate:**
>
> - the renewed sense of possibility when we greet each other in the morning
> - the way a spark of laughter can change the tenor of a classroom
> - how learning a new game brings people together
> - how we nod when we say thank you
> - how we crinkle our eyes to show friendship
> - the way friends leave less space between each other and can share a joke without saying a word
> - that we all need to dance and sing
> - how we straighten our gaze when solving an interesting problem
> - the way natural beauty causes us to pause
> - that few gifts are more treasured in a school day than receiving art from a student or a hot cup of coffee from a teacher.
>
> *Adapted from my Hanoi school visit journals in November 2020*

These truths are part of the universal magic of schools. While I did learn a few phrases in Vietnamese, more importantly I learned that it often doesn't take any language to communicate the most important things such as: *Thank you. Please. I see you. I value you. I'm happy you're here,* and *I'm happy we're here together.*

Strategies for Practice

During my time in Vietnam, our middle school students tried to coach me on my language learning. They were patient, encouraging, and fascinated by the nuances I struggled to hear in their tonal home language. Despite our collective best efforts, these lessons usually resulted in wild fits of laughter and very little language progress on my end. Then again, the point of the lesson wasn't so much about language learning. It was about connecting. I remember one lesson standing in the doorway of a seventh grade math class. The students were again working with me on counting. "Simple," they said, "Một, Hai, Ba, Bốn, Năm, Sáu, Bảy, Tám, Chín, Mười. When counting to ten proved out of my reach, we tried just Một, Hai, Ba, Bốn. It still wasn't going well. I remember looking at their eager faces and desperately wanting to get it right.

One of the most important ways we *get it right* as educators is remembering that they're all kids and they're all our kids. The middle school students I worked with in Hanoi were curious about everything. As we worked together you could see both the lasting glimmers of early childhood and the new glimmers of the young adults they were becoming. "Let's try one more time." a seventh grader said, trying to hold a serious yet encouraging face. I furrowed my brow and before we got to Hai (two) we were both crying with laughter. These young people brought their unique lived experiences, their culture, and their beliefs to their classroom, and they were also very much like every group of seventh graders I've known and cared for across my career. Curious. Awkward. Kind.

> *One of the most important ways we* get it right *as educators is remembering that they're all kids and they're all our kids.*

Remember they're all our kids. Dr. Lisa Delpit's seminal text, *Other People's Children* (2006), explores the role of race and culture in the classroom. One of Delpit's central claims is that too often teachers regard students from culturally diverse or marginalized backgrounds as though they are other people's children. Educators and school leaders who see students as other people's children aren't likely to extend the same care, concern, and high expectations they would for their own children. They also aren't as likely to teach them the hidden curriculum around power and privilege. A bit later in this chapter, we will explore Dr. Milton

Bennett's work around intercultural competencies. To borrow his language, regarding students as other people's children falls under an *ethnocentric worldview.*

Kathy Ritter, a school leader and one of my personal role models, offered her school community an alternative ethnorelative philosophy. She frequently reminded us that "they're all our kids." This phrase was foundational to her philosophy of care and as a result it became foundational to our school's philosophy of care. As you commit to growing in your intercultural competencies, what does it look like to remember that all kids are our kids? How does this influence your learning conversations around discipline? How does this influence the ideas you say yes to? How does this influence the ways you show care and concern?

While working in Hanoi, I was struck by how teachers, students, and staff can communicate care without saying a word. Together, we can make our schools places where we show up for each other with concern, generosity, and grace.

Reflective Work for Continuous Learning

For nearly 50 years, Dr. Milton Bennett has been a thought leader in intercultural communication and competencies. In 1986, he created the Developmental Model of Intercultural Sensitivity (DMIS), which is used widely across sectors including education, business, and nonprofits. The DMIS has six stages, outlined below.

> **Intercultural Sensitivity as Developed by Milton Bennett**
>
> The DMIS gives leaders and learners vocabulary to recognize where they are in working across new cultural groups. The arrows show how we can use this knowledge to build common language and grow toward more ethnorelative practices.

> **DMIS**
>
> | Denial | Defense | Minimization | Acceptance | Adaptation | Integration |
> |---|---|---|---|---|---|
> | *STAGE 1* | *STAGE 2* | *STAGE 3* | *STAGE 4* | *STAGE 5* | *STAGE 6* |
>
> **Ethnocentric** →   **Ethnorelative** →
>
> **Key Vocabulary**
>
> - **Ethnocentric:** To evaluate and judge other cultures as "right" or "wrong" based on the standards of our own culture. Our worldview is shaped by our cultural beliefs, customs, and ways of being and we can cling to those even when they are in tension with the cultural situations we are navigating.
> - **Ethnorelative:** The belief that all cultures are valid. Our worldview is shaped by our relationships with different cultures and we integrate the lessons we have learned across cultures into our behaviors and patterns of being.

At our most ethnorelative moments, school leaders integrate complex cultural dimensions into our decision-making. Like all skills, growing in intercultural competencies requires practice, commitment, and exposure. In a 2017 paper, Bennett writes that "Movement through the stages is not inevitable; it depends on the need to become more competent in communicating outside one's primary social context" (p. 3). Said differently, we must commit to lifelong learning if we want to grow toward integration.

The Peace Corps is one of the organizations that trains volunteers in the DMIS.[1] In their *Culture Matters Workbook*, written for volunteers working in schools, the authors share that as you move to ethnorelativism, not only do your attitudes change, but your behavior does, too. This moving in and out of patterns of being is sometimes called *style switching*. This doesn't mean you give up your culture, values, and beliefs; instead you "integrate aspects of other cultures into it. In the integration stage, certain aspects of the other culture or cultures become a part of [your] identity" (Peace Corps, n.d.). The groups you work, learn, teach, and build community with affect who and how you are in the world.

Consider the following reflective questions about how the DMIS framework can support care across cultures in your school community.

1. **Grow toward ethnorelativism.** What teaching, learning, or leading experiences have most helped you grow toward ethnorelativism?
2. **Celebrate culture.** What specific cultural backgrounds are represented in your school community? How does your team include and celebrate these cultures in your school practices, customs, and traditions?
3. **Set specific learning goals.** As with all learning goals, it is important to be clear on your objectives and thoughtful in leaning on accountability partners.
    a. What phrases and actions do you want to avoid because they signal denial, defense, or minimization?
    b. What phrases and actions do you want to amplify because they signal acceptance, adaptation, or integration?
    c. What goals do you have for growing your school community toward ethnorelativism?

Note

1 Milton Bennett served as a US Peace Corps volunteer in Micronesia from 1968–1970.

References

Bennett, M. (2017). Development model of intercultural sensitivity. In Y. Kim (Ed.), *International encyclopedia of intercultural communication*. Wiley.

Delpit, L. (2006). *Other people's children: Cultural conflicts in the classroom*. The New Press.

Peace Corps. (n.d.). *Attitudes toward cultural difference: From ethnocentrism to ethnorelativism*. Paul D. Coverdell World Wise Schools: Culture Matters. https://files.peacecorps.gov/wws/interactive/culturematters/Ch6/attitudes.html

19

Progress Is a Team Process

School change often results from a chain reaction of believing in one another. With contributions from Karen Scales, this chapter builds on a powerful story of teacher leadership. The examples in this chapter illustrate change as a team process, persistence as advocacy, and the power of believing in each other to bring about new realities.

> **Key Concept:** Have faith in the good ideas that students and teachers bring to you.

When I started working on this chapter, I planned for it to be about supporting teacher initiatives, and I knew just the story I wanted to tell. This story is among my top ten favorite school history stories. It takes place several years before I started working at our university lab school, and has had a lasting impact on our approach to saying yes to students, teaching with rigor, and persisting through challenges. In introducing the following story, I would have said it belonged to veteran teacher and school leader, Karen Scales.

Karen, who graciously partnered with me on this chapter, respectfully disagreed. She helped me see that this wasn't really a chapter on supporting teacher initiatives, per se. Instead, it is a chapter on understanding change as a team process in schools.

"Like so many teacher initiatives," she says, "this one actually began as a student initiative."

In 1998, Karen was serving as a language arts instructor for the lab school, which was transitioning from a correspondence model into a comprehensive online high school. The school was preparing for their first accreditation review and the launch of their diploma program. Big changes were happening everywhere, and Karen was about to bring yet another new and impactful idea to the picture.

At the time, the school was housed in the university's extension department, and faculty also served as field reps across the state—meeting with students, counselors, and administrators to deliver updated course catalogs, gather data, and facilitate curricular and support service requests. Karen worked with about 20 schools in a rural region of Missouri. During her visits, high school students and their counselors kept asking if our school would please offer Advanced Placement (AP) courses. AP courses are college-level classes students can take in high school. They include exams that can count toward college credit. They also require a rigorous approval process by the College Board, making them less accessible in rural and under-resourced districts.

> "So much credit," she says, "goes to our school principal. Teacher initiatives don't happen without administrator support. It was our principal who pushed for funding. She asked the hard questions. She investigated. She had faith in this vision, and it wouldn't have happened without her."

Reflecting on that experience today, Karen shares, "Expanding educational access to rigorous coursework for students in rural areas was at the heart of this." All the field reps were hearing this growing call for AP courses, so they brought the request back to their principal, with Karen hoping to pilot the effort in language arts.

"So much credit," she says, "goes to our school principal. Teacher initiatives don't happen without administrator support. It was our principal who pushed for funding. She asked the hard questions. She investigated. She had faith in this vision, and it wouldn't have happened without her."

In 1999, Karen traveled to Kansas City to learn more about AP through one of the College Board's AP Institutes. She remembers digesting information about content, processes, and requirements. She also remembers that all the workshops were squarely focused on in-classroom activities. "The Socratic Seminar, for example, is a key instructional practice in AP. When I shared that we wanted to build a class online, everybody was stymied by how that would work in a school without classrooms." Karen laughs and says, "I was, too!"

Karen struggled to translate what she was learning at the institute to her school's new virtual space. "Everything about online instruction was still new, even to career distance educators. Remember," she says, "there really wasn't even video conferencing at this time." A fellow teacher at the AP Institute graciously offered to partner with Karen as a sounding board during one of the workshop sessions. She helped Karen start thinking about how AP might work in an online context by advising her to take a step back and to imagine her new course. She encouraged Karen to think first about her students—what she wanted for them, what connection might look like in an online space, and how she could build from there. Karen smiles remembering this partner teacher's advice, "She reminded me that teachers can make magical things happen out of an idea. They do it all the time."

After the AP Institute, Karen and her colleagues got to work. "We started thinking like engineers," she explained. She then outlined the three foundational elements they needed to get in place before presenting this dream as an achievable reality for the College Board.

- **Course Content.** "We took almost a full year after the AP Institute to write the course content. At this time, the team was still printing and binding course books to snail mail to students." The first AP course book was about 350 pages.
- **Master Schedule.** Up to this point, all courses in the online high school used rolling admissions. Students

worked independently and at their own pace. "That asynchronous schedule simply wasn't going to work with AP discussions and collaborative requirements." Karen remembers working around a table with faculty and staff, mapping out ideas on a whiteboard, when it finally occurred to her to challenge the premise: What if online AP courses *weren't* asynchronous? Although scheduled courses were a radical adjustment for the school's online master schedule, a new format was just the solution they needed to get students in cohorts that would facilitate the kinds of collaborative interactions necessary in an AP course. (You can read more about the power of rethinking the master schedule in Chapter 12.)

- **Interaction and Technology.** Next, the team had to find a way to leverage interaction between students. There was one text chat tool available at the time and email. "These were the only tools we had, and we wrote plans to leverage both."

Finally they sent their proposal off to the College Board for approval.

*****

Karen laughed when I asked what happened next. "Well, I saved our rejection letters. Those are amazing historic artifacts. The letters were supportive, but not optimistic. We received feedback that the content was great but that the kinds of robust socratic seminars, peer collaboration, and meaningful academic conversations that distinguish AP scholarship were still lacking."

So the team got back to work. Karen says both the College Board and our accreditation officers stuck with them. "Everyone was supportive, even when it seemed impossible." They reworked and submitted the proposal—three more times.

When the approval letter finally came a year later, Karen's principal called her. "I was at home," she remembers, "and the College Board had sent the letter to the main office. That was a special moment of celebration."

The approval came about three weeks before the semester would need to launch for the coming academic year. As Karen puts it, this realization was "simultaneously the most accomplished feeling of my professional career to date and the most terrifying."

To the best of our knowledge this was the first online AP course ever approved by the College Board. In Karen's telling, this served as a testament to the team that they could do hard things.

*****

"The great irony is," Karen paused for effect, "that after all that work on collaboration and dialogue, we had *one student* the first year. This meant there was no opportunity for her to collaborate with other students."

That student, who we will call Hannah, is the next leader in Karen's story. By this point in the book, you know what happened next. Hannah became one of Karen's most important teachers. She and Hannah were "the first AP team." They partnered through the collaborative elements of that course together. Hannah helped Karen see it in a new way, and together they took a deep dive into what was and wasn't working. "We iterated," Karen said, "and got the course ready for the next school year."

The next year, five students enrolled, and Karen says this is when "AP really got going. As a distance educator, this was the first time I had a group of students sharing experiences and talking together about their learning. It was beautiful."

*****

This was 25 years ago. Since then our lab school's AP offerings have grown into a robust and interdisciplinary program. Thousands of students have gone through these rigorous courses with our instructors facilitating conversations and collaborations across time zones and geographic borders. Karen continues to teach our AP English language arts courses and coaches new AP teachers. When they get stuck, she is now the friend who reminds them that we can do hard things and that educators can make magic happen, sometimes by simply imagining a new reality.

Key Strategies for Practice

Karen built on the ideas and support of many stakeholders. Leveraging this kind of distributed leadership helps us mobilize collective knowledge. These practices support comprehensive school reforms and improve instruction (Chrispeels & González, 2023; Mifsud, 2024). As Karen met with high school students in her rural area, she learned of a pressing need and acted on its behalf. As she will be the first to tell you, this advocacy and building work was a team effort. Change is often the result of a chain reaction of believing in each other. Wholehearted school leaders believe in the good ideas students and teachers bring to them and use their power to advocate for new realities.

Today, Karen's classes still include students who are studying in rural areas in the Midwest. However, now these young people also learn alongside peers studying from South Korea, Panama, and Turkey. These students have an array of technical tools to create multimedia projects and collaborate over text and video. While the reach and technology have both grown significantly, the heart of our AP discussions still carries remnants of that first early chat tool. As anyone who has sent a text message knows, an ellipsis can mean someone is thinking. In our case, those three dots signal forthcoming dialogue and connecting at a distance. Within those three dots is a world of possibility on which our online collaboration is built.

Below are a few strategies for leveraging the great ideas in your buildings.

1. **Listen to and believe in students.** When Karen heard that high school students in rural Missouri wanted AP courses, she jumped to try and make that happen. Inherent in her advocacy is a belief that the high school students who asked for AP courses were capable of learning at this level. This belief matters. Throughout this book we have explored the

importance of high expectations and the power of relationships. As Karen modeled, this belief is part of a broader worldview about learning. Wholehearted educators believe that young people are capable of achieving at high levels. As students share their academic goals and their hopes for curriculum, or extracurricular activities, we have the responsibility to listen, believe, and work to make these goals a reality.

Throughout this book we have explored the importance of high expectations and the power of relationships. As Karen modeled, this belief is part of a broader worldview about learning. Wholehearted educators believe that young people are capable of achieving at high levels.

2. **Support change as a team process.** School change is a team process. In Karen's story, student interest led to teacher advocacy, which led to administrative support, which then led to team learning and iteration. There were many stakeholders speaking into this initiative including the College Board, our accreditation officers, and a team of faculty and staff who sat around a conference table mapping out a new way forward. While the details of each school initiative are unique to your local context, a team approach is essential in making lasting change possible. As you support your team through change processes, ensure that many voices are included at every step along brainstorm and implementation.

Reflective Work for Continuous Learning

This is a story about how change happens in schools. In order for change to happen, school leaders must be open to imagining new possibilities and ready to venture new ideas. Imagination can be a powerful precursor to action. An important mentor in Karen's story is a teacher she didn't know well. That teacher encouraged her to imagine. Rather than giving direction or proposing her own answers, she simply protected thought space for Karen to work through what the AP program might look like. Ting Wang, Dianne Olivier, and Peiying Chen write that readiness for change is "multi-dimensional, multi-level, and multifaceted" (2023, p. 2). The story in this chapter offers strong examples of students, teachers, and administrators who were open to change. This openness made a new program possible.

Below are a few reflective exercises to consider historical and current change initiatives in your school. As always, you can work through these individually or with your leadership team.

1. **Mark your defining narratives.** Understanding our change origin stories can inspire continued progress and iteration.
    - What are the defining narratives on which your school or district was built? To the greatest extent possible, seek out original sources for these stories. Explore them with veteran teachers, administrators, and alumni. Ask questions and listen deeply.
    - How do these stories continue to impact policy, practice, traditions, and beliefs in your school?
2. **Use persistence + iteration.** Karen outlined a methodical approach her school took to get that first proposal ready for the College Board. This process took over a year from planning to submission, and then it was still met with rejection. Luckily, in Karen's case the team persisted. They tried, iterated, and tried again.
    - What are the conditions needed to support this level of persistence through challenge?
    - What are examples of times when your team has persisted to bring about a new initiative in your district or building?
    - How can you strengthen your team's resolve to see change initiatives through?
3. **Practice active imagination.** Creating space for teachers, students, and leaders to imagine is a powerful practice in building possibility. Moral imagination, which Pamela Joseph (2022) also called critical reflection, can help uncover

blind spots, lead to self-knowledge, and support new actions (Joseph, 2022). This liberatory imagination allows educators and school leaders to envision what can be without constraint (Holyoke & Tily, 2024).
- ♦ As a school leader, how will you cultivate space for imagination without judgment or limitations?

References

Chrispeels, J. H., & González, M. (2023). The challenge of systemic change in complex educational systems: A district model to scale up reform. In A. Harris & J. H. Chrispeels (Eds.), *Improving schools and educational systems* (pp. 241–273). Routledge.

Holyoke, E., & Tily, S. (2024). "Without boundaries, something great might just be created": Examining preservice teachers' radical imagination through becoming writers and teachers of writing. *Teaching/Writing: The Journal of Writing Teacher Education, 12*(1), 1.

Joseph, P. B. (2022). Cultivating moral imagination through teacher education. In M. A. Peters (Ed.), *Encyclopedia of teacher education* (pp. 333–337). Springer Nature Singapore.

Mifsud, D. (2024). A systematic review of school distributed leadership: Exploring research purposes, concepts and approaches in the field between 2010 and 2022. *Journal of Educational Administration and History, 56*(2), 154–179.

Wang, T., Olivier, D. F., & Chen, P. (2023). Creating individual and organizational readiness for change: Conceptualization of system readiness for change in school education. *International Journal of Leadership in Education, 26*(6), 1037–1061.

20

Expand Learning, Reduce Barriers

Be open to discovering genius in your students and school communities. With a focus on inequities in identification for gifted services, this chapter introduces readers to "Nala," a high school refugee who teaches her class about life, death, violence, and grace. This student leader also reminds administrators of their essential role in closing opportunity gaps, expanding learning, and reducing barriers to participation for culturally and linguistically diverse students.

> 💡 **Key concept:** Be open to discovering genius in your students and school communities. Actively work to reduce opportunity gaps in educational programming.

> As a matter of urgency, it is incumbent upon the field of gifted education to end with expediency the longstanding concern regarding the underrepresentation of CLD [culturally and linguistically diverse] students in gifted programs… Where underrepresentation persists, efforts must be continued to conceptualize, formalize, and implement effective strategies on behalf of CLD students.
> (National Association for Gifted Children, 2021)

For several years I ran an equal opportunity gifted program at a large public high school. This program gave me the ability to reimagine representation in gifted services. In my program, we didn't rely on standardized identification. Instead, all were welcome. If you wanted to take advantage of gifted services, they were available to you. I also engaged in outreach and recruitment efforts to make sure our historically and continuously under-identified student populations knew about these services and that they were welcome here. This is how I got to know a student we'll call Nala.

Nala and her family had recently resettled in the United States. As refugees, she, her mother, and siblings had escaped violence in their home country, the Democratic Republic of the Congo, and had made the long and difficult journey to our city in the Midwest. The US chapter of the United Nations Human Rights Commission reports that "the displacement situation in the Democratic Republic of the Congo… is the most complex and long-standing humanitarian crisis in Africa" (2023). After resettling, Nala's mother got a job in health care. Her work started early in the morning and so Nala joined the zero block program I ran out of our gifted center. This program was a no-credit open time for study and social emotional learning. I started zero block 90 minutes before the first bell each day. The program included time for studying, talking through goals, and planning for the week or day ahead. I played soft jazz music through the speakers and made tea for the students who stopped by to start their day with me. It was my favorite time of each school day. For much of zero block, my gifted program students and I were among a small group of students in the building.

One morning late in the fall, Nala and I were drinking tea together and talking through an upcoming assignment in her English class when a small group of students ran into the room panicked. The students shouted that there was a bird trapped in the lofted atrium that connected our Social Studies and English hallways. Nala and I followed them to the hall, and sure enough, a small red bird was perched in the rafters. Soon, our commotion caught the attention of Mr. Jim, one of our early morning custodial staff. He joined us in looking up at the bird and wondering what to do next.

"Well," Mr. Jim said, patting his legs decisively, "I guess I'll go get the ladder."

Nala turned to me and told me she knew what to do. I wasn't sure what she meant, so I waited with the group until the custodian came back with a tall ladder and a broom. He was visibly nervous about heights, and I could tell the student crowd wasn't quelling his nerves. I tried my best to keep the group quiet as he climbed the ladder slowly, pausing at each rung, and looking down. When he made it to the top of the ladder, he looked up into the rafters, only to find he was still several feet away from the bird. As if in jest, the bird tweeted and flew to another beam. We groaned. Mr. Jim asked a student to pass him the broom. A student passed it up. Nervously, Mr. Jim tried to hoist the broom above his head, but even with the added height, his efforts were fruitless. He wasn't close, and even if he were, it was clear the bird wasn't going to just hop onto the outstretched broom.

Just then, Nala spoke up. Her voice was calm and clear, "Stop. You're scaring him."

The custodian climbed down the ladder, looked at Nala, and looked back up at the bird. "What would you suggest?" he challenged.

"Let me climb up there. I know what to do."

"I can't do that." said Mr. Jim, creating an impasse. "Students aren't allowed on the ladder."

We all stood there looking up. A couple minutes passed. No one else had any ideas.

Nala tried again, "Let me go up there." she said.

The custodian looked at me, and I nodded. I told him we would steady the ladder.

Mr. Jim relented, and Nala climbed confidently to the top. She, too, was still several feet away from the bird. A boy asked if she wanted the broom. "Shhhh," she hushed him. "Of course not. I am going to talk to him."

And then she began talking to the bird in Swahili. Her cadence was melodic. It sounded more like a song than a conversation.

We watched entranced, and after about 30 seconds, the bird flew toward Nala's outstretched hand.

The crowd hollered and the bird flew straight back to the rafters.

"Shhhh...." Nala hushed us all again now with a soft edge in her voice. "He won't come to me if he is scared," she explained in English. We complied.

Then she started her melody again, and again the bird flew toward her hand. Nala took a careful step down one rung of the ladder. The bird followed. Then she took another step and another. The bird hovered just above us when a young man picked up the broom and swatted at it.

Like a fighter jet, the bird zoomed down the hall. We ran after him. The bird flew into an open classroom. We ran into the room. Then the bird flew straight into a closed window and collapsed with a soft thud on the floor. We gathered around the bird, and all of us, including me, looked to Nala for guidance.

Again she said, "I know what to do."

Gently, she sighed. "This too," she explained to us, "is part of life." She bent down and picked up the bird delicately, wrapping him in a gray sweatshirt. "We will need to bury him," she said, "and say some words to help him pass." The students nodded solemnly and followed her to a tree in front of our school. I watched from the classroom window as Nala led the group in a short service. A few students lowered the bird into a hole they had dug, covered him with fall leaves and dirt, and walked back into the school building together.

*****

Like me, I suspect that our small student group and Mr. Jim still think of this experience. That said, it also bears mentioning that it didn't spread across our school the way other legendary acts sometimes do. Without ever discussing it explicitly, we knew that the bird, Nala's lessons, and our collective experience belonged just to us.

The US Committee for Refugees and Immigrants (2020) reports that:

> The situation in the Democratic Republic of the Congo... is one of the most enduring and complex humanitarian crises in the world. The country is simultaneously experiencing armed conflicts, food insecurity, forced displacement, and multiple recurring epidemics, including cholera, measles, and intermittent outbreaks of Ebola.
>
> (p. 1)

Nala brought to school different lived experiences than her peers, Mr. Jim, or me. We would never fully understand many of these experiences. The US Chapter of the UNHRC reports that women and girls are especially vulnerable to the ongoing humanitarian crisis in the Democratic Republic of the Congo (2023). Early one morning, before most students had arrived, Nala drew on her lived experiences and a rich cultural wisdom to help us navigate a surprising situation. As a result, she taught us about life, death, and our connection to nature. Nala knew at a deep level that fear and violence were not the way forward and she also taught grace to those who hadn't yet learned this lesson.

> *Early one morning, before most students had arrived, Nala drew on her lived experiences and a rich cultural wisdom to help us navigate a surprising situation. As a result, she taught us about life, death, and our connection to nature. Nala knew at a deep level that fear and violence were not the way forward and she also taught grace to those who hadn't yet learned this lesson.*

Strategies for Practice

Dr. Paris Django's work on *culturally sustaining pedagogies* calls for practices that honor the inherent wisdom our students and families bring to our classrooms (Paris, 2012; Paris & Alim, 2014). In his words, "Culturally sustaining pedagogy seeks to perpetuate and foster—to sustain—linguistic, literate, and cultural pluralism as part of the democratic project of schooling" (Paris, 2012, p. 93). In my own work, I often refer to school as a community project. By this, I mean that our policies, practices, traditions, and curricula must be both informed by and responsive to our communities, including the family, local, and global groups to which we belong. This work isn't just theoretical, it's practical. The Institute of Educational Sciences (2020) writes that culturally sustaining schools commit to these three criteria:

1. Supportive school leadership—authentically partner with families and community members.
2. Safe and inclusive school culture and climate—address bias-related incidents constructively and celebrate the strengths of diverse student backgrounds.
3. High-quality, culturally sustaining curricula—teach for representation and learning.

Throughout this book, we have explored the need for asset-based approaches and for global and intercultural competencies. Paris writes (2012) that the "long struggle against dehumanizing deficit approaches to education and toward humanizing resource approaches has never been easy." Yet in order to rewire our schools for courage, justice, learning, and connection, we must engage in this work. We must, as Paris puts it, point "toward an education that honors and extends the languages and literacies and practices of our students and communities in the project of social and cultural justice" (p. 96).

In a 2020 interview with the Texas Gifted Education Family Network, Dr. Joy Lawson Davis, a leading scholar on gifted equity, shared:

> According to research, there are countless... *students from culturally diverse backgrounds who are missing out on services* because of biased identification practices, teachers who don't recognize and believe in the high intelligence creativity of these students, and lack of funding to fully support comprehensive program changes needed to ensure equity and access for all students with high potential. Schools can do more to support these students by changing their identification practices, *providing cultural*

competency training for teachers, and ensuring that school leaders are culturally competent, as well [my emphasis].

Students from historically and continuously marginalized backgrounds, including Black, Latine, and Indigenous students, students from lower-income families, multilingual students, especially refugee and immigrant students, and twice exceptional students (or those with both disabilities and gifted identities) are under-identified in our gifted and advanced programs (Hemingway, 2022; Long et al., 2023). School leaders can play an important role in remediating this pressing equity issue. Below are practical strategies for school leaders to reduce barriers to identification and participation in gifted and advanced programming, and to further the work of equity for our culturally and linguistically diverse students.

1. **Audit participation in your academically advanced programs.** Examine your specific school context. What racial, ethnic, cultural, linguistic, economic, and ability diversity is present in your school community? Compare this to the identification and participation demographics of your gifted and advanced programs, including formal gifted programming, advanced math, world language, honors courses, and also programs like AP (Advanced Placement) and IB (International Baccalaureate). What gaps do you need to fill to achieve participation parity? For instance, if 16% of your school population is African American, what work do you need to do to ensure that African American students also represent at least 16% of your Advanced Placement enrollments? Once you are clear on your school's specific gaps, you can work purposefully to close them.

For a few years, one of the districts I worked at partnered with Equal Opportunity Schools (EOS). EOS uses a research-based four-phase model to address the enrichment opportunity gap (2024). I am adapting this model here for consideration as you engage in remediating access gaps in your own contexts.

- **Write Support Plans Based on Relationships:** Analyze equity barriers and opportunities as described above. Identify trusted adults who will help champion equity and student success and who have strong relationships with target students. Develop a staff and student support plan for change.
- **Champion Equity:** Engage in professional learning, work purposefully to strengthen and understand student belonging, lived experiences, and growth mindset in your schools. Identify target students who are missing services and opportunities commensurate with their abilities and needed to reach their full potential.
- **Examine and Evaluate Educator Practices:** Facilitate conversations to sustain shifts in school culture related to equity; review school data that might inform school insights on access, success, and advanced coursework.
- **Build for Sustainability:** Continue efforts to support underrepresented students in advanced coursework. Continue professional learning. Continue efforts to close the opportunity gap.

2. **Utilize universal screening.** Universal screening, or testing all students for gifted programs, has been shown to dramatically reduce the bias associated with teacher or family referral systems (Lakin, 2016; Morgan, 2020). This strategy has led to dramatic increases in culturally and linguistically diverse identification. In a 2023 article, Scott Peters, Matthew Makel, and James Carter III cite the results of universal screening in a large Florida school district. When this district switched from a referral-based system to a universal screener, identification rates for Black and Latine students jumped by 74% and 118%, respectively. The Naglieri General Abilities Test (NGAT) is often regarded as a leading assessment instrument, because it was developed specifically to measure thinking (which differs from knowing) and to be language-free and more conscientious of cultural differences (Denver Public Schools, 2024; Selvamenan et al., 2024). Given this research, several states in the United States are now mandating universal screening.

Sometimes this is coupled with funding for assessments. For those states that don't have funding support, universal screening does require a fiscal investment. As you are considering resources, these equity and impact data build a compelling case as part of a strategy for expanding learning and reducing barriers.

3. **Build gifted equity into your professional learning plans.** The great US poet Maya Angelou is credited with saying, "I did then what I knew how to do. Now that I know better, I do better." The stories and exercises in this chapter point us to ongoing learning about equity, basis, and barriers to educational programs. In my work in schools, I have found that this kind of knowledge is power. When we know better, we do better through new policies, practices, and initiatives. In the context of this chapter that includes professional learning on the nature and needs of gifted learners, the persistent underrepresentation of culturally and linguistically diverse students from our advanced programs, and antiracist and culturally competent teaching and assessment measures. As you set your professional development priorities for the next school year, these topics are important to consider.

Reflective Work for Continuous Learning

So many of Nala's gifts—persistence, humor, calm demeanor—couldn't be measured on a standardized assessment. She had lived through unimaginable experiences and arrived in my classroom filled with light and ready to challenge anyone to a dance off. Nala's gifts crossed multiple domains—language, leadership, mathematical thinking—and our gifted program was immeasurably richer for her involvement. Some afternoons Nala's mom, Ms. O, would come by after school to visit. She often arrived in her hospital uniform, weary from a long day. We would hug, and Nala had taught me how to greet her in Swahili. Then I would make us coffee. If Nala was in the room, sometimes she would translate for us. In addition to Swahili, the family also spoke

French, Lingala, and Tshiluba. On many of these afternoons though, Ms. O and I just sat together. English wasn't worth the effort after a long day at work; it was better just to be with a friend.

During one of these afternoons together, it started snowing. Nala and a group of friends ran into the gifted room, bright snowflakes clinging to their hair and coats. Ms. O and I smiled at the high schoolers and she stood to wrap her bright scarf around her neck and over her box braids. I pulled on my own heavy coat and we walked outside with the group. We stood not far from the tree where months ago Nala had helped her classmates bury a small red bird. Ms. O and Nala turned their faces to the sky so that the snow fell across them. They held hands and giggled.

******

Below are several reflective exercises to work through on culturally sustaining pedagogy, reducing barriers, and expanding access to learning.

1. **Engage in asset mapping.** Throughout this book, we have explored the need for asset-based approaches in student support and academic programming. Asset-based approaches begin from a place of celebrating strengths. At the individual student level, this might look like calling out gifts and talents. At the community level, Ivis García writes that asset-based work comes from the recognition that community development is a community process. This means community members must be valued for investing "their gifts and themselves in the process" (2020, p. 70). García continues, "it is better to start the process of development from within the community—that is, from the inside out." This philosophy reminds us that school is a community project. To celebrate and leverage the resources and gifts in your school and local communities, activist and educator Dr. Dena Simmons (2012) recommends identifying organizations, leaders, and teachers in our communities with whom we can partner.

- Create an asset map of your local community. Highlight the social, economic, educational, health, and faith-based organizations that are engaged in care, teaching, and leadership work.
  - Which of these organizations do you already partner with and learn from?
  - Which do your students access?
  - What does reviewing this list reveal about the strengths in your communities? How can you better support the great work happening in your local community and leverage new partnerships to build bridges and networks for ongoing care?

2. **Celebrate your school community's cultural and language landscape.**

According to 2020 research by the National Education Association, "By 2025, 1 out of 4 students across the nation will be an English learner (EL)." In a 2023 article for Education Week, US Secretary of Education Migel Cardona asks:

> Why is it that in 2023, in many school systems in our country, we treat our English learners as students with deficits—rather than assets in a globally competitive world? Bilingualism and biculturalism is a superpower—and we at the Department of Education will work to help our students become multilingual.
>
> (Najarro, 2023)

- What languages are present in your school communities?
- How can you grow in learning more about these language traditions and supporting others in your school community to do the same?
- In what ways are you helping to sustain and celebrate the different cultures present in your school communities?
- What lessons have you learned from the multilingual learners of your community?

3. **Action plan for equity.** This chapter included specific recommendations for reducing barriers to participation and expanding learning in your advanced and gifted programs. Write two immediate action items that you and your leadership team will commit to completing this semester. This might include data work, identifying teacher coaches or other equity champions, scheduling professional development, meeting with student advisors, exploring universal screening, etc.

References

Denver Public Schools. (2024). *Gifted & talented.* https://gt.dpsk12.org/o/gifted/page/universal-screening

Equal Opportunity Schools. (2024, January 27). *Our approach.* https://eoschools.org/eos-in-schools/approach/

García, I. (2020). Asset-based community development (ABCD): Core principles. In R. Phillips, E. Trevan, & P. Kraeger (Eds.), *Research handbook on community development* (pp. 67–75). Edward Elgar Publishing.

Institute of Education Sciences. (2020). *What is culturally sustaining pedagogy?* Regional Educational Laboratory (REL) Pacific. https://ies.ed.gov/ncee/rel/regions/pacific/pdf/REL_CulturallySustainingPedagogy_508.pdf

Lakin, J. M. (2016). Universal screening and the representation of historically underrepresented minority students in gifted education: Minding the gaps in Card and Giuliano's research. *Journal of Advanced Academics, 27*(2), 139–149.

Long, D. A., McCoach, D. B., Siegle, D., Callahan, C. M., & Gubbins, E. J. (2023). Inequality at the starting line: Underrepresentation in gifted identification and disparities in early achievement. *AERA Open, 9,* 23328584231171535.

Morgan, H. (2020). The gap in gifted education: Can universal screening narrow it? *Education, 140*(4), 207–214.

Najarro, I. (2023, May 3). The debate over English learner terminology, explained. *Education Week.* www.edweek.org/teaching-learning/the-debate-over-english-learner-terminology-explained/2023/03

National Association for Gifted Children. (2021). *Identifying and serving culturally and linguistically diverse gifted students*. https://cdn.ymaws.com/nagc.org/resource/resmgr/knowledge-center/position-statements/identifying_and_serving_cult.pdf

National Education Association. (2020). *English language learners*. www.nea.org/resource-library/english-language-learners

Paris, D. (2012). Culturally sustaining pedagogy. *Educational Researcher, 41*(3), 93–97. https://doi.org/10.3102/0013189x12441244

Paris, D., & Alim, H. S. (2014). What are we seeking to sustain through culturally sustaining pedagogy? A loving critique forward. *Harvard Educational Review, 84*(1), 85–100.

Peters, S. J., Makel, M. C., & Carter III, J. S. (2023). Gifted education advances school integration and equity. *Phi Delta Kappan, 105*(3), 50–54.

Selvamenan, M., Paolozza, A., Solomon, J., & Naglieri, J. (2024). A pilot study of race, ethnic, gender, and parental education level differences on the Naglieri General Ability Tests: Verbal, nonverbal, and quantitative. *Psychology in the Schools*. https://doi.org/10.1002/pits.23304

Simmons D. (2012, August 29). Guest blog: Emancipatory education: Dena Simmons on teaching for social justice in middle school. *Feminist Teacher*. https://feministteacher.com/2012/08/29/guest-blog-emancipatory-education-dena-simmons-on-teaching-for-social-justice-in-middle-school/

Texas Gifted Education Family Network. (2020, September 21). *Interview with Dr. Joy Lawson Davis*. Gifted Education Family Network. https://giftededucationfamilynetwork.org/2020/09/21/interview-with-dr-joy-lawson-davis/

US Committee for Refugees and Immigrants. (2020). *The crisis in the Democratic Republic of the Congo. USCRI backgrounder*. https://refugees.org/wp-content/uploads/2020/12/USCRI-Backgrounder_DRC.pdf

US chapter of the UNHRC. (2023, December 23). *Democratic Republic of the Congo refugee crisis explained*. www.unrefugees.org/news/democratic-republic-of-the-congo-refugee-crisis-explained/

 ## Concept Study: The Cognitive Triangle as a Support Tool

Emotions (feeling), cognition (thinking), and behaviors (actions) are not separate processes. Instead, they are coordinated and interrelated functions and structures in the brain. In the 1960s–70s, Dr. Aaron Beck revolutionized psychotherapy (or talking therapy)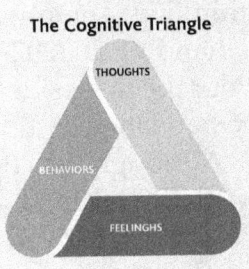
by developing *cognitive behavior therapy (CBT)* (Beck & Fleming, 2021). Today CBT is the most widely practiced and researched psychotherapy in the world (David et al., 2018). It is based on the cognitive triangle.

Although school leaders are often fortunate to partner with talented school psychologists, counselors, and other mental health professionals, our role (and often theirs, as well) is not to facilitate therapy. That said, as we continue building our own support repertoires we can learn from these professionals. This concept study builds on lessons I have learned from working with a talented psychologist who has supported many students in my care.

Dr. Greg Holliday ("Doc Holliday") is a talented and compassionate psychologist. Over the years, he has supported several students in navigating complex situations. In 2015, we worked closely together to support a group of gifted high school students, including a young man we'll call Paul. Paul, a profoundly gifted student, was struggling with mental health concerns. Doc Holliday and I met with him after school on several occasions. I remember one afternoon with particular clarity.

Paul felt stuck and we did, too, when Doc Holliday drew the cognitive triangle on the back of a classroom worksheet. The cognitive triangle is an accessible model for processing the relationships between cognition (thinking), emotion (feeling), and behavior (actions) (Chand et al., 2023). Doc Holliday asked Paul to consider the three sides of his pencil-drawn diagram, which he had labeled: thoughts, feelings, and behaviors.

Although the cognitive triangle is usually presented with thoughts at the top, Doc Holliday encouraged Paul to start anywhere he liked. "The point," he shared, "is that these are all interrelated." We can start with a negative thought and then move to the feelings that thought elicits and then move to the behavior resulting from these thoughts and feelings. We can also start with a behavior and use the cognitive triangle to better understand the thoughts and feelings that resulted before and after this action.

The profound power I saw in this simple exercise came next with its invitation for revision. As we have explored throughout this book, agency and authorship are some of our most important tools in supporting student growth and learning. Doc Holliday shared that while Paul may have started with a negative thought, this framework can be used to consider how his feelings and behaviors might shift if he rewrote that thought positively. For example, if Paul started with this negative thought: "I am just not smart enough to take AP Calculus." he might play with a true revision that says something like, "Mr. K believes I am capable of taking AP Calculus," or "I've done well in all my math classes leading up to this one."

That day, Paul had a breakthrough. No, his anxiety didn't go away. Instead, his breakthrough came, as they so often do, in incremental realizations. For Paul, this included learning that he has agency over his thoughts, feelings, and behaviors and that he has the power to rewrite his own story. As we continued talking, Paul also remembered what may be the most important truth of all—that he is not alone.

The student we were working with that day, who isn't named Paul, also wasn't struggling with math or even imposter syndrome. He was struggling with friendships, connection, and identity. The details of his story, including his revision, belongs to him. Since that afternoon session, I have used the cognitive triangle in my own work with students and teachers. I have also leaned on it as a personal reflective tool. I share it here with the hope that other school leaders might find similar value in this model.

That day, Paul had a breakthrough. No, his anxiety didn't go away. Instead, his breakthrough came, as they so often do, in incremental realizations. For Paul, this included learning that he has agency over his thoughts, feelings, and behaviors and that he has the power to rewrite his own story. As we continued talking, Paul also remembered what may be the most important truth of all—that he is not alone.

Questions for Consideration

1. What are the lessons or tools you have learned from working with your school psychologists, counselors, or other mental health professionals?
2. Since breakthroughs often come in incremental realizations, it is easy to miss them. Consider the last few courageous conversations you have had

with students, faculty, or staff. Are there any incremental realizations you noticed in those conversations that you now want to celebrate and continue to build from?
3. Try it out. What is a challenging or negative thought you are struggling with? Work your way around the cognitive triangle to process your thoughts, feelings, and behaviors, and then take time to also work through the power of a revision.

Important care note. If you or anyone you are working with is in danger of harm to themselves or others or is struggling with recurring negative thoughts, please seek professional mental health support. You can also find more information on mandated reporting on pgs. 94–95. Mental health support is integral to the Wholehearted Leadership themes of courage, learning, justice, and connection. Just as Paul learned, you, too, are not alone.

References

Beck, J. S., & Fleming, S. (2021). A brief history of Aaron T. Beck, MD, and cognitive behavior therapy. *Clinical Psychology in Europe, 3*(2), e6701. https://doi.org/10.32872/cpe.6701

Chand, S. P., Kuckel, D. P., & Huecker, M. R. (2023, May 23). *Cognitive behavior therapy*. StatPearls Publishing. www.ncbi.nlm.nih.gov/books/NBK470241

David, D., Cristea, I., & Hofmann, S. G. (2018). Why cognitive behavioral therapy is the current gold standard of psychotherapy. *Frontiers in Psychiatry, 9*, 4.

Continuing to Lead for Learning and Connection

Adela and her family had recently arrived from Mexico when she barreled into my first-grade classroom. Adela was the boldest language learner I have ever met. She was animated and confident as she experimented with the English language. When she joined our class, I conducted some diagnostics to assess her academic skills in both English and Spanish. Carefully she counted from one to five in English, raising one small finger with each number. "Can you count any higher?" I asked her. She drew her eyebrows together and looked at me with confusion.

"That was great!" I tried again, "Can you count any higher?" I raised my own hands to try and explain *higher*. She smirked and raised her fist high above her head and then counted from one to five again raising each finger as she said the new number. We laughed, and I suspected this was a great preview for the year ahead.

A couple months later, Adela was helping me carry a large stack of math manipulatives from our upstairs classroom to the kindergarten wing downstairs. "Maestra, this is much boxes. We should prolly take the alligator." Since then, I can't tell you how many times I've grinned stepping into elevators imagining that I am riding a mythical alligator to my destination.

Adela's playful boldness helped her learn quickly. She delighted in her mistakes and kept right on talking to teachers and peers even when the topics she wanted to talk about required vocabulary she hadn't yet learned. Adela's stories—and I have so many of them—remind me that all great teaching, and likewise, leadership, is an exercise in reciprocity. At its best, teaching and learning is a courageous feedback loop fueled by reciprocity. There are many young people I want to be like "when I grow up" and when it comes to language learning, Adela is one of them.

She also understood a fundamental truth about learning that is well supported by psychology and neuroscience research. As

Adam Grant writes in his 2023 book on hidden potential, "Comfort in learning is a paradox... Accelerating learning requires...being brave enough to use your knowledge as you acquire it" (p. 33). Grant's research on *polyglots*, people who speak six or more languages, points to those who continued learning or in some cases started learning new languages well into adulthood. "According to a growing body of evidence, the decline in the rate of language learning around age 18 is not a feature of our biology. It's a bug in our education" (p. 26). Instead of leaning into imperfect and growing attempts, too often many adults wait for some elusive mastery. The irony is that waiting for mastery delays it. Instead, we need to be more like Adela. We need to play and experiment with the concepts we are learning. We need to take risks and maybe even ride a few alligators along the way.

****

As school leaders, we are barraged with decisions each day. Our choices about leadership, policy, practice, and the initiatives we say yes to all have a lasting impact on student and staff outcomes. The Wholehearted Leadership Framework offers a compass for navigating these decisions with purpose and integrity. Central to this framework is consistent, supportive relationships. Throughout these chapters, I have offered specific examples of the ways relationships can help us rewire our schools. As we close this section, I want to remind school leaders that this intentional work isn't just for our students—building intentional relationships and a culture of support is just as important for the teachers and staff in our schools. Supported faculty and staff are more equipped to care for students and more likely to stay in their school communities.

In their research on teacher retention in rural schools, Matthew Frahm and Marie Cianca (2021) write that administrative support is a consistent and critical component of retaining effective educators. Both superintendents and school principals are cited in their research, with school principals having unique proximity to shaping the culture and conditions that support teachers and staff including "creating schedules, providing resources, facilitating collaborative interactions, and establishing community partnerships" (p. 3).

A 2021 research brief from the Learning Policy Institute at North Carolina State University reported that principal leadership was a strong and significant factor of teacher retention. Drawing on extensive data across North Carolina, the authors Barnett Berry, Kevi Bastian, Linda Darling-Hammond, and Tara Kini found that the support and trust a principal extends to their teachers is among the most important conditions for teacher retention and collective efficacy (Berry et al., 2021).

In my own school community, our culture of support (Berry et al., 2021; Frahm & Cianca, 2021) has contributed to teachers and staff staying at our school. Many of our faculty and staff have worked for our school for more than ten years and several as many as 20 or even 30 years. This means that, as professionals, we, too, have grown up together. We have seen our own children matriculate from elementary to secondary school and onto college and trade schools. We have celebrated marriages and milestone anniversaries. We have been there for each during the loss of parents, siblings, and grandparents. We have been there for each other in sickness, divorce, and hospitalizations. We have been there for graduations, new certifications, and academic accomplishments. Wholehearted leaders recognize that working together often also means doing life together. This relationship work may be incremental and is different from the ways you do life with a spouse or family, but it is life and joy, celebration and sadness, and growth and change all the same. This is the work that holds us together. When we take a long view and look back, this is also often the work that helps us heal. As we invite our faculty and staff to be authentically themselves—to grieve, to heal, to celebrate—we give our students permission to do the same.

School leaders are pulled in many directions. Leading for connection and learning means no matter what direction we are pulled in, people are always our first priority. School leadership sometimes reminds me of the Cherokee folk story about two wolves. In the story, a young boy goes to his grandfather for advice on how to respond to someone who has done something unjust. The grandfather explains that we all have two wolves inside us. One is quick to anger and do harm. The other is committed to harmony, justice, and no harm. The grandfather shares that sometimes it is hard to live with both wolves because both want to control us. The child asks, "Which wolf wins in the end?" The grandfather responds. "The one I feed."

> *As we invite our faculty and staff to be authentically themselves—to grieve, to heal, to celebrate—we give our students permission to do the same.*

Relationships feed hope. Connection feeds courage. Learning feeds growth. Bravery feeds justice. When we choose courage, justice, learning, and connection, it is our students, and therefore our communities, who win.

References

Berry, B., Bastian, K. C., Darling-Hammond, L., & Kini, T. (2021). *The importance of teaching and learning conditions: Influences on teacher retention and school performance in North Carolina*. Research Brief. Learning Policy Institute.

Frahm, M. T., & Cianca, M. (2021). Will they stay or will they go? Leadership behaviors that increase teacher retention in rural schools. *The Rural Educator, 42*(3), 1.

Grant, A. (2023). *Hidden potential: The science of achieving greater things*. Penguin.

The Brave Leadership Needed to Rewire Our Schools

This book has offered stories from a place of becoming. In the opening, you read about a meeting I held in two chairs facing a desk that I was hesitant to take my place behind. While I have come a long way from that first day, those mahogany desk moments have persisted throughout my leadership practice. Recently, I had to share some difficult news with a large group of educators in our school system. The announcement came in the form of a faculty meeting, and I remember hesitating for just a moment when it was time to step in front of that theater curtain. The Wholehearted Leadership Framework offers us a compass for these moments and other challenges, conflicts, and micro-ethical decisions. It helps us find a way forward.

Just as I was on that first day meeting with a teacher lead and looking at the desk, I continue to be struck by the responsibility of school leadership. This work matters. It is complicated and important. It can (and does) save lives.

These chapters celebrate the professionalism of school leadership. A week after I took my first administrative position for our university lab school, I started a folder titled: Autoethnography. Thus began my first school leadership reflective journal. This journal was my safe processing space. It was where I went to work out the big questions about leading. It was where I reflected on the lessons I was learning, where I celebrated students and teachers, and where I wrote about the areas I still had to grow in. It was a safe, quiet place that was all mine.

While all reflective practices are helpful, this book with its over 300 questions celebrates the power of intentional reflection *with* your team. This is a practice that has transformed my leadership. It is also one that I have had to work at by moving beyond my own safe journal. Today, I have kept up my reflective practice, but I have moved it outside of a singular folder in my Google Drive. Now much of my reflective practice is shared on collaborative documents with colleagues. I keep several team and two-way journals and collaborative "white boards" with members of our leadership and administrative teams. I use text chats to work out challenges in real time with colleagues and advisors who workshop blossoming ideas, ask important questions, bring new perspectives, refocus conversations, and co-create solutions and processes. Writing continues to be a powerful sense-making tool for me, and during my time in administration I have learned that writing as dialogue has a unique ability to help us create, co-create, and recreate wholehearted solutions (Freire, 1970).

Poet-activist, Beth Strano (2023), writes that the idea of *safe space* is a myth. Strano calls for work that exists, just like our schools, in real contexts that are messy and complicated. My original reflective journal may have been a safe space but only because it existed in isolation. A few years ago, I remember meeting with Antwaun Smith, who has advised me on many difficult situations. I told Antwaun that I was frustrated there was so much conflict in school leadership work. He smiled and told me, "Kathryn, if you want to avoid conflict, you have to avoid relationships. All relationships have conflict." I have thought about this often since. With practice, now I sometimes find myself leaning into conflict as a way to hear what different perspectives can teach me. This kind of deep listening invites us to engage in productive struggle. While I can't prevent conflict completely, as a leader, I play an important role in helping our school community navigate conflict through authenticity, belonging, and high expectations.

Leaning into conflict is not the same as leaning into injustice. In fact, leaning into conflict requires leaders to practice the courage, connection, and learning necessary to rewire our schools for justice. In our lessons on antiracism, I shared about the importance of leveraging a "pedagogy of discomfort" (Boler, 1999). In the proceedings for a 2023 International Conference, Raghavendra Gudur writes that pedagogies of discomfort can offer us a transformational teaching approach to "challenge students' existing beliefs, assumptions, and comfort zones in order to encourage critical thinking." Gudur continues that this methodology can create "the necessary learning environment to foster intellectual and emotional discomfort as a means of encouraging students to confront and question their preconceived notions, biases, and limitations." A pedagogy of discomfort isn't just for young people. It is for all of us. This book has encouraged brave leadership. By the nature of our work around justice and inclusion, this work is often uncomfortable. It is in this discomfort that we do some of our most important learning. When we learn from conflict, we learn from each other.

Much like my reflective practice, insight can be multiplied when we lean into relationships. The stories I have shared throughout this book are relationship stories. In working on these chapters, I discovered that everything important I have learned about leadership, I have learned through relationships. Relationships, as I have shared, are the heart of great teaching and great leadership. They are also the tether of the Wholehearted Leadership Framework. In every component of the framework, relationships are listed as a key concept. Courage, learning, connection, and justice start and are maintained through our relationships with each other.

The shift from "safe space" to "brave space" is more than just semantic (Arao & Clemens, 2023). In brave spaces, community members commit to inclusivity and dialogue. In these co-created learning environments, leaders support members in taking healthy risks, including emotional risks. Here students and staff have the agency to make their own decisions about participation, challenge, and disclosure (Arao & Clemens, 2023; Ali & NASPA, 2017). This practice affirms that leading for courage, justice, learning, and connection are what it means to be an effective leader. This means, if a leadership practice doesn't align to our moral compass or work for one or more of our student populations then it doesn't work for our school. Brave spaces require us to center morals and justice in all our decisions.

In a 2017 policy article for the National Association of Student Personnel Administrators (NASPA), Diana Ali writes that "oppressed students are unlikely to experience truly risk-free spaces, even within the confines of resource centers, on friendly campuses, or in the most inclusive classrooms" (Ali & NASPA, p. 7). We saw this with Jayden and Hank in the chapter on antiracism. We read about this in Anthony Ploggers's advocacy work to support members of the LGBTQ+ community and in Matt Miltenberg's work to help students stand up to bullying. This brave work calls on us, our teams, and our students to lead with heart. Wholehearted leadership recognizes the historical and continuous harms of oppression and marginalization while also inviting radical hope (Fishman-Weaver, 2017) and imagination.

******

Writing a book is a didactic experience. Working on this one affirmed for me that teaching and learning are ubiquitous. One of our greatest strengths as school leaders is our ability to think broadly and humbly about our own professional learning communities. The stories in these chapters reminded me of the importance of mentorship and friendship. They reminded me of the incredible human beings I get to learn from and "do school" with each day. In this book you read about teacher leaders like Karen Scales whose advocacy radically expanded access to rigorous coursework. You read about community leaders like Kaci Conley whose work has furthered inclusion and accessibility in her school communities. You read about district leaders like Dr. Jill Brown and Dr. Susan Deakins whose bravery helped build a new elementary school. You read about student leaders like Mariah, Sam, and Lacie who helped address sexism and discrimination in an extracurricular activity they loved.

When I started writing this book, I knew that wholehearted leadership meant keeping students and those who support them at the center of every decision. What I didn't yet realize was how many of the important lessons I've learned about leadership were taught to me by our students and their families. I think of seven-year-old Luiza taking me by the hand on my very first day and leading me upstairs to a classroom that would change my life and transform our school community. I think about Jamal and everything he has navigated through foster services in elementary and middle school, and how today, I get to see him thrive in high school. I think of the ways Amari is showing her middle school teachers a new way to think about student support. I think about Nala teaching her class about life, death, crisis, and grace. I think about the fifth graders tending to Brazilwood trees in their school garden. While this is a book for professionals, it is these young people who are the protagonists of this story.

Who are the Jamals, the Nalas, and the Luizas in your school communities? As you implement these action plans and reflective exercises, what lessons are you learning from student leaders like these? With hope, the Wholehearted Leadership Framework has offered you a values-based approach for cultivating the conditions needed to lead for courage, justice, learning, and connection. This is not an algorithm, but a living work. It comes to life in thousands of different contexts, in small moments of connection, in classroom doorways, cafeterias, and food drives. It comes to life in saying yes to great ideas, and celebrating the genius in your schools and communities. It comes to life by being brave enough to learn from others, by asking for help, by iterating, and by seeking a new way forward. It comes to life in relationships, in keeping students and those who support them at the heart of your work in every decision, every day.

References

Ali, D., & National Association of Student Personnel Administrators (NASPA). (2017). *Safe spaces and brave spaces*. www.naspa.org/files/dmfile/Policy_and_Practice_No_2_Safe_Brave_Spaces.pdf

Arao, B., & Clemens, K. (2023). From safe spaces to brave spaces. In L. Landerman (Ed.), *The art of effective facilitation: Reflections from social justice educators* (pp. 135–151). Routledge.

Boler, M. (1999). *Feeling power: Emotions and education*. Routledge.

Fishman-Weaver, K. (2017). A call to praxis: Using gendered organizational theory to center radical hope in schools. *Journal of Organizational Theory in Education*, 2(1), 1–14.

Freire, P. (1970). Chapter 3. In *Pedagogy of the Oppressed*. The Seabury Press.

Gudur, R. R. (2023). Teaching empathetic design through the pedagogy of discomfort. Presented at the 25th International

Conference on Engineering and Product Design Education. Barcelona, September 7–8. https://researchprofiles.canberra.edu.au/en/publications/teaching-empathetic-design-through-the-pedagogy-of-discomfort

Strano, B. (2023). Untitled poem by Beth Strano. *Facing History & Ourselves.* www.facinghistory.org/resource-library/untitled-poem-beth-strano

For Product Safety Concerns and Information please contact our EU representative GPSR@taylorandfrancis.com
Taylor & Francis Verlag GmbH, Kaufingerstraße 24, 80331 München, Germany

www.ingramcontent.com/pod-product-compliance
Lightning Source LLC
Chambersburg PA
CBHW052220300426
44115CB00011B/1760